S0-BVY-833

A History of Top Management in Japan

A History of Top Management in Japan

Managerial Enterprises and Family Enterprises

Hidemasa Morikawa

2001

OXFORD
UNIVERSITY PRESS

Oxford New York
Athens Auckland Bangkok Bogotá Buenos Aires Cape Town
Chennai Dar es Salaam Delhi Florence Hong Kong Istanbul Karachi
Kolkata Kuala Lumpur Madrid Melbourne Mexico City Mumbai Nairobi
Paris São Paulo Shanghai Singapore Taipei Tokyo Toronto Warsaw

and associated companies in
Berlin Ibadan

Published by Oxford University Press, Inc.
198 Madison Avenue, New York, New York 10016

Library of Congress Cataloging-in-Publication Data

Morikawa, Hidemasa, 1930–
[Toppu manejimento no keieishi. English]
A history of top management in Japan : managerial enterprises and family enterprises / by Hidemasa Morikawa.
p. cm.
Includes bibliographical references and index.
ISBN 0-19-513165-7
1. Industrial management—Japan—History. 2. Executives—Japan—History. 3. Family-owned business enterprises—Japan—History. I. Title.

HD70.J3 M598413 2001
338.0952—dc21 00-066953

1 3 5 7 9 8 6 4 2

Printed in the United States of America
on acid-free paper

PREFACE

In Japan, many of the top managers of large enterprises join their companies upon graduating from university (some join in mid-career) and are promoted as they accumulate knowledge and experiences before becoming top managers. Both the number and percentage of these types of top managers have increased since the Meiji era, and, along with the lifelong employment and seniority based promotion systems, this is a fundamental characteristic of the Japanese corporate system.

I began my study of salaried managers in Japan, particularly salaried managers who had risen to their positions through promotion, in the early 1970s. Prior to that, I had studied the business history of *zaibatsu* in Japan. However, after I began examining the roles of salaried managers in *zaibatsu* and their roles in top management as key factors in the development of these organizations, I focused on salaried managers, particularly promoted salaried managers in large enterprises, both those in *zaibatsu* and those who were not. Much to my surprise, a similar study was going on almost simultaneously in the United States. Professor A. D. Chandler, Jr., was also studying large enterprises in which salaried managers make decisions at the highest levels of management and the significance of these types of companies in the history of business in the United States. It was in the article "Seedbed of Managerial Capitalism," in *Managerial Hierarchies* by A. D. Chandler and H. Daems, published in 1980, that Dr. Chandler clearly defined large enterprises run by top managers who are salaried managers and who own little or none of the company's stock as managerial enterprises. In *Visible Hand*, an earlier work by Chandler published in 1977, however, Chandler had yet to clearly define the term "managerial enterprise."

While often referring to Dr. Chandler's study, I pursued my own investigations into salaried managers in Japan but did not use the concept of managerial enterprise in my book *Nihon Keieishi (Japan's Business History)*, published in 1981, or in my presentation at the Ninth International Economic History Congress, B9 Session, held in Budapest in 1982. At that time, some researchers were applying Dr. Chandler's managerial enterprise concept to enterprises in which salaried managers were top managers, and others to enterprises with developed managerial hierarchies, even though Dr. Chandler himself did not differentiate between these two applications of the term. In 1985, at the Twelfth Fuji Conference organized by the Business History Society, I used the concept "managerial enterprise" to refer to large enterprises where top managers who make decisions at the highest organizational levels are salaried managers. At the conference, I was assigned the role of project leader and delivered a keynote report. Those joining in the discussion at that time included Dr. Chandler, T. Gourvish (United Kingdom), H. Kaelble (Germany), W. Lazonick (United States), and H. Daems (Belgium). One of the topics under discussion was the definition of the term "managerial enterprise," and the concepts it implied. Dr. Chandler supported my view that a managerial enterprise is an enterprise whose top managers are salaried managers.

It was around this time that the theme of my study shifted slightly to embrace a comparison of managerial enterprises and family enterprises. Although I mainly examined Japanese enterprises, I also tried to conduct surveys in the United States, Europe, and other Asian countries. Furthermore, I not only studied *zaibatsu* enterprises up to 1945 and the end of World War II but also tracked their course into the 1990s. This book is based on my views about managerial enterprises and compares managerial enterprises and family enterprises primarily using Japanese examples, as well as some from overseas. In writing this book, I was guided and greatly encouraged most notably by Dr. A. D. Chandler, Jr., and Dr. Keiichiro Nakagawa. My thinking on the topic was also greatly stimulated by engaging discussions with many of my friends, particularly those younger than myself. These friends include Dr. Jeofferey Jones of Reading University and Dr. Alice Amsden of M.I.T. I would like to express my gratitude to all those who were so helpful to me.

This book was first published in 1996 by the Japanese publishing company Yuhikaku Publishing. My friend Dr. Akira Kudo read the book and recommended publication of an English version for foreign readers. He then kindly introduced me and my book to Dr. Toyoshi Onji and Mr. Herb Addison of Oxford University Press. Thanks to the kind assistance of these individuals and the generosity of the Daido Life Insurance Company, which provided funds for the English translation, Oxford University Press has published this English version, and I am greatly appreciative of this opportunity and the warm support from all these people. Finally, I would like to thank Mr. Steve Ziolkowski of TransPac Publishing in British Columbia, Canada, for translating and editing this difficult book, which I hope will contribute to an understanding of the history of business in Japan.

Yokohama, Japan H. M.
2000

CONTENTS

LIST OF TABLES AND FIGURES

TRANSLATOR'S NOTE

As with any translation, the greatest effort has been made to stay true to the meaning of the original text while attempting to make the read as smooth as possible. I hope this effort has been successful but, if not, the responsibility is mine and not that of Professor Morikawa.

In terms of transcriptions of Japanese words and phrases, I have followed the Hepburn system and kept the long vowels of Japanese short in order to aid readability and to conform to other romanizations of Professor Morikawa's works.

As many readers will know, Japanese names follow the surname/first name model that is common to most Asian countries. In this book, however, the order has been reversed and the names of Japanese people follow the Western first name/surname order.

Names of Japanese companies, organizations, and other institutions have in most cases been rendered only in roman letters and have not been listed by their English names (if they have one), since many older Japanese companies did not have English names and we sought consistency in the tables that list so much useful information in this book.

Books and/or articles only published in Japanese have been romanized followed by an unofficial translation (in parentheses).

Finally, I would like to thank Professor Morikawa for his able and quick assistance in the translation. I would also like to offer my sincerest thanks and appreciation to Alan and Uta Bryce and my wife Kimiko for their hard work with the translation of *A History of Top Management in Japan*. This book would not have been translated without them, and if there are any errors, they are mine.

Steve Ziolkowski
British Columbia, Canada

A History of Top Management in Japan

CHAPTER ONE

Theoretical Problems Regarding Managerial Enterprises and Family Enterprises

Managerial Enterprises and Family Enterprises

In this book I have attempted to analyze the top management of leading Japanese enterprises as part of my research into the history of managerial enterprises and family enterprises, a project that has engaged me for many years. Managerial enterprises and family enterprises are both concepts proposed by A. D. Chandler, and, although I have based the development of my own postulations on Chandler's theoretical framework, I have, however, taken a different stance from Chandler and many Chandlerians.

Chandler's Classification of Enterprises

As is widely known, Chandler has classified enterprises according to their owners and managers. An explanation of Chandler's classification system and my views on it are outlined below.[1]

- *Individual enterprise*: An enterprise owned and managed by its founder that does not have a hierarchical management system.
- *Entrepreneurial enterprise*: An enterprise owned and managed by its founder that has hired salaried managers who are not owners and possessing a hierarchical management structure. The difference between an individual enterprise and an entrepreneurial enterprise is solely whether the enterprise has a hierarchical management structure, so both can be called a

"founder enterprise." Chandler does not mention this point, which is noteworthy.

- *Family enterprise*: An enterprise owned and managed by its founder and/or heirs of the founder. Although Chandler considers heirs to be family members and classifies enterprises jointly owned and managed by their founders and heirs as family enterprises, my views differ somewhat. I consider such enterprises family enterprises only after the founder retires or dies. As with founder enterprises, family enterprises are of two types: those with a hierarchical management structure and those without one.
- *Financial institution-controlled enterprise*: An enterprise owned and managed by a bank or financial institution.
- *Major-shareholder-controlled enterprise*: This is an original concept of mine and one not proposed by Chandler. The enterprise is jointly owned and managed by a few major shareholders. Chandler may have considered this type of enterprise to be a financial institution–controlled enterprise, but there is no firm evidence that he grouped things in this way.
- *Managerial enterprise*: An enterprise in which salaried managers who are not owners of the enterprise and who own none or little of its stock control its top management and make decisions at the highest level. The founder, the family of the founder, major shareholders, or financial institutions (representatives of these institutions) have delegated management authority to the salaried managers, and in some cases do not even have the right to appoint or dismiss top managers, and in effect do not have control of the enterprise.

Kocka's Classification of Enterprises

The classification of enterprises should be as simple as possible. Classifications that are too complex are impractical for analytical purposes, and it is certainly better to make classifications as simple as possible and to deal with them in a flexible way that is based on actual situations in real enterprises. Thus, I find myself at odds with classifications such as the "intermediate type," as proposed by the German, Jurgen Kocka. Kocka classified enterprises into the following three categories:

1. *Owner enterprises*: Enterprises in which long-term strategic decision making and daily management and administration decision making are done by the owners.

2. *Managerial enterprises*: Enterprises in which both types of decisions are made by salaried managers and only rarely by the owners of the enterprise's diversified assets.
3. *Intermediate enterprises*: Enterprises in which strategic decisions (particularly investment decisions) are still made by the founder, his family, heirs, and close friends, but most decisions regarding ongoing management and administrative matters are made by salaried managers.[2]

In my opinion, the intermediate enterprise classification is unnecessary. The core of top management's decision making includes strategic decisions and decisions on the long-term allocation of managerial resources, including investments. The classification of enterprises is based on who makes these decisions. Enterprises reflecting Kocka's proposed intermediate enterprise classification are founder enterprises, family enterprises, or, in other words, owner enterprises.

Chandler notes that in family enterprises, or in family enterprises in which hierarchical management structures emerge, the founder and his family make the strategic decisions, and salaried managers, who are middle managers or lower, make the decisions pertaining to daily operations. Here as well, the classifications should be simplified and enterprises should be classified, for example, as either owner enterprises or managerial enterprises.

Classification Specifications in More Detail—Family Enterprises

In order to apply Chandler's enterprise classifications to the historical analysis of enterprises, the classification criteria should be examined in greater detail.

First, the term "family enterprise" should not be applied to families running tiny operations solely for the purpose of making a modest living; rather, it should refer to profit-driven organizations in which management is ongoing and has specific goals. Second, to classify a family enterprise separately from a founder enterprise (individual enterprises and entrepreneurial enterprises) the enterprise's founder must be either retired or deceased. Third, it is important to remember that there are several stages in which family-owned/managed enterprises may develop.

1. The owner and top management of the enterprise is the family of the founder.

2. Although the family is the owner of the enterprise, the family and salaried managers constitute top management.
3. Although the family is the owner of the enterprise, salaried managers are entrusted with top management. The appointment and dismissal of managers, however, is still done by the family.
4. The family is the owner in name only. Salaried managers constitute top management, and the appointment and dismissal of salaried managers is done by salaried managers. The family has a figurehead role and rubber-stamps the decisions of top management.

Of the enterprises in the above four stages, those in (1) and (2) are obviously classified as family enterprises and those in (4) as managerial enterprises. The classification of enterprises in (3), however, is unclear. For now, I would like to classify them as family enterprises.

Based on the above points, a detailed description of a family enterprise is as follows: An enterprise that is owned and managed by the founder's family (sometimes in conjunction with salaried managers) after the founder has retired or died, or an enterprise in which management is conducted by entrusted salaried managers appointed and dismissed by the family.

Types of Salaried Managers

There are several types of salaried managers and the three key types can be described as follows:

1. Those promoted from within the company. This category includes people who started their careers with the company, and those who joined it after previously working elsewhere. The latter can be classified into different categories, depending on when they joined the company.
2. Top managers who move from company to company seeking ever-higher remuneration as executives. These people can be called "*wander vogel* managers."
3. Former high-level government officials recruited by the company to become top managers. Naturally, there are various opinions on what constitutes a high-level government official.

Let's assume that salaried managers fall into one of the above three categories. In Japan, most salaried managers fit into category

(1), and most of the remainder into category (3). *Wander vogel* managers, category (2), are the exception.[3] In the United States, however, the percentage of managers in category (2) is high, while in France the percentage of managers who are former high-level government officials, category (3), is high.[4]

When these salaried managers take over top management positions from various capitalists the company becomes a managerial enterprise. Salaried managers cannot establish enterprises by investing their own capital, so enterprises do not start as managerial enterprises.

Enterprises are established either by individuals or through joint investment. When an enterprise grows and becomes quite large, those established by individuals can be called founder enterprises and those established through joint investment can be called major shareholder-controlled enterprises. In joint investment situations, as a company grows there are generally major changes in the identity of the financiers because few enterprises can grow to be enterprises controlled by a few original major shareholders. Rather, as with cotton-yarn and spinning companies and railway companies in the Meiji era (1867–1925), several wealthy people who have made fortunes through their own businesses establish joint stock companies and, as major shareholders, share management authority. In such cases, as the founder cannot establish a company solely with his own capital, he asks his friends to invest. Thus it is common for the founder to become a top manager or, for the major shareholders who have invested as equals to establish the company, to have their representatives or agents become top managers. There have been few cases in which salaried managers are appointed as top managers at the outset and these are generally in companies of special concern to the nation or in third-sector companies.

According to the classification system described in this book, no enterprises begin as family enterprises or financial-institution controlled enterprises. These types of enterprises should be considered enterprises that were once capitalist enterprises. Since the goal of this book is not to classify capitalist enterprises, we should understand that managerial enterprises are established when the major shareholders of capitalist enterprises appoint salaried managers as top managers. In other words, managerial enterprises can be considered capitalistic enterprises in which the capitalists have entrusted noncapitalist managers with management authority.

How Top Management Is Appointed

Finally, I would like to discuss how capitalists—such as company founders, their families, major shareholders, and financial institutions—appoint salaried managers as top managers. In some cases this is done with written contracts and in others with verbal agreements. In the latter case, counterrevolutions in which the capitalists regain management authority may occur if the top management does not achieve expected results or personal relationships between the capitalists and the salaried managers deteriorate.

According to Shigeaki Yasuoka, in most cases the salaried managers of Japan's leading companies are appointed top managers by the capitalists in verbal agreements. I agree with Yasuoka's statement that "I have the impression that the power of managers of shops in the Edo era, of the *zaibatsu* in the Meiji era, or of companies (groups of companies) established after World War II was undefined and vague."[5] Is this, however, a phenomenon unique to Japan? Are contracts in other Asian countries and the West a form of glue that binds together capitalists and salaried managers? Regarding other Asian countries, we must wait until managerial enterprises there develop more fully in order to answer this. But, are there no cases in the West in which salaried managers become CEOs or receive top-management positions without clearly worded contracts? I tend to think that even in the West the degree to which managers can be independent from capitalists depends on the power relationships between managers and capitalists.

I do not entirely agree with Yasuoka when he says, "unless trends that support illegitimate systems based on nationality are understood, the power of managers cannot be understood."[6] I think that the issue of the power of managers should not be discussed in terms of culture but in terms of political dynamism, a perspective I elaborate on later in the book.

Requirements for the Establishment of a Managerial Enterprise

Reasons for Separation between Company Ownership and Management

The phenomenon Chandler defines as managerial enterprise has long been discussed from the perspective of the separation of ownership and management. When it comes to joint stock companies the view that the separation of company ownership and management occurs through the broadening of the distribution of shares has been widely accepted since A. A. Berle, Jr., and G. C. Means published their seminal work on this topic.[7] According to Berle and Means, when a joint stock company becomes large, individuals, the family, or a few major shareholders lose control over large amounts of shares, which they put on the market, broadening the distribution of the company's shares and increasing the number of minor shareholders. Minor shareholders are basically interested in share value and dividends—and some not even in those—and managers with little or none of the company's shares take over top-management positions.

To be honest, this well-known theory puzzled me for a long time. I understood the broadening of the distribution of shares (although I think there are some problems with the explanation as to how this occurs), but I was completely unable to understand how this leads to the separation of a company's ownership and management, or to the establishment of a managerial enterprise.

Chandler's Managerial Hierarchy

Chandler helped provide answers to the questions I outlined above. He emphasized that the development of a managerial hierarchy is a prerequisite for the establishment of a managerial enterprise, a theory that rang a bell with me. On the contrary, however, I did not think his explanation about how the establishment of managerial enterprises relates to managerial hierarchies struck one as the most logical. From a Japanese viewpoint, American scholars use a different form of logic, and I consider Chandler to be no exception. It is thus necessary to supplement his theory and to make its core more widely accessible so that it can be clearly understood by all. Below are what I consider some of the weak points in Chandler's theory.

First, Chandler explains that when a managerial hierarchy is formed, the founder, his family, major shareholders, and agents of financial institutions cannot fill all the managerial positions, which means that they have no choice but to hire salaried managers. This is how a managerial enterprise develops.[8] However, even when salaried managers are hired to fill positions in the managerial hierarchy it is still possible to keep them in positions below middle management, allowing the capitalists to continue to serve as the top managers and to control the company. Chandler himself refers to the possibility of a classification between strategic decision making by the owner and daily decision making by middle-level salaried managers (what Kocka described above as the intermediate form). Chandler's theory thus does not quite explain how a managerial enterprise develops in terms of a managerial hierarchy because the key issue with a managerial enterprise revolves around the identity of the top managers.

Second, Chandler notes that after a managerial hierarchy is established, capitalists, such as the founder, his family, the agents of financial institutions, and major shareholders who are not full-timers, cannot acquire the skills required to effectively control the managerial hierarchy in a management environment that is radically changing because of technological advances and expanding markets. The result is that the top-management positions are filled by full-time salaried managers with the required skills, which is how a managerial enterprise is formed.[9] However, it is still possible for capitalists, such as the founder, his family, the agents of financial institutions, and major shareholders, to continue serving as full-time top managers. Examples of this are easy to find. Even Chandler noted that there are full-time managers and part-time managers among members of founders' families, saying, "In the United States, by 1917 distinctions between in-house directors and outside directors started becoming clear. In-house directors are full-timers and include the elite salaried managers and members of the founders families who are also full-time top managers. Outside directors are part-timers and represent major shareholders, including family members who are part-time managers."[10] With this second point, Chandler's premise is that the capitalists are not full-time managers. Under this premise, managerial hierarchies can be closely related to managerial enterprises. If this premise is incorrect and there are both full-time and part-time capitalists, a managerial hierarchy cannot be a prerequisite for a managerial enterprise. Some research has been done on the fact that family enterprises strengthen their organizations with managerial hierarchies, a point that I will delve into later. To overcome some of Chandler's more ambiguous areas and to explain the inevitable relationship between managerial hierarchies and the establishment of managerial enterprises it is necessary to examine two aspects of managerial hierarchies: bureaucratic organizations and the network among skilled personnel. Again, I will discuss these points later in the book.

The essence of Chandler's theory is that a managerial enterprise is established when, in an ever-changing management environment, capitalists who have not acquired the skills required to manage the top managers of a large enterprise with a managerial hierarchy entrust salaried managers who have acquired these skills in the managerial hierarchy with top-management positions. In this sense a managerial hierarchy is one of the prerequisites for the establishment of a managerial enterprise. In his writings Chandler maintains his view that, along with a managerial hierarchy, the broadening of the distribution of shares is also a prerequisite for a managerial enterprise—until he wrote *Age of Managers*.[11] In subsequent works,[12] however, particularly in his latest book, *Scale and Scope*, he regarded the broadening of the distribution of shares to be a very minor point.[13]

A Dispute with Etsuo Abe

Etsuo Abe is another Japanese scholar who has spent time researching Chandler's work and theories. As to the ramifications of Chandler's work, however, Professor Abe and I have publicly disagreed and a brief analysis of the issues under dispute is outlined below.

Chandler's theory that the development of a managerial hierarchy leads to the formation of a managerial enterprise is in agreement with my views, and I have often expressed my opinion that the establishment of a managerial enterprise is unrelated to the concentration or the broadening of the distribution of shares. I have also noted that "even if a company is totally owned by an individual or a family, separation of ownership and management does occur, which means that such a company is capable of becoming a managerial enterprise."[14] Abe, however, disagrees with my views on this matter and holds the same position as Chandler did in his early days, noting that the establishment of a managerial enterprise should be explained from the perspective of both the broadening of the distribution of shares and the managerial hierarchy.[15] Abe has also discussed the sequence of the cause and effect of the broadening of the distribution of shares and the establishment of a managerial enterprise, an area which had long been ignored. According to Abe, the broadening of the distribution of shares is fundamental to the gaining of autonomy by salaried managers. Although I value his efforts in this area, I continue to disagree with his views and discussions between us are ongoing.[16] I will not report the contents of our discussions here in detail but will explain why I think the ideas espoused by Professor Abe are flawed.

How My Views Differ from Those of Etsuo Abe. First, I firmly believe that salaried managers cannot be autonomous. A joint stock company is owned by those who hold shares in it; salaried managers are simply entrusted with top-management positions by the company's shareholders and must ultimately bow to their wishes. In some situations, of course, these salaried managers may to all appearances have freedom, but this is due solely to the trust their employers have vested in them, and they are essentially nothing more than hired hands. When employers trust their salaried managers it's simply because they're satisfied with the results these salaried managers have attained, or that they perceive that these salaried managers have the potential to attain favorable results. When this is not the case, however, the trust vested by employers in salaried managers, which may be misconstrued as the granting of autonomy, immediately disappears.

Second, if we can image a scenario where a company's shares were completely decentralized and all the shareholders were only interested in dividends, yield rate, and the asset value of the shares (or, on the contrary, they were totally uninterested in these things), salaried managers could theoretically control shareholders' meetings and thus gain autonomy that way. This scenario is a far cry from reality, however. Share distribution surveys show that, regardless of the country and regardless of the timing, the distribution of shares is never a random event like the scattering of sand in the wind but more like a mixture of stones and sand. In other words, there are always major shareholders who command the authority to address the top management, in terms of both how the company is run and who runs it. Even when an enterprise grows and the number of shares issued increases, there is no decrease in the number of major shareholders—individuals or groups—with the authority to speak to top management. The authority of the major shareholders to address top management grows stronger in proportion to the increasing number of minor shareholders who are uninterested in the workings of the top management of the company in which they have invested. Therefore, no matter to what extent the distribution of shares is broadened, salaried managers cannot ignore the wishes of major shareholders; rather, they must satisfy shareholders and fulfill their expectations. In short, the idea of salaried managers obtaining autonomy is unrealistic and does not happen.

Given this, Abe's theory purporting that the broadening of the distribution of shares leads to salaried managers gaining autonomy and the establishment of a managerial enterprise is untenable.

Whether a company's shares are widely distributed or not, major shareholders always maintain pressure on salaried managers through one means or another and obstruct the emergence of managerial enterprises. But salaried managers should join the effort to persuade major shareholders to give up the idea of occupying top management and to accept its delegation to salaried managers. Still, it is these sorts of conditions that give birth to the formation of a managerial hierarchy. In other words, a managerial hierarchy is one where salaried managers who have management skills, are interested in company management, and possess appropriate amounts of information and experience appear at each level of management (top, middle, and lower) and through the human networks among them and in the labor force, these managers become established in their firms under the umbrella of their company's particular administrative mechanisms. Managerial enterprises are established in situations where owners realize that inserting such salaried managers into the managerial hierarchy and entrusting them with top-management positions is more advantageous than having the owners operate the company.

Are Managerial Hierarchies Simply Bureaucratic Administrative Mechanisms?

Chandler has noted that "only a managerial hierarchy brings about the separation of company ownership and management."[17] He has also noted that, according to his view, the only prerequisite for the establishment of a managerial enterprise is the formation of the managerial hierarchy. However, as I mentioned earlier, the context of his conclusion that "only a managerial hierarchy" can lead to the establishment of a managerial enterprise is somewhat unclear. According to my own interpretation of this idea, a managerial hierarchy is a human network within the framework of a particular administrative mechanism that has been established among salaried managers with management skills at various levels within an organization and could include salaried managers at the same level and salaried managers and other members of the labor force. Such a managerial hierarchy fosters salaried managers capable of becoming top managers and enables a capitalist enterprise to become a managerial enterprise. Chandler's interpretation, however, seems to take a different track and Chandler simply defines a managerial hierarchy as a bureaucratic administrative mechanism. If this is the case, it is unreasonable to conclude that a managerial hierarchy is a prerequisite for the establishment of a managerial enterprise, which means that his overall theoretical structure is less than perfect—a theory, perhaps one could say, with holes.

One argument against Chandler's views is that if a managerial hierarchy were simply a bureaucratic hierarchy it would not be difficult for the founder, the founder's family, or other capitalist managers, to stand atop the organizational hierarchy and command the rest of the troops. The authority to make commands and the obligation to obey them are clearly documented and, thus, even a capitalist manager who is both lacking in experience and deficient in knowledge has the authority to make commands. This is one of the ironic charms of a bureaucracy. If a capitalist manager realizes that he or she doesn't have sufficient experience or knowledge he or she can easily have middle managers formulate the plans which he or she can then decide on. H. C. Livesay has noted that there are many examples of founders' families effectively and successfully using bureaucratic administrative mechanisms that have been established within family enterprises.[18] Therefore, if a managerial hierarchy is the same as a bureaucratic hierarchy that can be established in both capitalist enterprises and managerial enterprises, it seems clear that it cannot be a prerequisite for the establishment of a managerial enterprise.

The second reason that it is unreasonable to conclude that a bureaucratic managerial hierarchy is a prerequisite for the establishment of a managerial enterprise is that, as Chandler notes in discussions on organizational capabilities in one of his recent books, *Scale and Scope*, skills in conjunction with physical infrastructure make up one of the most important driving forces in the development of modern industry.[19] If Chandler thinks that there is no relationship between managerial hierarchies and management skills networks, then I see no alternative but to conclude that his theoretical structure must be considered very loose.

The Hardware and Software of Managerial Hierarchies

I would like to emphasize that I am by no means suggesting that the managerial hierarchies Chandler discusses are either bureaucratic administrative mechanisms or human networks. I think instead that we should look at managerial hierarchies as unions that combine bureaucratic administrative mechanisms and human networks. The distinction between bureaucracies and networks is not a matter of bureaucracies being formal structures and networks informal ones. Rather, it is more like the difference between hardware and software.

To continue this metaphor, a bureaucracy (which is essentially a set of regulations that clearly authorizes superiors to issue commands and then obligates subordinates to follow them) is the hardware of a managerial hierarchy. It is the box into which the control functions must fit. But, as we know, hardware alone cannot drive a computer and organizations cannot truly and fully be run by the frame bureaucracy. It is the people, the software, who actually buy into the bureaucracy to make it work. Even when a bureaucracy is in place, if superiors give directives that go unheeded by their staff, anarchy results purely because the software of the organization, the managerial hierarchy, is not functioning as planned. The only reason that subordinates follow orders is that they agree to acknowledge their place in the hierarchy of a company's management.

The software of a managerial hierarchy consists of the networks established among a company's managers at the top, middle, and lower levels of their firm. Moreover, these networks also include all managers in the company, other members of the labor force, and skilled workers. In other words, software is a kind of mutually agreed trust or a set of shared values or information into which everyone buys. Without this software, orders would languish unobeyed. It is essential to remember the human side of organizations and to realize that workers follow orders merely because they agree to and not because the bureaucracy demands it. In fact, workers like to assert their humanity and differentiate themselves from cogs in a machine or sheep in a flock by balking at orders from their managers that they consider to be threatening, to either their physical well-being or their psychological welfare. In *Heishi ni Kike (Ask the Soldiers)*, a report on Japan's Self-Defense Forces, author Takao Sugiyama notes that, "When a commander is unable to gain an understanding of his troops inside of three months, it invariably means that the subordinates have come to their own conclusions about the commander's mettle in only three days."[20]

The software that drives an organization is the trust and mutual respect that develops among management and workers gained through an understanding of each other's skills, experiences, and knowledge, funneled through the human networks that make up all organizations. In this respect, a managerial hierarchy is a prerequisite for the establishment of a managerial enterprise.

It is interesting to note the differences between enterprises that function successfully with capitalists in top-management positions and ones that become bogged down when capitalists occupy high-level management posts. The factor that separates these two situations is usually the background of the capitalist. In the organizations that work, there are usually internal human networks that remain accessible to capitalist top managers, although, as a rule, there are not many top-level capitalist managers who are welcomed freely inside the networks that make up the management hierarchy. The major exceptions to the isolated capitalist top manager are those who founded their own company and helped create the networks of which we speak, although such individuals may find more and more network doors closing as their company becomes larger and more successful.

The human networks of companies are, in many ways, invitation only and contain their own sets of rituals that make them impenetrable by outsiders, whether they are major shareholders, members of the founder's family, or representatives from some financial institution. Only those who have been through the network know the effort and grit required, and it's therefore only natural that high-status top managers would feel uncomfortable and seek out salaried managers to take over management positions that might be handled more deftly.

A managerial hierarchy contains features of the human networks developed among skilled personnel at various levels—and, as we've noted, this hierarchy is not simply a bureaucratic administrative mechanism. As we've also stated, the development of a managerial hierarchy is also a fundamental prerequisite for the establishment of a managerial enterprise. Although Chandler does not explicitly convey this idea, his views seem to be gradually merging with mine, as evidenced by his ideas on organizational capabilities in his book *Scale and Scope*. At the risk of sounding bold, I hope that I've been the first into this new area of analysis and consider my ideas on the subject to be some of the most advanced in the field.

Misunderstanding Chandler's Views

Many people in Japan and other countries think, quite wrongly, that Chandler has limited his areas of discussion to the development of bureaucratic pyramids in large enterprises. Chandler, of course, considers bureaucratic organization important, but his views are certainly not limited to this. There are also many people who consider managerial enterprises to be developed forms of managerial hierarchies that are tantamount to bureaucracies. At the twelfth Fuji Conference held in 1985, one participant put forward the notion that enterprises in which bureaucratic pyramids have been developed are managerial enterprises, regardless of whether their top managers are capitalists or salaried managers. Chandler opposed this view, saying that a managerial enterprise is a large enterprise in which salaried managers constitute top management, and that a managerial hierarchy is a prerequisite for the development of managerial enterprise.[21] Moreover, Chandler has consistently maintained this opinion and that his objective has not been to write about the history of the development of the bureaucratic pyramids. Why have these misunderstandings occurred? In my view it is because Chandler's theory lacks a clear explanation of how a managerial hierarchy leads to the establishment of a managerial enterprise.[22]

CHAPTER TWO

The Transition from a Family Enterprise to a Managerial Enterprise

The Transition from a Founder Enterprise to a Family Enterprise

Handing over an Enterprise to Descendants

After a founder has been successful in his or her business and is confident about its future, there comes a time when he or she has to decide to hand over its ownership and management to a designated heir. The first possibility to consider when handing over the company is whether or not the heir is an appropriate one. If not, the founder might consider the supplementary, or alternative, approach of handing the firm over to a family member who is not the obvious heir, such as a wife (husband), siblings, or other children. Moreover, in the event that the heir has a health problem or is considered too young, the founder would also expect support from other close associates or family members in helping the heir execute his or her ownership and management responsibilities. As one might expect, in most cases the founders of a company make great sacrifices to build up their firm. As one might expect, burdens and sacrifices are usually made also by the founder's family, and behind every successful founder there is usually a hardworking and dedicated family. Thus it is only natural for founders to hope that their family and heirs will take over the business. As a result of this sort of thinking and natural turn of events, some other potential succession candidates are left out of the picture.

Although there are many different factors in the succession process (such as the company's financial and business circumstances, the character and values of the founder, and the personalities and capabilities of family members), the transition from a founder enterprise to a family enterprise generally takes place in the manner outlined in the above paragraph. The process is essentially a natural one, where the founder first goes about selecting and grooming the successor with an eye to the transfer of top-management responsibilities while attempting to maintain the company's centripetal force.

Succession Timing

Even when a founder decides to hand over ownership and management of his company to his family and has found an appropriate successor within the family (usually his designated heir), the transition from a founder enterprise to a family enterprise is not an easy one and often is fraught with difficulties. Many of the problems revolve around the fact that most company founders are extraordinary people. They are people who have built a business up from nothing and are usually possessed of extraordinary ability and dynamic personality. Such people are also usually competitive in spirit and natural leaders. Most founders pride themselves on the hard work that has gone into making their company a success, and they are also possessed of long experience at the center of the action and in management. Such individuals also often take on legendary status within their company and employees often treat the founder's statements as almost a kind of stricture that defines the company's culture. In other words, they are a hard act to follow.

If such a founder dies naturally while his company is still a success, he and the company are probably very fortunate indeed. This, of course, is not always the case. Indeed, it is not unusual for a founder to maintain confidence in his abilities and his authority into ripe old age, even while his powers to think rationally and make judgments are diminishing. As a result, decisions can easily get made that harm the company, and the founder may unfairly intervene in personnel matters to ensure the entrenchment of "yes" men. Another common scenario is when a founder who has outlived his usefulness suddenly mixes his private affairs with company business, which lowers employee morale and creates unwieldy and unnecessary problems. There can be no doubt that the transition from a founder enterprise to a family enterprise is a complex one.

But these problems can be avoided, and the key to doing so is to have the family plan the succession in advance and, if need be, persuade the founder to resign before irreparable damage gets done and hurts the business everyone has worked so hard to build.

Family Enterprises as Legal Entities

When a family takes over ownership and management of a company from its founder, it is usually assumed by all that the enterprise will continue to exist for generations to come. Since the assets and management of the enterprise handed over to the heir are not his private property, he is not permitted to dispose of them at will, ensuring, most believe, continuity. The same reasoning applies to other members of the family since, despite the fact that the enterprise is a family one, the family is not just a group of individuals who can do as they wish. Although there are no legal barriers that prohibit family members from treating the enterprise as their own private property, there are family enterprise customs that block them from doing so.

It should be understood that family enterprises do have strict rules that facilitate their continued existence. Although these rules, or customs, are not particular to Japan, I would like to use some Japanese examples to help expand our analysis and understanding. In the family precepts of merchants in the Edo era, which were widely introduced by Matao Miyamoto and others, there were a number of stipulations that prohibited family businesses from being treated as the private property of their owners. For example, the Konoike family had precepts stipulating that any family heir must observe the family precepts until the transfer of the enterprise to the next legitimate child. The same family precepts contained a condition that the heir must regard the family estate as something entrusted to him from his ancestors (the family precepts established in 1723).[1] These family precepts clearly illustrate the concept of a family enterprise as a legal entity and of a nature that is beyond the realm of any individual.

In Japan, the idea of restricting an heir from making self-interested, arbitrary decisions about the assets and management of the family business was not restricted to the Edo era. Even in the Meiji period, the family business was thought of as an organization that belonged to the founder's family (including ancestors and descendants) as an entity that existed for the purpose of providing security to the clan. In fact, when an heir created problems through either bad behavior or general incompetence, the right to inherit the business was stripped from him, a process formally known as disherision.

According to Dr. Matao Miyamoto, merchant families in the Edo era were entities that shared many of the same characteristics as a juridical person. As such, since the family considered the family's income more important than the income of any individual family member, management was sometimes transferred to a head clerk, which resulted in a separation of management and ownership that seems strikingly similar to the modern appointment of salaried managers to run family businesses.[2]

On this point, however, my own views do not match those of Miyamoto. I believe that there are two issues here that need to be separated and discussed on different levels: the issue of one individual's value in a family versus the welfare of the whole clan, and the issue of how management responsibility gets transferred to employees from outside the family. In defense of his position Miyamoto uses a Mitsui family document that dates back to the time of the Mitsui Bank's establishment and indicates that Mitsui employees were considered part of the clan's extended family. The document, dated 1874, does not in my view draw such conclusions but instead simply explains that employees must be treated in the same manner as family members. Furthermore, it should be pointed out that the document in question, which describes the restructuring of the Mitsui family as planned by Rizaemon Minomura, was later discarded. It strikes me that a single document should not be extrapolated to infer the management principles of Edo-period merchant families, although the document is admittedly of historical interest.

The Essential Characteristics of a Family Enterprise

Discussions about what actually constitutes a family enterprise usually feature criteria such as self-financing, personal management (referring to a management style or structure where a single individual is in sole command), and an overemphasis on the importance of blood relations, all areas that do not necessarily constitute the essence of what makes up family enterprise since these characteristics are ones not limited to family enterprises. As mentioned earlier, the overemphasis on the importance of blood relations can be regarded as harmful to a family enterprise and, as such, cannot go on indefinitely. Also, the idea that a family enterprise is an unfragmented, united body is problematic since there are any number of cases where the founder's family is divided into several groups, which often results in the breakup of the original family enterprise into pieces with ownership and management of different sections of the company going to one group or another. The newly formed entities then result in the establishment of any number of businesses, all of which, it should be pointed out, are family enterprises still linked by blood if not by common purpose. The situation occurs in other countries as well, of course; in Korea, for example, when related family enterprises come together and form a single, loosely unified group, the group is then classified as a family enterprise.[3] In conclusion, I would like to stress that a family enterprise is one that is owned, managed, and inherited by the family of its founder.

The Development and Limits of Family Enterprises

An Example of a Well-Developed Family Enterprise—The DuPont Company

The business world has borne witness to a number of companies managed by founders' families that have developed into some of the world's leading enterprises. Although these companies are neither founder enterprises nor managerial enterprises owned by the founders' families, family enterprises in the strictest use of the term still represent a phenomenon worthy of further investigation. One good example of this phenomenon is the DuPont Company, the integrated chemical manufacturing giant. Dr. Katsuyuki Ozawa has this to say about DuPont and the du Pont family (although some early members of the family spelled their name "de Pont," the spellings have been consistently rendered "du Pont" throughout this book):

> For 165 years, from the time of the company's founding until its 11th president stepped down in 1967, the positions of company president and chairman were occupied solely by members of the du Pont family (meaning that they were either direct descendents or the spouses of direct descendents). Therefore, until quite recently the du Pont family not only owned the company but was also responsible for its management at the highest levels.[4]

During that 165-year period, the DuPont Company was definitely a family enterprise (according to even the strictest definition) for

130 years, dating from the time its founder, Eltere Irénée du Pont, stepped down from the company's top post, a position he had held for 35 years. For 165 years the DuPont company never stopped growing nor relinquished its position as the world's top chemical company. Examining some of the details, we find that Charles B. McCoy, DuPont's twelfth president, was married to a niece of Walter S. Carpenter, Jr., the ninth president and, given the fact that Carpenter was a nephew of the du Pont brothers (who were the company's sixth to eighth presidents, respectively), it could be said that DuPont retained its classification as a family enterprise right up to the time of its twelfth president. However, as Ozawa has pointed out, after that time and event, DuPont began showing the colors of a managerial enterprise even though the du Pont family still maintained tremendous influence over the company.[5] Notwithstanding, it is highly significant that DuPont continued to develop as a family enterprise for 130 years.

Another Example of a Well-Developed Family Enterprise—The Rothschilds

The Rothschild family enterprise has a longer history than even that of the du Pont family, dating back to the time when Mayer Rothschild, the founder of the Rothschild empire, established a financial business in the Jewish district of Frankfurt, Germany, in the late 1760s.[6] Mayer Rothschild's five sons joined him in the family business, and, amazingly, in the 1780s the five boys combined to set up five bases in five major European cities; it was from these locations that they embarked on successful business careers. The company's history thus dates more than 200 years. The five cities included Frankfurt (eldest son), Vienna (second son), London (third son), Naples (fourth son), and Paris (fifth son). Although the family line of the eldest son provided no sons or continuance, and the business in Naples ceased operations, the family's spread of success was unprecedented; there is no other example of one ancestor begetting so many family branch businesses that became so successful and intertwined that they formed an international network for over 200 years, a network in which information was shared, knowledge exchanged, and capital employed. Since these enterprises were driven by the power of the family, they can be confidently regarded as one type of family enterprise. Despite this, however, reference materials do not easily reveal exactly how the Rothschild family developed their businesses. Several questions remain: Were the Rothschilds really able to maintain a "family enterprise" for over 200 years? (And has the family both owned and managed the company for that long?) Has the scale of the company gone beyond the point where the family is simply attempting to preserve its assets? The mystery, I'm afraid, remains. Answers to these questions and others like them seem almost impossible to obtain.

Other Well-Developed Family Enterprises

Let's assume for a moment that the Rothschilds' business does meet our criteria as to what constitutes a family enterprise, and one that has continued to grow. One reason to allow such speculation is that examples of the long-term development of family enterprises, such as those of the du Ponts and Rothschilds, are few and far between and difficult to come by. In the United States, developed family enterprises are best represented by Ford, J. P. Morgan, the Mellon Group (Alcoa and others), Sears, Roebuck and Company (Rosenwald family), Reynolds (tobacco), Procter & Gamble, Kresge (retail), and Heinz (foods). Companies like McDonald's and Walt Disney have too short a development period to be considered in the league of the others mentioned. To look at other specific cases, the Rockefeller family has significantly lowered the percentage of stock it holds in leading companies such as Exxon, while the Firestone family and the McCormick family have almost completely divested themselves of their holdings in Firestone Tire and International Harvester, respectively.

Chandler has stated that the United Kingdom is one country where family enterprises have remained in continuous existence to a degree greater than in other countries. The reasons behind this, Chandler says, are low economic growth, the low level of organization of large enterprises, and an emphasis on personal management. European scholars (including British scholars) of management history, however, have expressed different views on the makeup of family enterprises.[7] These scholars have noted that family enterprises developed widely not only in the United Kingdom but also in Germany and played major roles in the second industrial revolution, greatly contributing to the technological progress that followed it. However, in expressing their views, many of these same scholars seemed to have confused what Chandler called founder enterprises with family enterprises. If the truth be told, there has not been much research done on successful founder enterprises that later evolved into family enterprises (without becoming managerial enterprises), albeit ones run by the founders' families after the founder either stepped down or passed away.

Looking at Europe as a whole, we find there are not many examples of large family enterprises that have managed to continue developing into the modern day, despite the level of importance placed on such family enterprises by European management history scholars. The major reasons for this dearth of continental family enterprises include the post–World War II nationalization of the family enterprises that cooperated with the German war regime (e.g., France's Renault), breakups resulting from the bifurcation of Germany (e.g., Zeiss of Germany), and the nationalization of major industries under socialist governments. There are, of course, some examples of successful family enterprises, including Pilkington (glass) of the United Kingdom; Siemens (electronics) and Tissen (steel) of Germany; Michelin (tires), Peugeot (automobiles), Saint Gobain (chemicals), and de Vandel (steel) of France; Geigy (pharmaceuticals) of Switzerland; Pirelli (tires) of Italy, and Heineken (beer) of the Netherlands.

The Long-Term Development Difficulties Facing Family Enterprises

An analysis of family enterprises in the United States, Europe, and Asia, including Japan, reveals that the continuous development of any family enterprise lasting over 100 years must be considered very rare indeed. The reasons for this are as follows:

1. The growth period of a family enterprise is usually linked to the period when the business momentum generated by the company's founder is still in effect. Unless family enterprises manage to change this dynamic and strategy, the family firm usually ceases to grow.
2. What often appears to be the long-term development of a family enterprise is actually not the rapid expansion of existing business or the development of new business but actually just the preservation of assets and business handed down through the family.
3. Even if a family enterprise is considered to be in a state of long-term growth, top management is often directed by salaried managers with the enterprise being operated under their guidance. In such cases, the enterprise should be considered a managerial one and not a growing family enterprise, and we should be careful to compare like with like.

As we have mentioned, most founder enterprises are started by individuals of extraordinary ability and, even then, growth does not come easily. Bearing this in mind, it should really come as no surprise that most family enterprises are unable to continue successfully for generation after generation, and although some families are blessed with gifted members, there is no guarantee that they will either be drawn to the family business or that some unforeseen circumstances will not get in the way.

The Limits of Family Enterprises

As mentioned above, the percentage of family enterprises with people from within the family who can live up to the standards set by the company founder is naturally and unavoidably very low. Furthermore, the pool from which to draw the next generation of leaders is also limited, and, above and beyond this, the fact that they are family members can, ironically, work against them. What I mean by this is that any family member who aspires to follow in the founder's footsteps is under more than considerable pressure. Those of mediocre talents tend to rely on the momentum of the founder's success and may either be too lazy or merely incapable of rising above their given station. On the contrary, talented successors may try desperately to supersede the legendary founder and, in doing so, either fly too close to the sun or hit the wall put in place by those who remain in awe of the founder and are unwilling to step outside the boundaries imposed by the founder's legacy. Loyalty is not an easily transferable commodity, and, as many successors have found, it is a sharp, double-edged sword.

The second reason family enterprises and nominated successors fail to succeed is, again ironically, often due to the success of the business. Thanks to the founder's successful efforts, his family has become wealthy. The generation following the founder has had a taste of material wealth, often received a good education, and frequently has been exposed to the wide world beyond the boundaries of the family enterprise. Such circumstances are perfect breeding grounds for the "prodigal son," an heir who develops a deep interest in the arts or other fields but not in the family business. This phenomenon has been called the ***Buddenbrooks*** effect, a term suggested by L. Hannah.[8] Yet even if those destined to succeed to the family business rein in their desires for freedom away from the family, they are often unsuccessful because their spoiled youth makes them mentally or psychologically unfit to be a top manager.

They may be arrogant. They may be narrow-minded. They may have grown up only with privileged friends like themselves and know little of "real" people and the real world outside the ivory tower. Once again, the potential for failure is enormous.

Yet, the above scenarios do not spell certain gloom. Often the still-wet-behind-the-ears successors may be given effective family support, and such assistance usually increases the chances that the family enterprise can continue on the course of self-preservation, growth, and development. Despite this optimistic note, however, we should not forget that there's a limit to the human resources within any family and the people capable of providing support may just not be there.

Personal Management

The shortage of human resources is not the only factor that limits the growth of a family enterprise. There are numerous examples to demonstrate that the operation of many family enterprises is based upon a mutual trust among the blood relatives. Although one might surmise that trust is an admirable quality, the overreliance on trust can lead to delays in the establishment of formal organizational structures, or an overemphasis on what might be termed extremely ad hoc management structures. For example, some family enterprises might even hold "board of directors meetings," but owing to the power of the clan-leading CEO these meetings are but mere formalities with important matters decided by the CEO (a family member, of course) or by the CEO in conjunction with family members close to him. Key management decisions in such cases are often made in unstructured ways for unsystematic, family-related reasons.

A. D. Chandler has attributed setbacks in the development of the British economy (relative to that of the American and German economies) to the culture of personal management distinctive to the family enterprises found widely in the United Kingdom, and he has concluded that the British economy is essentially one of individualistic, or personal capitalism.[9] At the same time, however, it is important to note that some European management history researchers (including some from Britain) have been critical of Chandler for placing too much emphasis on family enterprises, particularly their use of personal management, as the reason for declines and periods of stagnation of the British economy that started in the late nineteenth century. One example of a dissenting voice is that expressed by Roy Church in his article, "The Family Firm in Industrial Capitalism: International Perspectives on Hypothesis and History."[10]

I think that Church and other researchers are dissatisfied with Chandler for his criticism of British family enterprises without having fully examined the extensive research done by British scholars of management history, a viewpoint I can well understand. However, we also should keep in mind that Chandler looks at family enterprises in comparative contexts, contrasting family enterprises with enterprises that employ salaried managers and thus use different managerial hierarchies. Church and other researchers critical of Chandler take the position that family-owned enterprises are not peculiar to the United Kingdom and cite examples such as Germany (or Japan, for that matter). What may be different, however, is the dynamic quality of the postwar German and Japanese economies, and the criticism of Chandler may just be the result of using a different frame of reference.[11]

In his studies, Chandler has also looked at the interactions between the owners of family-run German business and salaried managers, and the functioning of the managerial hierarchies that existed within this context.[12] What Chandler has referred to, however, when considering similar issues, is the Japanese *zaibatsu*.[13] Interestingly, the *zaibatsu* (with a few exceptions) actually helped contribute to the growth of the Japanese economy without being affected by the harmful aspects of personal management, largely owing to the roles and performance of the salaried managers, who were both well educated and rewarded for their competence by being promoted and becoming part of the managerial hierarchies. *Zaibatsu*, it should be made clear, were not simply family enterprises. Some *zaibatsu*, such as Mitsui and Sumitomo, were actually managerial enterprises because salaried managers were given top-level decision-making powers by the families. Although Church has referred to my book *Zaibatsu* in the work mentioned above, discussion of this important point is missing.

The Limitations of Church's Views

As we have seen, Roy Church has been critical of Chandler regarding the role of family enterprises in the historical ups and downs of the British economy. Church has also concluded that the business structures within the economies of the United Kingdom, Germany, and Japan between World War I and World War II were very similar. Church even notes that there's seemingly little difference in the decision-making rationales of family enterprises and managerial enterprises in each of these countries, and that if there are any disparities in the functions of the family enterprises in each country, they are mainly attributable to cultural differences.[14] I must say, however, that I question whether Church fully understands the true difference between family-owned enterprises and family enterprises. Although Church states that a number of family-owned enterprises, both large and small, developed in Germany, the United Kingdom, and Japan between World War I and World War II, and in the post–World War II period, and contributed to economic growth in each country, I have strong suspicions that quite a few of these businesses were actually family-owned enterprises in which salaried managers were in charge of top management with the enterprises run under their command. In Church's analysis, there seems to be no provisions for a category of enterprise owned by the family and managed by salaried managers.

By this point, it should seem clear that families that continually attempt to retain top-management positions and authority are essentially signing a death warrant for their enterprise. The odds against their succeeding are huge: there is a chronic shortage of suitable successors and individually driven management (which we've termed "personal management") has its own insidious effects destined to make the enterprise less competitive over the long term. We will come back to this topic later.

At the same time, however, I do not wish to suggest that family enterprises are hopeless and have no future. Some European family enterprises have certainly been around for a long time, as Church and others have pointed out. But it is important to determine whether they are active, growing businesses, or just ones that merely exist for the sake of existing.[15]

Crises in Family Enterprises

If the goal of a family enterprise is simply to stay in business and avoid bankruptcy, its goal is certainly much more achievable than if the objective is growth and development. That is, of course, assuming that the family business has not been burdened with a totally irresponsible or incompetent heir in the role of top manager or that some feud has not torn the family apart. Although there seems to be no reliable information about whether the number of family enterprise failures caused by family disputes is greater than those caused by incapable heirs, I can state categorically that there's no easy way to prevent disputes from erupting within a family over a company's assets and its management. In some cases, blood is *not* thicker than water, especially if money and power are involved.

There are many examples from the past and present and from all over the world that show that establishment of family rules concerning a family firm's assets and management is the most effective way of preventing disputes from arising within the family. One example is the Mitsui clan, where Takatoshi Mitsui and his descendants managed to maintain the Mitsui family's business thanks to the family management systems established by their ancestors, including Takatoshi.[16] Although significant effort is required, it is possible (albeit difficult) for family enterprises to carry on through any number of generations. Bad luck, of course, sometimes comes into play and this bad luck usually takes the form of an incompetent or untrustworthy heir.

Efforts to Preserve Family Enterprises

Needless to say, key factors in management environments, such as the market and technologies, are constantly changing. This is also true of the life cycles of the products and services offered by companies. Even if the goal of the company is not to grow but simply to maintain its status quo, managers of family enterprises must be sensitive to the changing world, changing markets, new information, and the latest trends. What's more, these managers must not only be aware of these changes but must also act in response to them.

Let's now look at some examples—and some contrasts. Toraya was a company that had made sweet bean jelly for an astonishing 400 years. From their humble origins, Toraya made the following changes: they adopted partial automation; they began distributing their products through department stores; they got involved in exporting; and they even began creating some new products (such as *Yokan* de Paris, a French twist on a traditional Japanese sweet) to cater to their export market. A Japanese confectioner with a similarly long history (370 years) but a different approach was the Fujimura Company. Yet despite the similarities in age, Fujimura has taken a completely different approach. They have firmly maintained their traditional approach to the production and the selling of their products in shops. What these two companies *do* have in common is that both are doing their best to preserve the family business.[17] Although both approaches have their difficulties, if the goal of a family enterprise is to preserve itself and its business, even with a minimal growth rate, this objective can be achieved by family members' handing down the skills accumulated over years of experiences without having to rely on a layer of salaried employees.

Cooperation and Conflict between the Family and Salaried Managers

The Significance of Salaried Managers in Family Enterprises

If the goal of a family enterprise is development, there are a number of reasons that it is undesirable for the company's top management to be composed solely of family members. First, unlike the founder and salaried managers, the founder's family does not usually have as much interest in, information about, or experience with the management of the company. Second, in many cases, although some family members try to overcome their shortcomings by working for the family enterprise while they are young in order to satisfy their interests, acquire information, and gain experience, as explained above, they are at a considerable disadvantage in comparison to the founder. While the founder had to scratch and claw his way to the top of the heap and learn firsthand about the survival of the fittest, those who follow have far easier—but less valuable—experiences. Third, although a family might produce an extraordinary, charismatic, larger-than-life figure in the form of their company's founder, such individuals are few and far between, especially in one family. Numerically, the odds work against families because most families just do not have a large enough pool of candidates to pick up where the founder left off. For this reason, salaried managers offer a more likely route to a successful future; put simply, there are just so many more of them.

Given the above, if a family enterprise wants to grow and move beyond mere existence, cooperation with salaried managers, particularly those engaged as top-level managers, becomes necessary. At this stage, the overall framework of the family enterprise is still intact and the enterprise has not yet become a managerial enterprise, or one in which the salaried managers are delegated the overall power of top management. Within the family-enterprise structure, the cooperation of salaried managers at the top level can be obtained by reorganizing top management and by sharing the positions among the family members and salaried managers.

The DuPont Example

I would now like to look at the example of the DuPont Company. Let's travel back to the beginning of the twentieth century, when T. Coleman du Pont was appointed as the DuPont Company president, Alfred was appointed vice president (and manager of the Black Powder Department), Pierre was appointed manager of the Treasury Department, and Francis was appointed manager of the Smokeless Powder Department. With this arrangement, four of the seven positions on the Executive Committee, including CEO, were occupied by the du Pont family and the rest were occupied by salaried managers. The three salaried managers were Hamilton Barksdale, Dynamite Department manager; J. Amory Haskell, manager of the Sales Department; and Arthur Moxham, manager of the Development Department (as of 1903).[18]

By around 1910, the position of CEO was separated from the Executive Committee and a new system was established, one in which the CEO was selected from the du Pont family and most Executive Committee members were selected from among the salaried managers. Excepting the CEO (Coleman du Pont), the acting president (Pierre du Pont), and one Executive Committee member (Lammot du Pont, manager of the New Black Powder Department) of the seven Executive Committee members, all the top-management positions were occupied by salaried managers (as of 1914).[19] This structure remained virtually unchanged even after World War I. With Irénée du Pont as CEO, two out of the nine Executive Committee members were from the du Pont family (the other being Lammot du Pont, the chairman), and six of the 11 Finance Committee members were from the du Pont family (as of May 1919).[20] As we can see, the du Pont family managed to have their cake and eat it too. There was cooperation between the founder's family and their salaried managers, yet the position of the family as owners and controllers was not threatened. DuPont's long and successful development as a family enterprise owes much to this arrangement between family and managers who came from beyond the boundaries of the du Pont family.

Conflict between the Family and Salaried Managers

In the management of family enterprises, it is by no means a given that good and cooperative relationships exist between the family and salaried managers. In fact, it's more natural for the family and salaried managers to distrust each other to a certain extent and for conflict to be ongoing.

It is an axiom of human relationships that the best and most cooperative relationships are those that have both sides making a concerted effort to have the relationship work. In recent years, business managers have become more aware of this axiom, and it is becoming more unusual for a founder's family to regard their salaried managers either as mere followers who can be led by the nose or as threats to the family's assets if the family is not constantly on guard. Another factor that has influenced the relationship between family owners and hired managers is industrialization. When industrialization is advanced, family enterprises tend to be larger, salaried managers tend to be better educated and have greater management and technical skills, and the family's ideas about how to approach its enterprise are more sophisticated. The result of this advancement is that conflicts should decrease and cooperation improve.

The source of much conflict is the deeply inbred idea that a family enterprise is a family asset inherited from the founder, and one that should be passed down from generation to generation forever. If a family is committed to this line of thought, the tendency is to think that management should be totally controlled by the family. After all, the family owns the company, the thinking goes. Paired with this belief is the idea that salaried managers should never rise above middle or lower management.

Circumstances change, however, when a family enterprise grows larger and its management becomes more complex. The family might suddenly find itself unable to handle the top-management chores and has no choice but to have salaried managers join their top-management team. At this stage, it's still quite common for the family to believe the situation is only temporary, and that it is family only who should rightfully occupy the top-management positions. An example of this possessive mentality in family enterprises is when the founder has become seriously ill or died and the successor is not yet ready to take over the business. In this case, a salaried manager is often appointed CEO, albeit as a temporary measure;

when the successor matures (with the salaried manager becoming responsible for teaching the designated heir how to become CEO) the salaried manager serving as CEO is then expected to relinquish his post to the successor since, after all, the salaried manager is from outside the clan.

In the case where a family enterprise regularly integrates salaried managers into the company's top management (although not as CEO since this would jeopardize the company as a family enterprise) there is often ample distrust and worry on the part of the family. It may suspect that these managers are taking imprudent risks, that they are expanding too fast, and that they are spending too much on risky investments and are looking for ever-higher salaries. The fear in this case is based on the survival instinct, because the family is usually well aware that bad investments could mean the end of their enterprise and a loss of assets.[21] Such fixed ideas on the part of a founder's family are not easily discarded, so it is quite normal for salaried managers and founder families to have relationships characterized by conflict.

Conversion from a Family Enterprise to a Managerial Enterprise

Comparisons of Family Enterprises to Managerial Enterprises

Discussions of whether family enterprises are superior to managerial enterprises or vice versa draw wide interest from a range of individuals, both management scholars and nonresearchers alike. I too have an interest in this issue and have noted publicly that there are limits to family enterprises in terms of their management potential and that, for the long-term development of their enterprises, families must rely on salaried managers. For family enterprises to develop and grow continually, they have no other choice than to become managerial enterprises. Having said that, however, I am not prepared to argue that managerial enterprises are superior to family ones.

As might be expected, family enterprises tend to place a priority on benefits to the family, while the actions of managerial enterprises are based purely on economic motives. Also, there are those who believe that the managers of managerial enterprises are better educated than those of family enterprises, and in family enterprises there is constant conflict within the family concerning assets and management. For these reasons, some contend that managerial enterprises are superior to family enterprises. There is a counterargument, however, that says that family enterprises are superior because salaried managers of managerial enterprises are interested only in protecting their positions and remuneration and that family enterprises have a lot of inherent advantages, such as cohesiveness, strong ties, loyalty, and quick decision making. What's more, the assumption about managers of managerial enterprises being better educated has been challenged.[22] Discussions of the superiority of the two types of enterprise is thus meaningless, as it is impossible to make simple generalizations about their characteristics.

If we were to look for hard evidence favoring one or the other kind of enterprise, we would be hard pressed to come to any certain conclusions. We can't, for example, demonstrate that the decision-making processes of family managers in family enterprises are totally conservative, as some believe. By the same token, we can't prove that all decision making in managerial enterprises is done through laborious and time-consuming discussions that inhibit dynamism. In the end, much of management decision making and action comes down to human qualities that are monopolized by neither family enterprises nor managerial ones. Selfishness, a tendency to gamble on risky investments, a desire to own land, a love for hobnobbing with the rich and famous, flexibility, a strong and unique corporate culture—these qualities are relentlessly egalitarian and can be found anywhere regardless of management structure or type of enterprise.

Some management history researchers in various countries compare family and managerial enterprises by saying that managerial enterprises dynamically adjust to changes in technology and the market by establishing bureaucratic systems composed of middle and lower managers and technical and marketing experts. Family enterprises, on the other hand, do not establish such bureaucratic systems, which inhibit the formation of a strong organization.[23] However, as Harold Livesay emphasizes and as the examples of DuPont, Matsushita, and Sony demonstrate, family enterprises can have bureaucratic systems.[24] As I described earlier, the challenge for family enterprises is to coexist with networks of skilled people, but this is an issue that should be discussed separately.

It is meaningless to compare family enterprises with managerial enterprises in terms of superiority. In Japan, Bridgestone, a family enterprise, is the leader in the tire business, while a managerial enterprise, Kao, is the leader in the toiletry business. What's more, the second-place company in the toiletry business is Lion, a family enterprise. Such examples are common, so these discussions about superiority are not constructive. I think the most important thing to examine is the type of enterprise that can generate the most economic growth.

The Superiority of Managerial Enterprises as a Trend

I would like to emphasize the following points once again:

1. From the perspective of executive-level human resources, the talent pool for salaried managers is much larger than that of any founder's family.
2. Generally, members of the founder's family grow up in a less stressful environment than do salaried managers.
3. A founder's family cannot escape from believing in the importance of the family name and the need to maintain the family's assets and tends to think that profits belong to the family, which owns the business. Salaried managers are free from such constraints. These variations result in policy differences between family enterprises and managerial enterprises in diverse areas, including dividends and taxes.
4. Generally, after the founder's death, salaried managers, particularly those who have worked at every level in the managerial hierarchy and have polished their management skills, have a better understanding of the day-to-day operations of the company than do members of the founder's family.
5. If the top manager makes a major mistake or becomes a source of conflict within the company through arbitrary management practices, he must be replaced. In such situations, a salaried manager is easier to replace than a member of the founder's family (it is even more difficult when the top manager is the founder).

These points do not suggest which of these two types of enterprise is superior; each company has different characteristics based on the environment within it and the personality and capabilities of its top manager. Factors that are negative for some companies can be positive for others.

Some managers of family enterprises are well aware of their weaknesses. As Werner Siemens has noted, "Making money is a lot of fun. But making money does not guarantee survival in terms of the continuation of the family system."[25] Siemens realized that in a family enterprise, profit making and long-term goals can run contrary to each other. In examining the relationship between family enterprises and managerial enterprises, it is evident that the latter has more potential for long-term growth. In other words, managerial enterprises have a better chance of attaining long-term results that correspond to economic growth. Therefore, family enterprises seeking long-term growth convert to managerial enterprises, so I think it reasonable to conclude that managerial enterprises dominate capitalist economies.

Conversion to Managerial Enterprises

Chandler has noted that one method for examining the development of managerial enterprises is to focus on the evolution of managerial hierarchies in integrated industrialized enterprises, the largest and most complex managerial hierarchies.[26] Chandler's noting of this method shows that in his discussions on managerial enterprises, he focuses on their managerial hierarchies and vertical integration. According to Chandler, in the United States and Europe vertical integration takes place in industrialized enterprises in the order of foward integration followed by backward integration. The integration of research and development does not often occur. In addition, enterprises expand their activities through multinationalization and by increasing their product lines. Vertical integration encourages the formation of large, integrated production departments and distribution departments that are capital intensive and centralized. This integration requires economy of scale and the rapid flow of throughputs (processes between the raw materials suppliers and end-users) and a managerial hierarchy in which human resources in a wide range of jobs are combined at various levels.

If a labor-intensive industrialized enterprise is without integrated departments and doesn't need a managerial hierarchy of highly skilled personnel, either the founder's family, bank agents, or major shareholders can maintain power to control top management. Once a managerial hierarchy is formed, however, even these powerful groups can no longer maintain power. Chandler explains that this is how a managerial enterprise in which salaried managers control the top management is formed.[27] Despite this explanation, some questions remain. Why can the capitalists not control the top management under a managerial hierarchy? Why do salaried managers need to make top-level decisions? As Chandler offers no clear answers to these questions, I have constructed my own views based on what Chandler has noted and the context of his reports.

A managerial hierarchy is not simply a bureaucratic system or a communications route for commands and reports; rather, it is a complex hierarchy of people with management and technical skills, including top, middle, and lower managers, technicians, and other members of the labor force. Chandler is also aware of this.[28] For a company to survive and grow in an environment characterized by expanding markets, rapid technological progress, and severe competition, its managerial hierarchy must be effectively utilized. To ensure that this hierarchy is used effectively, the top manager must be a person with the following qualities:

1. Able to handle a rapidly and dramatically changing management environment—in other words, a person with foresight and the ability to make correct judgments and decisions.
2. Has a concept of the company's long-term growth, a clear philosophy and goals, and a technological orientation.
3. Able to coordinate large groups of managers and technicians under a managerial hierarchy; is trustworthy, logical, and inclined to share information and values.

Unless people with the above qualities become top managers, family enterprises are destined to be unable to grow in severe, competitive business environments.

At the same time, people with the above skills are rare finds. Although it's difficult to find such people even in a large labor pool such as that of salaried managers, finding such people in a founder's family is an even greater challenge. Of the three categories of qualities that we've defined as requisite for top managers, it's possible that some family members may have qualities (1) and (2), even if they may lack sufficient information or on-the-job experience. The qualities in category (3) are the most difficult to foster among members of a founder's family. Given this, salaried managers have a much better chance of becoming top managers because they have been trained and promoted for a long time within the managerial hierarchies and can be comfortable with the managerial hierarchies necessary to compete in severe, competitive environments. In other words, it should come as no surprise that family enterprises seeking continuous growth and development often feel a compelling need to become managerial enterprises.

Variations

To recap briefly, the above section discusses some of the most common ways that managerial enterprises develop from former incarnations as family enterprises. Once again, much of my research on this subject has been based on the model developed by Chandler. Naturally, there are also atypical ways in which family enterprises are transformed into managerial enterprises.

Let's look at some of those transformation patterns. One such case is when a family enterprise faces dramatic changes in its management environment before having a chance to form some kind of managerial hierarchy. In this case, the family company usually resorts to custom and continues with its long-established way of doing business. Crisis is often the result. To avoid such traps, the family enterprise must act quickly and appoint salaried managers capable of solving these problems. In this scenario, however, the family enterprise often becomes a managerial enterprise almost overnight, such as the case of the Mitsui *zaibatsu*.[29]

Of course, crisis situations are not the only way in which managerial enterprises are formed. In Japan alone there are plenty of cases of enterprises that began as managerial enterprises, with accompanying managerial hierarchies developing as the firm's top salaried managers employ well-educated people as middle and lower managers.[30] In order to understand variations in the formation of managerial enterprises, it is necessary to take a more in-depth look.

Managerial hierarchies are not always formed because of the need for vertical integration. There are many forms of cooperation between the founder's family and top salaried managers, and managerial enterprises are not the de facto result when a founder's family totally populates its top-management positions with salaried managers. In some cases, the family and the salaried managers run the business cooperatively. In others, salaried managers have full-time positions and family members part-time ones. In another variation, sometimes the family entrusts top management to salaried managers but maintains the right to appoint and fire salaried managers.

The ultimate form of managerial enterprise, in which salaried managers are responsible for the management of personnel, is not a structure that develops very quickly. Moreover, there are examples of managerial enterprise that are far more complex in their makeup and how they're created. Imagine, if you will, a case where the founder's family appears to give full top-management responsibility (including the right to appoint and dismiss lower-level managers) to their salaried managers but in reality maintains its influence and implement its rights in unofficial ways. Another example of the complicated interplay that can take place between family and managerial enterprise is when a family that holds a majority of the company's stock decides to reclaim the top-management roles formerly entrusted to their salaried managers.[31] These situations will be discussed in more detail later.

The Examples of the Zaibatsu

We have been examining the various processes by which companies are transformed from family enterprises into managerial enterprises. In Japan prior to the Second World War, there were a few other significant variations on this process, most notably that of the *zaibatsu*. Let us now take a few moments to explore this theme.

My views concerning the *zaibatsu* system have drawn comments from researchers outside of Japan, a fact of which I'm most appreciative. Having said this, however, as in the example of Church, above, it can be problematic to enter into such discussions when it may be that the understanding of my views is not complete. First, not a few of these researchers have misconstrued *zaibatsu* as a flexible organization in which a large family enterprise is successfully allowed to grow while the family maintains overall control.[32] Although such types of *zaibatsu* do exist, there are many other types as well. Some *zaibatsu* (Mitsui, Mitsubishi, Sumitomo) conform successfully to the above definition while others (Asano, Yasuda, Suzuki) do not. Furthermore, the different ways in which *zaibatsu* developed is another indicator of their heterogeneous nature. Mitsui and Sumitomo, for example, became managerial enterprises. Suzuki became a managerial enterprise controlled by an outside financial institution. Mitsubishi was being transformed into a managerial enterprise where cooperation between family and salaried managers was the order of the day, and others like Asano and Yasuda stubbornly maintained their status as family enterprises. From these examples alone it should be clear that *zaibatsu* took on many forms and, as a next step, in the following section, I'd like to explain how both *zaibatsu* and other large enterprises became part of a trend toward the development of managerial enterprises.

Perspectives on Newly Industrialized Countries

Issues

Above, we have been examining enterprise transformation processes: founder enterprises transforming to family enterprises, and family enterprises changing into managerial ones—both processes, I believe, that are universal. Having said that, however, we have only examined European, North American, and Japanese cases, so it is now necessary to take a look at the newly industrialized countries in East Asia and Southeast Asia before categorically declaring that the process is universal. And although there is, of course, an argument for examining the formerly communist countries, the collapse of communism is still so recent that the situation in many of these countries is still so much in flux that accurate analysis is, for the present time, essentially impossible.

Viewpoints from Ryuichiro Inoue

Dr. Ryuichiro Inoue is a highly respected researcher of *zaibatsu* and enterprises in the newly industrialized countries of Southeast Asia, and I have drawn on some of his research results in my discussions of business enterprise in the area.[33] Inoue's studies have focused on the rapid advance of industrialization in the newly industrialized countries of Southeast Asia during the 1970s and 1980s. In particular, he also looks at the *zaibatsu* and private enterprises in these economies, both of which were driving forces in the industrialization process. Although these enterprises conducted their activities in their own ways and handled governments and foreign capital using different methods, the desire to internationalize and increase foreign investment was common to all of them. When discussing these non-Japanese Asian *zaibatsu*, Inoue referred to my definition of the term, saying "that it [the definition] applies to most of the *zaibatsu* in Asia."[34] At the same time, Inoue also noted that one of the most distinctive characteristics of Asian *zaibatsu* is that the *zaibatsu* families maintain closed ownership and control over their operations.[35] The power of the family, even if *zaibatsu* are thrown into the equation as a type of family enterprise, is remarkable. According to Inoue, the reason for this level of control is that the founders are for the most part still in power or, alternatively, the founders' progeny have just inherited the businesses. Since most Asian *zaibatsu* were founded and developed after World War II, attrition has yet to take its toll and the exclusive management of the *zaibatsu* by their founding families is still common.[36]

Despite the above examples, there are cases in the Asian context where managerial power is not centered purely on the founder. Key posts may be given to the founder's family and/or salaried managers, or the business may be operated under a council system. Inoue also notes that, recently, when management gets handed over from founder to family, one of two things tends to happen. The first is that the top-management post goes to someone in the family who is capable enough to handle the job. The second is that the family appoints reliable salaried managers to powerful positions where part of their responsibility is to assist the successor in the development of the business and the successor's management skills.[37] In other words, although the strong family management system is still distinctive, the managers of family enterprises have become more professional and they are also hiring more highly educated and capable employees.

According to Inoue's analysis, it seems clear that the trend in Asia is for family enterprises to gradually become managerial enterprises. Inoue explains this by noting that Asian *zaibatsu* are committed to accepting foreign capital and technology in order to become more high tech, have a greater heavy-industry focus, and be more export oriented. With the intense globalizations of economies and resultant competition, the *zaibatsu* are faced with little choice. To facilitate the changes necessary to keep up international competition, Asian enterprises face the challenge of finding capable personnel. These people must be international in outlook and be advanced in terms of both management and technical ability. Proof of this contention rests in the fact that highly educated people who have studied overseas are in great demand.

It seems certain that there are enterprises in India and other countries in East and Southeast Asia that are striving to become more international and more industrialized. To succeed in the current competitive environment, a company must hire and train its key personnel. What these enterprises need are top managers who have advanced management, technological, and marketing skills. When these managers take their place on the broad stage of global business, their first task is to build human networks and a business structure that can utilize those networks. In other words, what is needed are competent managerial hierarchies. If, in the process, family enterprises fall by the wayside and are transformed into managerial enterprises, so be it. Progress is a demanding taskmaster and the facts of the new world order of business add an urgency unlike anything that the business world has ever seen.

Perspectives on Managerial Enterprises

In his book on Asian enterprises, Inoue introduced some 32 Asian companies. Given the fact, however, that this research was published in 1987 (and that no Indian enterprises were included), I have taken the step of reexamining the situation based both on Inoue's research results and that of other researchers. Table 2.1 shows representative Asian *zaibatsu*.

As table 2.1 shows and as Inoue has noted, the enterprises listed are generally eager to hire or promote well-educated salaried managers. Most of these enterprises, however, allow salaried managers only to become middle managers (or top managers of subsidiaries), very few of them allow salaried managers to become head office CEOs. As family enterprises hire more well-educated people who've gone to school in the United States, Japan, and other developed countries, it reflects well on the family and their business and even encourages family managers to better educate themselves. What's more, these skilled and educated employees help create the kinds of networks that can lead their companies into the future.

Based on his examination of specific examples from Thailand, Dr. Akira Suehiro has noted that the families themselves do not facilitate the conversion to managerial enterprises.[38] Despite this resistance, the networks of highly educated managers and technicians hired by a family enterprise may nonetheless become a driving force in transforming the family business into a managerial enterprise. The influence of networks should thus not be underestimated.

In his book, Inoue has written about Byung-Chol Lee, who was chairman of the South Korean giant Samsung in 1987. Inoue notes that Lee showed a penchant for replacing incompetent family members of the management team with salaried managers. By taking this action, Lee not only removed unproductive managers but also separated the family capital from company management, which helped upgrade the company's human resources. As a result, Samsung became well known in the business world for its innovative personnel policies. Thirty years after the 1956 adoption of an open employment system (in which even the company chairman was in-

Table 2.1. Representative Asian *Zaibatsu* (groups)

Country/ Region	No.	*Zaibatsu* (group)	Primary Businesses	Leader	Promotion of Salaried Managers
Hong Kong	1	Ka-Shing Li	International conglomerate, real estate	Ka-Shing Li (founder)	
	2	Y. K. Pao	Marine transport, commerce, finance, real estate, others	Y. K. Pao (founder)	
Taiwan	3	Taiso	Plastics-processing, others	Yung-Ching Wang (founder)	**
	4	Tatung	Electricity electronics, machinery, others	Tei-sei Lin II	**
	5	Tainan Spinning	Foods, fibers, others	Multiple investors	**
Korea	6	Daewoo	Automobile parts and other machinery, trading, securities, others	Woo-Jung Kim (founder)	****
	7	Lucky Goldstar	Chemicals, electrical/electronic machinery, others	Jagyon Gu (2nd)	***
	8	Hyundai	Automobiles, iron manufacturing, heavy industry, including shipbuilding	Ju-Young Chung (founder)	**
	9	Samsung	Electronics, trading, others	Gon-Hi Lee (founder's third son)	**
Thailand	10	Bangkok Bank	Banking, insurance, investment trusts, soft drinks, sugar-refining, others	Small group of sons of the late Sophonpanich Chin	*
	11	CP Group	Agribusiness (feed, chemical-fertilizers, broilers, others)	Chiarawan On (founder) family	**

(*continued*)

Table 2.1. *(continued)*

Country/ Region	No.	*Zaibatsu* (group)	Primary Businesses	Leader	Promotion of Salaried Managers
	12	Saha Group	Toiletries, shoes, apparel, foods, electronics, others	Chokwatana Tiam (founder) family	**
	13	Siam Cement	Cement, engines, paper, cathode-ray tubes, plastics, others	Royal family of Thailand	**
Indonesia	14	Liem	Fibers, real estate, commerce, others	Liong Sioe Liong (founder)	**
	15	Astra	Automobile sales, agriculture, forestry, fisheries, real estate, finance	William Suryadjaya (founder)	**
	16	Rodamas	Chemicals, electric machinery, others	Siong Kie Tan (founder)	**
	17	Bakrie	Steel, finance, plantations, others	Abrizal Bakrie (2nd)	**
The Philippines	18	Ayala	Finance, real estate, agriculture, others	Jaime Zobel Sobel IX	**
	19	Soriano	Steel piping, beer, finance, others	Andres Soriano III	**
Malaysia	20	Kuok	Sugar-refining, flour, cement, hotels, marine transportation, others	Robert Kuok (founder)	
Singapore	21	OCBC	Banking		*
	22	UOB	Banking, securities, real estate, hotels, others	Wee-Cho Yaw II	**
	23	Khoo Tech Puat	Hotels, real estate, banking, others	Tan Sri Khoo Teck Puat (founder)	

(continued)

Table 2.1. (*continued*)

Country/ Region	No.	*Zaibatsu* (group)	Primary Businesses	Leader	Promotion of Salaried Managers
India	24	Tatas	Iron manufacturing, others		**
	25	Birlas	Cotton, others	G. D. Birlas (founder)	**

Notes: The symbols in the far right column represent the following:
* = An enterprise that appoints (or has allowed) salaried managers to top-management positions in the head office.

** = An enterprise eager to hire well-educated people, but one that doesn't appoint them to head-office top-management positions. At best, these highly educated salaried managers can become vice presidents, department managers, or subsidiary presidents.

*** = A family enterprise not particularly eager to hire well-educated people.

**** = An enterprise in which the family and general investors either cooperate with or are in opposition to each other. Salaried managers have a low status.

Sources: 1–10, 14–23: Ryuichiro Inoue, *Asia no Zaibatsu to Kigyo (Asian Zaibatsu and Enterprises).*

6–9: Tamio Hattori, *Keieishi Gakkai Dai 29 Kai Taikai Hokoku, Dotaikai Hokokushu, (Report of the 29th Conference of the Management History Society, Report of the Conference)* 1993.

10–13: Akira Suehiro and Makoto Nanbara, *Thai no Zaibatsu Family Business to Keiei Kaikaku (Zaibatsu in Thailand—Family Businesses and Management Reform)* (Dobunkan, 1991.)

24–25: Shoji Ito, "India," in *Sekai no Zaibatsu Keiei (Zaibatsu Management around the World),* Shinichi Yonekawa eds. (Nihon Keizai Shinbunsha, 1981).

volved in hiring) its influence was still apparent. Of 149 managers within the Samsung group, 104 had been promoted from within the group, while only 37 had been recruited from outside.[39]

Although Thailand CP Group has maintained family control over the entire group, it has also introduced a departmental division system in which nonfamily members are appointed as department managers. Also, group policy clearly stipulates that investment and personnel are the responsibility of departmental managers.[40] Furthermore, some of the organizations' highly educated, elite technical people have been appointed as head-office vice presidents, where they're in charge of the technical fields in which they specialize. To conclude, after looking at examples of family enterprises in some of Asia's newly industrialized countries, we have seen that the same sorts of relationships between managerial enterprises and managerial hierarchies that exist in other countries can also be observed here.

CHAPTER THREE

Development of Managerial Enterprises in Japan

Salaried Managers on the Board of Directors

In this chapter I present several tables and explain some basic facts pertaining to long-term trends in the development of managerial enterprises in Japan. Table 3.1 shows the number of salaried managers on the boards of directors of large, leading enterprises in 1905, 1913, and 1930 (respectively), as well as the board membership percentages that these numbers represent. A definition of the term "large, leading enterprise" is contained in the notes.

Salaried Managers in 1905

In 1905 there were 75 large, leading enterprises, and in as many as 47 of them (over 60%) no salaried managers attended board of directors meetings. If the number of former bureaucrats who were invited to become directors, but who were not large shareholders, is included in the number of salaried managers, 33 enterprises out of 75 large, leading enterprises had no salaried managers attending directors meetings. There were 22 enterprises (32, if former bureaucrats are included) in which one salaried manager attended the meetings and only five enterprises in which two or more attended.

At the turn of the twentieth century, the status of employees at enterprises in Japan (even white-collar employees) was still low. To have a more concrete understanding of this situation, let's now have a look at the example of Kyozo Kikuchi, who was a product of that era.[1] After graduating from the Mechanical Engineering Department of the Institute of Engineering, Kikuchi joined the navy and the Osaka Mint Bureau. He then entered the Hirano Spinning Company under the condition that he go abroad to study. Kikuchi was likely to receive such consideration because he was one of the few university graduates working in the cotton spinning industry in those days. After studying in the United Kingdom (where he worked in a factory by day and studied at Manchester Technical School at night) and returning to Japan, he was offered jobs by two companies, the Amagasaki Boseki Company and Settsu Boseki Company, and he joined both while staying at Hirano. He worked for three companies (Hirano, Amagasaki, and Settsu) as both a manager and head of engineering. Although he was much in demand, his social status as an engineer was not high and Hirano had a corporate rule that stipulated that engineers were not to become executives. Kikuchi was disappointed with this corporate policy and felt, it seems with some justification, that it was very unfair.[2] In June 1893, however, he was appointed director of Amagasaki through the efforts of Motonosuke Fukumoto, the president of Amagasaki, who was both a wealthy man and, for Osaka, unusually progressive. In 1901 Fukumoto resigned and appointed Kikuchi president despite objections and rival candidacy from large shareholders and other executives.[3] Even though Kikuchi was a great asset to the spinning industry in this period, he would have been thwarted in his attempts to become a director and subsequently president of a company except for the efforts of a progressive, open-minded capitalist in the form of Fukumoto. The numbers in the 1905 column in table 3.1 clearly indicate the low social status of white collar employees at that time.

Large-Shareholder Executives Working for Several Enterprises

The stock company system was introduced to Japan relatively early and progressed quickly compared to developed western nations. (A national bank founded in 1872 was the first basic stock enterprise.) Such initiative was quite understandable for a developing country eager for rapid economic growth. However, since Japan had long been a country closed to foreigners under a policy of isolation, and one that did not accumulate wealth through foreign trading, the stock company system developed in a rather distinctive manner. Although a number of stock companies in various fields were founded in rapid succession, there was a limited number of wealthy people capable of providing the working capital necessary

Table 3.1. Number of Salaried Managers on Boards of Directors of Large, Leading Enterprises

		Number of Salaried Managers					
Year	Number of Large Enterprises	0	1	2 or More	2 or More up to Half the Total	Over Half	Unknown
1905	75	47 [33]	22 [32]	5 [9]			1 [1]
1913	115	48 [39]	38 [39]	29 [37]			
1930	158	15 [11]	27 [17]	113 [127]	71 [75]	42 [52]	3 [3]

Notes: The following enterprises (unlimited partnerships, limited partnerships, and stock companies) are considered large, leading enterprises in each of these years:

1905: Enterprises with paid-up capital of at least 1 million yen (at least 2 million yen for banks).

1913: Enterprises with paid-up capital of at least 1.5 million yen (at least 3 million yen for banks, electricity companies, and mining companies).

1930: Enterprises with paid-up capital of at least 10 million yen (at least 20 million yen for banks and electricity companies).

The numbers in square brackets show totals including former bureaucrats.

for these companies. Furthermore, of these wealthy people, the most powerful avoided joint investment with nonfamily members and established multienterprise groups called *zaibatsu*. In some cases *zaibatsu* assisted in the founding of stock companies through joint investment, but in most cases they avoided joint investment and insisted on closed family involvement. As a result, the number of investors providing large amounts was very limited, with one wealthy person investing in several companies and becoming a large shareholder in each. In other cases, several wealthy people invested in one company and became large shareholders. After these types of individuals and groups invested, their concerns were solely focused on financial security and building their assets. Their objectives were clearly not on improving the management of newly joined stock companies but on family businesses in which they had invested in the hopes that they would grow and become prosperous.

Takeo Yamabe, a former director of Osaka Boseki Company and an engineer who had become president of the company in 1898 (and whose career paralleled that of Kyozo Kikuchi's), noted that most investors of that time were concerned only with profits and that some were not interested at all in the long-term economics of their companies.[4] These wealthy people doubled the directorships of several companies because they were large shareholders in them and were thus able to impose their wills on the organizations. Such concurrently serving, large-scale shareholding executives were common in the prewar period. As Yamabe has noted, they only wanted quick returns and had totally different interests from other full-time employees. Furthermore, since they were not full-time managers but directors of several companies, they were very busy and could not focus on the management of an individual company. Quite naturally, in terms of experience and information, they couldn't compete with other employees, especially middle managers.

Although these wealthy investors were not passionate about the companies they invested in and felt little responsibility, they did not want to give up their positions because of the profits and public exposure they derived from them. After 1905, however, the management environments of large, leading enterprises became more difficult and many of these executives struggled as top managers before relinquishing their positions. Although they were reluctant to give up their directorships, they tried to avoid positions of responsibility such as president and senior managing director—positions that required them to go to the office frequently. Instead, they entrusted these positions to salaried managers who were middle managers. In other words, until around 1905 the management environment was so simple that even executives who were large shareholders of several companies could serve as quasi part-time directors with the assistance of middle managers and mid-level engineers.

Salaried Managers in Traditional Zaibatsu

Thus far we've examined stock companies founded through the joint investment process. In this section, we will now examine how salaried managers gained higher posts in *zaibatsu* that were owned and controlled exclusively by wealthy families or groups. Before undertaking this discussion it should be noted that *zaibatsu* could be divided into two groups: traditional *zaibatsu* founded in the Edo era, such as Mitsui and Sumitomo; and new *zaibatsu* founded in the Meiji period. In many large merchant families in the Edo era it was common for founders' families to entrust management to their employees. Founders' families were owners but not top managers, and top-level decision making was made by the chief clerk. This sort of situation was in place at Mitsui and Sumitomo when the third- or fourth-generation heads of families inherited their respective businesses.[5]

The head clerk was generally someone who had gradually climbed the ladder from a low-level position while learning various aspects of the business, such as basic trading, money exchange, and finance. These individuals were, as a rule, not well educated and whose skills were mainly reading, writing, and calculating with an abacus. They could conduct business while dealing with regular customers using static systems in which technology remained unchanged. However, after Japan opened its doors to foreign countries and embarked on the process of modernization and industrialization, companies could not continue to operate successfully without making changes. Thus, starting around the 1890s, old-type salaried managers began to be replaced by well-educated salaried managers. Two of the best examples of this social and business phenomenon were Rizaemon Sanomura of the Mitsui family and Saihei Hirose of the Sumitomo family. Both of these men realized significant achievements in their respective companies in the challenging business environments that characterized the beginning of the Meiji period, when virtually all business had to undergo significant change. Having said that, however, these two men also generated considerable confusion within their companies. In short, although these two men predicated change in the business world, they were not well-educated top managers equipped with the knowledge required to lead modern enterprises in the new era.[6]

At Mitsui, Hikojiro Nakamigawa, Takashi Masuda, and Takuma Dan became top managers, while at Sumitomo Sadatake Iba, Teikichi Tanabe, Kinichi Kawakami, and Masaya Suzuki assumed this role. They were all well educated (some had even studied abroad), new-generation salaried managers who hired well-educated people in sync with the new era to form layers of managers-to-be. Most of these men, however, do not appear in the columns for 1905 in table 3.1.

Hikojiro Nakamigawa of Mitsui died in 1901. The executives of the Mitsui Bank in 1905 were Takayasu Mitsui as president, Senkichiro Hayakawa (a former bureaucrat) as managing director, and Shogoro Hatano, member of the board of directors. Takashi Masuda was managing director of the Mitsui Family Executive Office, the head office department that controlled Mitsui businesses (all businesses were unlimited partnerships prior to 1909). The executives of the Mitsui Trading Company were Hachirojiro Mitsui, president, Senjiro Watanabe, managing director, and Giichi Ida, member of the board of directors. Only Takuma Dan, who was also managing director, appears in table 3.1.

Although Sumitomo had various businesses, it was slow in organizing the various tentacles into the form of a company. The Sumitomo Bank was founded in 1895 but, under commercial law, could not be considered an official bank. Even at Sumitomo, the Sumitomo Bank was considered a business department that was part of the head office. Sumitomo's head office became an independent controlling organization in 1909, but it too was not a legal company. The Sumitomo Bank, however, did finally become an official company in 1912. The 1913 column of table 3.1 lists Kichizaemon Sumitomo as president, Kinkichi Nakata as managing director, and Masaya Suzuki and Kankichi Yukawa as members of the board of directors. Sumitomo's head office finally achieved company status in the form of a limited partnership in 1920.

Although Sumitomo was slow in organizing into a company, its businesses developed remarkably well. In particular, after Kinichi Kawakami, a director, Shunpei Uemura, head of the Document Bureau, Rokuro Fujio, head of the Computation Bureau, and Tetsujiro Shidachi, head of the Western Branch, all joined the Sumitomo Bank from the Bank of Japan, its management improved. In 1905, following Mitsui and Daiichi, it became the third largest bank in Japan in terms of deposits and loans. It should be noted that Rokuro Fujio was particularly well skilled in the fields of bank management, and corporate finance and accounting. He had learned banking from A. Allan Shand, and from 1874 onwards Fujio served first as a middle manager in the Ministry of Finance and then at the Bank of Japan.[7]

Salaried Managers in the New Zaibatsu

Salaried managers also made remarkable achievements in the new-type *zaibatsu* that accumulated wealth during the turbulent period of political and economic change that was one of the defining characteristics of the early Meiji era. These circumstances were particularly evident at Mitsubishi and Furukawa, where the founders (Yataro Iwasaki and Ichibei Furukawa, respectively) died before the middle of the Meiji period. In *zaibatsu* in which the founders were actively involved in the business until the Taisho era or the beginning of the Showa era, the founders had considerable influence on their own businesses. As an example, we can look to table 3.1 (the 1905 column) and see that, for Yasuda Bank, Yasuda Shoji and Okura Gumi, the only members of the board included on the list, are the founders and their families. However, those companies did employ graduates from the Imperial University and attempted to use their academic training to meet the needs of the times. Interestingly, most of them took those people into their families and did not have them join the top management as salaried managers. These examples were Teiichi Iomi (who later became Zenzaburo Yasuda) of Yasuda, Kokinji Takashima of Okura, Kumema Ito (Kumema Okura), and Motojiro Shiraishi of Asano, who were taken into the founders' families.

After the founders of Mitsubishi and Furukawa died, these companies became family enterprises. At Mitsubishi, Yanosuke (Yataro's brother), Heigoro Shoda (the husband of Yataro's niece), and Ryohei Toyokawa (Yataro's cousin) were in charge of the top management, albeit in cooperation with a crew of well-educated salaried managers.[8] At Furukawa, Junkichi Furukawa (Ichibei's adopted son) died two years after Ichibei had passed away in 1903. Since Toranosuke, Ichibei's son and Furukawa's third president, was still young and not really capable of fulfilling the role as top manager, people from various fields, such as chief clerk Choshichi Kimura, salaried manager and engineer Rikusaburo Kondo, politicians Kei Hara, Kunisuke Okazaki, Kaoru Inoue, and Eiichi Shibusawa, were involved in one aspect or another of top management. As one might guess, the Furukawa *zaibatsu* was in a state that could easily be termed chaotic.[9]

The number of salaried managers in the new *zaibatsu* is not included in the 1905 column in table 3.1. Family enterprises such as Mitsubishi and Furukawa had salaried top managers, but at Mitsubishi the bank, the coal mine, and the shipbuilding businesses were not established as independent companies until World War I, while at Furukawa, Furukawa Kogyo (Furukawa Mining Company) had been founded in 1905. Given this, with the exception of Mitsui, it can be concluded that the *zaibatsu* did not organize themselves into companies until 1905.

Changes in Large Enterprises at the End of the Meiji Era

By 1913 the situation surrounding the top management of large enterprises had clearly changed. There were 48 companies (39 if former bureaucrats are included, and all numbers in parentheses below refer to the inclusion of former government bureaucrats) with no salaried managers on the board of directors, which accounts for 42 percent (34%) of the 115 companies in total. There were 38 companies (39 companies) with one salaried manager, an increase of 16 (seven companies) over 1905, which accounts for 33 percent (34%) of the total. There were 29 companies (37 companies) with at least two salaried managers, an increase of 24 companies (28 companies), which accounts for 25 percent (32%) of the total.

From 1905 to 1913 (between the Japan-Russian War and World War I), which is considered to be the late Meiji era by Matao Miyamoto and Takeshi Abe, salaried managers established their presence at the directors' meetings of large, leading enterprises.[10] In this period, both the internal and external environments of large, leading enterprises changed dramatically and the top managers had to face any number of complex, difficult problems. As we have seen, it was becoming increasingly difficult for the capitalists who were working full time in top-management positions to take on anything more or new. These capitalists, who had originally installed themselves essentially to protect their investments, had little experience and even less information about the detailed workings of their companies. Something had to give.

The difficulties that the large, leading enterprises had to face included changes in how business was conducted, the development of new industries, the introduction of new technologies, and new market opportunities (such as the urbanization and westernization of consumers' lifestyles, expansion into overseas markets, etc.). There was also the intensification and concentration of competition to deal with, the expansion and bureaucraticization of management systems, and the development of stock company systems and modern securities markets. Social concerns also entered into business since labor movements were increasing owing to changes taking place in the employment system. Also affecting labor was the standardization of compulsory education and the advancement of education systems, which were improving the overall educational standards of the country. Finally, western companies were coming to Japan. It was a time of massive change, one that the business world had no choice but to address.

Rise of the Need for Salaried Managers

I have briefly explained the background related to the active advancement of salaried managers to the boards of directors of large, leading enterprises for the eight-year period from 1905 to 1913. However, the inability of non-full-time managers who were also large shareholders to adjust to dramatic changes in markets, technology, and the financial environment is not the only explanation for why so many salaried managers became board members. In this period, the management of many large, leading enterprises led by non-full-time managers collapsed or remained stagnant for extended periods, and these enterprises let salaried managers who had been successful at other companies join them. Good examples of such people include Raita Fujiyama, who was recruited to become president of Dai Nihon Sugar after the company almost sunk into bankruptcy, and Eiichi Shibusawa, the introducer who formulated plans to rebuild the company. Fujiyama, in particular, demonstrated superior management skills in helping Nakamigawa reform Mitsui.

As one of his management tasks, Fujiyama was actively engaged by the Mitsui Bank to help take over Oji Paper, which also resulted in the removal of Shibusawa, the chairman of Oji Paper, and Heizaburo Okawa, its managing director. Although Shibusawa must have held more than a little resentment for Fujiyama, he still took the bold and unusual step of recruiting Fujiyama to help rebuild Dai Nihon Sugar. Fujiyama, who left Mitsui after the failure of Nakamigawa's industrialization policy and Nakamigawa's death, now had another opportunity to demonstrate his management skills.[11] Other examples of this newly emerging class of top managers included Ginjiro Fujiwara of Oji Paper, who came from Mitsui Co.; Toyotaro Isomura of Hokkaido Tanko Tetsudo, who came from Mitsui Co.; Tatsukichi Suganuma of Osaka Dento, who came from the Yamaguchi Bank; and Seizo Ida of Kirin Beer, who came from Sanyo Railways.

Some salaried managers were helped by the class of middle managers who, through ability and hard work, was subsequently promoted and won top-management positions. A good example is Sanji Muto, who had battled against Kyugoro Suzuki, when Suzuki had tried to buy up shares that had been released by the Mitsui Bank in an attempt to become the top manager of Kanegafuchi Boseki. When Muto became the managing director of Kanegafuchi, he promoted the following middle managers as directors: Narazo Takatsuji, Masazumi Fuji, Ryokichi Kagao, and Takeshi Yamaguchi. It is evident that many salaried managers became top managers in the eight years starting in 1905, and this rise can be seen as an attempt to compensate for the shortcomings of executives who were large shareholders. Ginjiro Fujiwara (senior managing director of Oji Paper), Tsunezo Saito (managing director of Mie Boseki), Sumisaburo Uemura (vice president of Dai Nihon Beer), Hanji Soma (senior managing director of Meiji Sugar), Matazo Kita (managing director of Nihon Cotton), Keijiro Hori (vice president of Osaka Shosen), Mitsuhiro Ota (managing director of Keihan Railways), and Tatsukichi Suganuma (senior managing director of Osaka Dento) all actively played strategic leadership roles in their respective companies after 1913.

From the Taisho Era to the Beginning of the Showa Era

Table 3.1 shows that, from 1913 to 1930, more salaried managers were becoming board members of large, leading companies. In 1930, out of 158 companies only 15 (11 if former bureaucrats are included, and all numbers in brackets below refer to the inclusion of former government bureaucrats) were without salaried managers on their boards of directors, which amounts to 9.5 percent (7%). In 1913, this figure was 41.7 percent (33.9%), and, as well, there were 27 (17) companies that had only one salaried manager as a member of the board, which amounts to 17 percent (10.8%). There were another 113 (127) companies that had at least two salaried managers as members of the board, a percentage of 71.5 percent (80.4%), a huge increase when compared to the 25.2 percent (32.2%) of 1913.

Looking at the figures more closely, we find that there are two categories of companies that had at least two salaried managers: those with at least two salaried managers that amount to 50 percent or less of the total number of board members; and those with at least two salaried managers that amount to over 50 percent of the total number of board members. In other words, the first category refers to companies where salaried managers played a smaller role and the second category to companies where two or more salaried managers made up more than half of the top management team. The first of these categories contains 71 (75) companies, while the second contains 42 (52) companies, which amounts to only 26.6 percent (32.9%) of the total number of large, leading companies. Given this, it can be concluded that although a significant number of salaried managers became top managers in the period that lasted from World War I until the recession in the Showa era, this time span should be considered merely the transitional period for this long-term trend.

The reasons for the significant growth of managerial enterprises during this later period are considered to be the same as those for the period 1905 to 1913. The reasons it was necessary to increase the number of managing directors, however, became more different. This increase was triggered by several factors: the expansion of the scales of businesses and expansion of business activities, both of which were functions of the changing economy around the time before, during, and after World War I; the amalgamation of enterprises and the development of more complex management systems during and after World War I; and the recession after the war. At Oji Paper, for example, the number of managing directors increased from 5 to 13, at Asano Cement from 6 to 11, at NEC from 3 to 10, at Nihon Cotton from 5 to 10, at Sumitomo Bank from 4 to 9, and at Nihon Woolen from 4 to 9.

During this period, numerous companies took on the form of more modern corporate organizations and established boards with an increased number of directors. These companies include Odakyu (established in 1923) with 11 directors, Mitsubishi Shipbuilding (established in 1917) with 9 directors, Mitsubishi Mining (established in 1918) with 9 directors, and Toyo Cotton (established in 1920) with 9 directors. The increase in the number of directors did not always coincide with an increase in the number of salaried managers, however. For example, at Asano Cement, both when there were 6 directors and 11 directors, all of the directors were either members of the Asano family or representatives of investors who had close relationships with the founder, Soichiro Asano. At NEC and Nihon Woolen, the additional board members were also large shareholders.

At Odakyu, Mitsubishi Shipbuilding, Mitsubishi Mining, and Toyo Menka, which were established with large numbers of board members, the percentage of directors who were salaried managers was high. This was particularly true at Toyo Menka, where eight out of the nine directors were salaried managers and one was also a large shareholder. Generally, the salaried managers who became top managers of large enterprises founded in the Meiji era, and that steadily grew in the pre– and post–World War I periods, were middle managers who had been promoted from within. These, it should be pointed out, were men who developed their management skills while they were middle managers. Nihon Cotton, for example, had a president named Matazo Kita who had been promoted from the position of middle manager, and 9 out of the 10 directors were promoted salaried managers as well. More examples of companies in which numerous middle managers were promoted as top managers (as of 1930) are listed below. Note that in many of these companies the presidents or vice presidents were salaried managers who also had considerable influence.

***Note: The first number in the series indicates the total number of directors. The second number refers to the number of directors appointed from within the company, including presidents and vice president, who, if applicable, are named.**

- *Toyo Boseki*: 11–9. Vice president: Otokichi Shoji
- *Kanegafuchi Boseki*: 9–8. President: Ryokichi Nagao (Nagao was appointed as a salaried manager from within the company, but Sanji Muto, a former president, played the most important role in promoting middle managers. Muto retired in 1930.)
- *Nisshin Boseki*: 8–6. President: Seijiro Miyajima
- *Osaka Godo Boseki*: 8–5. President: Kota Akiyama (The ideas of founder Fusazo Taniguchi had a great influence regarding the promotion of salaried managers.)[12]
- *Naigai*: 9–7. President: Ayazo Takei
- *Nihon Cotton*: 10–9. President: Matazo Kita
- *Oji Paper*: 13–9. President: Ginjiro Fujiwara
- *Dai Nihon Beer*: 10–7. President: Kyohei Magoshi
- *Dai Nihon Sugar*: 8–6. President: Raita Fujiyama
- *Meiji Sugar*: 10–6. President: Hanji Soma
- *Mitsukoshi*: 9–8. President: Masao Kurachi (I think the decision to promote a number of middle managers was primarily made by Hibi Osuke, who developed Mitsukoshi Gofukuten into a department store. He had been senior managing director since the establishment of Mitsukoshi Gofukuten in 1904 and then became its chairman in 1913. He retired in 1918.)
- *Toho Gas*: 6–5. President: Sakura Okamoto

The Top-Management Structure in Zaibatsu *Enterprises*

In this section I would like to examine how directorships were structured at the head offices of the *zaibatsu* and their direct affiliates. The first thing to note is that there are some interesting contrasts among the *zaibatsu*.[13] Although I have embarked upon explanations of *zaibatsu* in other books and reports, I outline the different types here again both for purposes of clarity and for those who have not read my works. My definition of a *zaibatsu* is the following: a multidimensional business group that has developed under the exclusive ownership and control of its founder or his family. Another definition, this one by Shigeaki Yasuoka and others, defines a *zaibatsu* as a Konzern—a system for controlling stock companies in which a family-owned holding company was developed and diversified into several business fields through the vehicle of stock issues.[14] Unfortunately, I must disagree with this definition based on the fact that *zaibatsu* existed before such a system became established, which was around 1910. Also, Yasuoka, Hiroaki Yamazaki, Juro Hashimoto, and Haruhito Takeda have all stated that being an oligopoly is another distinctive feature of the *zaibatsu*, but once again I am forced to disagree. First, it is impossible to prove that all businesses under any or all *zaibatsu* are oligopolies. Second, a *zaibatsu* is not simply a multidimensional business group. For example, even if a family manages a retail shop, restaurant, and parking area, the unit cannot be called a *zaibatsu* since a *zaibatsu*, taking general logic into account, must consist of businesses that are of considerable significance to the national or local economies. Although Takeo Kikkawa has questioned the difference between the importance (or overall influence) of a business and its being an oligopoly, I contend that they *are* different.[15] Business influence is an issue concerned with the role and position of the businesses in the economic system while an oligopoly is obsessed with domination of the market. I think the term oligopoly is used too readily, and the above example is, I believe, a case in point.

Let us now look in detail at how some *zaibatsu* were structured in actual practice. In the Mitsui *zaibatsu*, the heads of 11 Mitsui families (except the head family) became the presidents of direct affiliates, including a bank, a trading company, and a mining company. Of the executive directors, three or four were salaried managers who had been promoted, and the rest of the directors were all heads of the Mitsui family, representatives of the Mitsui Unlimited Partnership (head office), representatives of subsidiaries, top salaried managers of Mitsui, and direct affiliates of the Mitsui Unlimited Partnership. At Mitsui Unlimited Partnership, Hachiroemon Mitsui, the master of the head family, became president. He was also a member of the three-member command committee; the remaining members were the heads of other Mitsui families. The Mitsui Unlimited Partnership directors of the board, however, had a slightly different structure since its members consisted of salaried managers: the managing director, two senior directors, and two regular directors.

At the Mitsubishi *zaibatsu*, the chairman and senior directors of direct affiliates were salaried managers. The board of directors consisted of Koyata Iwasaki, president of Mitsubishi Limited Partnership (head office); Hisaya Iwasaki, head of the Iwasaki head family; Kusuyata Kimura, general director of Mitsubishi Limited Partnership; one or two representatives of other direct affiliates;

and salaried managers of those direct affiliates. At Mitsubishi Limited Partnership, Koyata Iwasaki became president but the general director, two senior directors, and two regular directors were salaried managers. Hisaya Iwasaki did not assume any of these posts.

At the Sumitomo *zaibatsu*, there was one chairman for all direct affiliates, a salaried manager who was the general manager of Sumitomo Limited Partnership, the head office of which functioned as the holding body, or controlling arm, of the organization. The senior directors and executive directors were salaried managers of each direct affiliate while the regular directors were Kichizaemon Sumitomo (head of the Sumitomo family), representatives of other direct affiliates, and salaried managers of those direct affiliates. At Sumitomo Limited Partnership, the head of the Sumitomo family became the president while the general managing director, senior director, executive director, and auditor were salaried managers.

As complicated as the above examples may seem, they do serve to demonstrate that there was a variety of structures and organizational modes for boards of directors. Despite this, there are some common features worth recognizing. The salaried managers of each direct affiliate were in charge of top-level decision making and their decisions were checked by the family of the *zaibatsu*, the head office, and other direct affiliates. In addition, although the head office was led by the family of the *zaibatsu*, the opinions of the salaried managers carried significant weight (in the case of Mitsubishi) or the salaried managers were in charge of management (as with both Mitsui and Sumitomo). At Mitsui (an unlimited partnership and the head office of the Mitsui *zaibatsu*), after salaried managers made decisions at board meetings (consisting of salaried managers), their decisions were reported to the president and members of the command committee, who were representatives of the Mitsui family. The president, the master of the head family, however, only attended about 50 percent of the committee meetings, and even when he did, he rarely objected to decisions made by the board.[16]

The situation was almost the same at the Okura *zaibatsu*, an unlimited partnership where the only directors of Okura Gumi (Okura Group), which functioned as the head office of the *zaibatsu*, were President Kishichiro Okura (son of founder Kihachiro) and Vice President Jukuro Kadono, Kadono being a salaried manager who acted as Kihachiro's right-hand man. At Okura Mining, which was a direct affiliate of Okura Gumi, five of the seven directors (including one senior director) had long worked as salaried managers, while the others were salaried managers working in other direct affiliates, although Kadono, who represented Okura Gumi, became chairman. In short, salaried managers were more numerous than family and theoretically could have, if push ever came to shove, held sway over family wishes.

Compared to the four other *zaibatsu* we've just looked at, the Furukawa *zaibatsu* was the most family-oriented *zaibatsu*. At Furukawa (an unlimited partnership and the central office of the Furukawa *zaibatsu*), Toranosuke, the head of the Furukawa family, became president, and Manjiro Yoshimura and Suekichi Nakagawa, both Furukawa family members, occupied two of the six regular directors' positions. The head of the board of directors, one general director, two senior directors, and three regular directors were employed as salaried managers at Furukawa, while one regular director was a salaried manager of Furukawa Mining. At Furukawa Mining, the Furukawa family (Toranosuke, chairman, and Yoshimura, president) was in a dominant position vis-à-vis the salaried managers. Three of the five directors were salaried managers from the head office and only two salaried managers of Furukawa Mining became directors.

The Yasuda *zaibatsu* and Asano *zaibatsu* were cast with a stronger family pale than that of the Furukawa *zaibatsu*. At Yasuda Hozensha, an unlimited partnership, the controlling head office of Yasuda, Zenjiro II (who headed the Yasuda clan) was appointed chairman, and four of the seven directorships were occupied by masters of the Yasuda family. Three boardroom seats were occupied by salaried managers and two by former bureaucrats. At Yasuda Bank, Zenjiro Yasuda was president and, like elsewhere in the broad Yasuda organization, two of the four directors were heads of branches of the Yasuda family. The vice president and a regular director of the bank were salaried managers, dispatched from Yasuda Hozensha. The other regular director represented several large shareholders, and four senior managing directors were salaried managers promoted from within Yasuda Bank.

The Asano *zaibatsu* had the strongest family element of any of the above *zaibatsu* we have looked at. At Asano (the head office of the Asano *zaibatsu*), the president and all four managing directors were members of the Asano family. At Asano Cement, the primary direct affiliate, there weren't even any salaried managers. Although Monjiro Suzuki, the managing director of Asano, and Kiyota Kaneko, of Asano Cement, appeared to be salaried managers, they were actually members of the Asano family because Suzuki was the husband of founder Soichiro Asano's daughter, and Kaneko was the husband of Soichiro's granddaughter.

It is believed by some business management theorists that if a *zaibatsu* family completely controls or holds all of their *zaibatsu* company's stock, the autonomy of its salaried managers is guaranteed.[17] However, as the examples of Yasuda and Asano suggest, this generalization is not strictly accurate and is one that should be avoided.

Engineers as Directors

As table 3.2 shows, it is estimated that there were 478 salaried managers employed in large Japanese enterprises at the director level or above in the year 1930. Of this total, 170 (35.5%) were engi-

Table 3.2. Educational Background of Top Salaried Managers of Large Enterprises in 1930

Graduates of Institutions of Advanced Education	Number	Total Number	%	Total %
Imperial universities		194		40.6
Imperial University of Tokyo	163		34.1	
Others	31		6.5	
Law	64		13.4	
Engineering	123		25.7	
Agriculture and science	7		1.5	
Advanced commercial colleges		89		18.6
Advanced engineering colleges (including high schools)		28		5.9
Other specialized colleges		11		2.3
Private universities		70		14.6
Keio	40		8.4	
Waseda	8		1.7	
Others	22		4.6	
Studied abroad		9		1.9
Law and business	5		1.0	
Engineering	4		0.8	
Specialized schools		10		2.1
Business	6		1.3	
Engineering	4		0.8	
Others		43		9.0
Unknown		24		5.0
Total		478		100.0

Source: H. Morikawa, *Nihon Keieishi (Management History in Japan)* (Nihon Keizai Shinbunsha, 1981): 148.

neers, the majority of whom were university graduates (usually from one of the Japanese imperial universities) and had bachelor's degrees in engineering. To be more specific, in 1930 one-fourth of the salaried managers of large enterprises had bachelor's degrees in engineering. Salaried managers who were engineers constituted about 36 percent of the 478 salaried managers of the 158 large, leading enterprises, which included not merely engineering-related occupations but also banks, trading companies, insurance companies, and department stores. Particularly when compared to the West, this figure is nothing short of astonishing.

As a newly industrialized country, Japan was under pressure from western enterprises and was striving to successfully industrialize through capitalist enterprises. To achieve this, companies felt compelled to recruit engineers who were university graduates, train them, keep them, and motivate them by offering them promotions. In Japan at that time, classroom instruction and on-site training were closely combined in advanced technology education institutions, and this approach was useful in helping advance technology in Japanese industry. Moreover, this approach heightened the practical skills of the young engineering corps and was instrumental in creating personal and professional networks among the engineers and on-site operations people. It should be noted that engineers who were knowledgeable about actual production sites and had connections with on-site technical people constituted about 36 percent of the top managers of large enterprises in the 1930s, an important consideration when examining the international characteristics of Japanese corporate systems.[18]

Shareholder Power

A number of salaried managers were promoted to top-management positions from 1913 to 1930, though not on a large scale. This small scale indicates that large shareholders still had considerable power. The following statement by Dr. Tetsuji Okazaki supports this view:

> In non-*zaibatsu* enterprises, over 20% of the managing directors were large shareholders (at least among the top 10 stockholders) who were not family members. Considering that some of the large shareholders who were not even among the 10 largest became directors, this percentage could have been even higher. In non-*zaibatsu* enterprises large shareholders joined management essentially in order to monitor managers. In *zaibatsu* enterprises,

> however, there were not many cases in which large shareholders who were members of the family became directors. The ratio of large shareholders who were directors was lower than in non-*zaibatsu* enterprises even if the directors sent over from head office were included in the shareholders. In *zaibatsu* enterprises, the percentage of directors who had been promoted was the highest.[19]

There are some errors and misunderstandings in Okazaki's views, however. For example, the non-*zaibatsu* enterprises Okazaki referred to include the Nissan *zaibatsu* and Asano *zaibatsu* enterprises, and he overlooked the fact that the large shareholders who were family members controlled the board of directors at Yasuda and Asano *zaibatsu* enterprises as well. But I agree with Okazaki's view that the system in which shareholders monitored management was in place up to 1935. Below is a list of data I would like to add to Okazaki's analysis:

- *Nihon Petroleum*: Four of the 10 directors were salaried managers. President: Keisaburo Hashimoto (a former bureaucrat); Senior Director: Montaro Tsuge (who joined the company in mid-career); Directors: Jiro Tanaka (a former bureaucrat); Seikichi Mizuta (who had been promoted); the other six were large shareholders (including Shintaro Ohashi).
- *NKK*: Two of the nine directors were salaried managers: Kaichiro Imaizumi and Nagahisa Matsushita (both of whom were promoted). The other seven were large shareholders. President: Heisaburo Okawa; Vice President: Motojiro Shiraishi; Director: Shintaro Ohashi).
- *Toyo Seitetsu*: One of the nine directors was a salaried manager. Executive Director: Keinosuke Nishino (one of the few *wander vogel*–type salaried managers who became presidents of Teigeki, Tokyo Kaijo Kasai, and Shirakiya). The other eight were large shareholders (President: Seinosuke Go; Vice President: Kumakichi Nakajima; Director: Shintaro Ohashi).
- *NYK*: Five of the 12 directors were salaried managers: Vice President Noboru Oya and four promoted salaried managers. The other seven were large shareholders (President: Kenkichi Kagami, who was also the president of Tokyo Kaijo Kasai; Director: Shintaro Ohashi).
- *Tokyo Electric*: Six of the 15 directors were salaried managers (four of the six were promoted salaried managers and two were former bureaucrats). The other nine were large shareholders (Chairman: Seinosuke Go; President: Shohachi Wakao; Vice President: Ichizo Kobayashi; Director: Shintaro Ohashi).

The above five enterprises were all non-*zaibatsu* enterprises. NKK and Nippon Yusen Kaisha had distant relationships with the Asano *zaibatsu* and Mitsubishi *zaibatsu*, respectively, in terms of capital and human resources. At these enterprises, large shareholders were very influential and promoted salaried managers failed to gain much power.

Shintaro Ohashi was a director at all five enterprises, and he owned and managed Kobunkan (publishing) and Kyodo (printing), both of which were businesses owned by his family. Ohashi, however, also invested in a number of other enterprises and became a director in each of them with the goal of pursuing profits and improving his social status.[20] Seinosuke Go, chairman of Tokyo Electric and president of Toyo Seitetsu; Shohachi Wakao, president of Tokyo Electric; and Seishichi Iwasaki, president of Iwaki Cement, were similar to Ohashi in terms of both the breadth of their participation and the types of goals they were pursuing. In many stock companies in prewar Japan, there were any number of executives who were, simultaneously, large shareholders with considerable power.

The payment of high dividends was the most obvious and important result of the company monitoring performed by large shareholding directors. Okazaki has noted that under the management monitoring by shareholders, enterprises in the prewar period allocated a large share of profits to dividends. Figures compiled through a sampling of enterprises from 1921 to 1935 show that the average dividend amounted to a whopping 70 percent.[21] It seems obvious now that it was the large shareholding executives who should be blamed for the high dividend demands and attempts to raise stock prices. Here were corporate directors who should have been building up capital reserves for future company development but were more intent, it seems, on lining their own pockets. That these individuals were "monitoring" management seems almost ludicrous in retrospect; somebody should have been monitoring them instead. Author Kamekichi Takahashi has severely criticized these individuals in his book *Kabushiki Gaisha Bokoku Ron (The Ruination of a Country by Stock Companies)*. According to Takahashi, the main factors in the collapse of company management are as follows: (1) the company's management approach is not based on the long-term goal of growing the business; (2) the financial base of the company is very weak; (3) the bogus settlement of accounts and dividends is done almost openly; (4) the moral standards of the company have disappeared; (5) incompetent executives willingly seek and make tainted profits by performing dishonest acts; and (6) large shareholders are greedy tyrants keen to obtain large dividends that may and do send the company into decline. This type of company management is based on the following: the large shareholders' rough-and-ready approach to the pursuit of profits; and the corruption of executives.[22]

In his analysis, Takahashi was not simply criticizing large shareholders who doubled as executives but also executives who were controlled by the big shareholding players. In the less rigorously controlled times that Takahashi writes about, it was easy for capitalists to ride roughshod over undercapitalized growing companies by injecting them with money. Takahashi's book gives a lucid and fresh account that still has many applications and lessons that can be learned and used today.

Concerning Comments by Tsunehiko Yui

In my book *Nihon Keieishi (Japan's Business History)* I have noted that (based on figures in table 2 of that book), although the growth of managerial enterprises was quite rapid in the prewar period in Japan, in the period around 1930 these enterprises were still in the transition stage and truly rapid growth did not occur until after World War II. Commenting on these figures, Dr. Tsunehiko Yui has said that most of the data I collected related to banks and public companies (which had many non-full-time directors), such as electric companies, most of which were large enterprises. I cannot agree with him in the following two areas.[23] First, I think that Dr. Yui wanted to say that the growth of managerial enterprises would appear to have been greater if the data had ignored banks and electric companies, and that 1930 was not a transition period in the growth of managerial enterprises. We cannot, however, change the results by merely eliminating some of the enterprises from our subject of study. Second, if, as Dr. Yui suggests, we simply use manufacturing and mining companies as examples, in 1930, 77 of the 158 enterprises were manufacturing and mining companies: 52 of these manufacturing and mining companies had boards in which fewer than half the directors were salaried managers; 25 of them (32.5%) had boards on which more than half the directors were salaried managers; and 20 of them had boards on which more than two-thirds of the directors were salaried managers. Given this, even if we simply looked at manufacturing and mining companies, in 1930 the growth of managerial enterprises was in a transition stage.

Trends from the Beginning of the Showa Era to Today

Explanation of Table 3.3

Table 3.3 shows how managerial enterprises developed in the period from 1930, a time when managerial enterprises were in transition, to 1991.

The Chairman/President System and Managerial Enterprises

Table 3.3 also shows changes in the percentage of enterprises with a chairman/president system. Many large Japanese enterprises have both chairman and president positions, a system I would like to

Table 3.3. Changes in the Chairman/President System

	Number of Enterprises (A)	Number of Enterprises with the Chairman/President System (B)	B/A	Number of Enterprises Where the Chairman and President Were Promoted Salaried Managers (C)	C/B
1930	158	4	2.5%	0	0%
1943	433	83	19.1%	5	6.0%
1954	387	85	22.0%	25	29.4%
1974	305	148	48.5%	90	60.8%
1991	492	316	64.2%	194	61.4%

Notes: The figures for 1930 were derived from the *Shogyo Koshin Sho* (Commercial Inquiry Agency), *Nihon Zenkoku Shogaisha Yakuin Roku (Record of Company Directors in Japan)*. The enterprises counted were those with at least 10 million yen in capital (and at least 20 million yen for banks and electric companies). The figures for 1943 were derived from "Dantai Kaisha Shokuin Roku" (Record of Company Employees), an attachment of *Jinji Koshin Roku (Personnel Inquiry Record)*. The enterprises counted were those with at least 10 million yen in capital.

The figures for 1954 were derived from Keizai Oraisha, *Nihon Kaisha Shi Soran (Comprehensive Bibliography of the History of Japanese Enterprises)*. The enterprises counted were those with at least 300 million yen in capital.

The figures for 1974 were derived from Diamondsha, *Diamond Kaisha Shokuin Roku—Zen Jojo Kaishaban (Diamond's Company Employees Record—Complete Record of Listed Companies)*. The enterprises counted were those with at least 5 billion yen in capital.

The source for the 1991 figures was the same as that for the 1974 figures. The enterprises counted were those with at least 15 billion yen in capital.

Sources: Morikawa "Nihon no Top Management" (Japanese Top Management), in Tadayuki Itami, Tadao Kagono, and Motoshige Ito, eds., *Nihon no Kigyo System (Company Systems in Japan)*, Vol. 3 (Yuhikaku, 1993): 206.

call the "chairman/president system." Some enterprises also have the position of "advisor" (other than the chairman), a role that allows a company president to continue to hold decision-making power at the highest level even after retirement.

To conduct this survey I selected five years: 1930, 1943, 1954, 1974, and 1991. As to why these years were chosen, 1943 was the year the Munitions Company Law came into effect, 1954 was the year that heralded the start of Japan's rapid economic growth, 1974 was the year of the oil crisis, and 1991 was the last year of my research. The standards applied in the classification of large enterprises are described in the table notes and were based on no particular criteria.

My focus was to look at the process whereby salaried managers gained power under the chairman/president system by choosing enterprises in which the chairman and president were promoted salaried managers; I then calculated the percentage of these enterprises among large enterprises that had chairman/president systems. I limited my choice of enterprise to those whose chairman and president were promoted salaried managers and not former bureaucrats or *wander vogel*–type managers.

In 1930 there were four enterprises (2.5%) with chairman/president systems. The number and percentage of these enterprises continued to increase and, by 1991, they totaled 316 enterprises (64.2%). The number of enterprises whose chairman and president were salaried managers was zero in 1930 but climbed to 90 (60.8%) by 1974. In 1991, however, although 194 of the 316 enterprises had a chairman and president who were salaried managers, the percentage of these enterprises was only 61.4%, up only slightly from the 60.8 percent in 1974. These figures tell us that there was a significant increase in the number of chairmen and presidents who were former government officials or bureaucrats. Having said that, however, managerial enterprises whose top managers were promoted salaried managers were still numerically superior.

The percentage figures for such managerial enterprises increased greatly from 1943 to 1954 and then again from 1954 to 1974. In the first of these two periods, great changes occurred in the legal and financial infrastructure of Japan: the Munitions Company Law came into effect, *zaibatsu* families withdrew from top-management positions because of the dismantling of the *zaibatsu* by the Allied occupying forces, tax systems were reformed (for example, property taxes and inheritance taxes were significantly increased and the

War Profits Tax was established), and agricultural reform was carried out. In the second of the two periods mentioned, founder enterprises frequently became family enterprises and founders' families were often seen to withdraw from family enterprises.

Effects of the Munitions Company Law

The Munitions Company Law, enacted in December 1943, stipulated that those responsible for production in munitions companies must be appointed only by the order of the government, and that representatives of these companies must assume responsibility for the operation of the companies for the government (Article 4). The law also stipulated that imperial commands had the greatest authority regarding how the operation of munitions companies was carried out and how the shareholders meetings, including decision making at these meetings, were conducted (Article 14). The sum effect was to make the operation of munitions companies free from the control of regular commercial law and decisions that were usually imposed by and at shareholder meetings.[24]

Mr. Osamu Nagashima summarizes the objectives of the Munitions Company Law in this way: (1) to allow the government to directly intervene into a munitions company's organization; (2) to make corporate activities free from conventional laws and regulations; (3) to establish systems for designating particular people responsible for production; (4) to compensate for losses accrued as a result of government strictures and to guarantee profits; and (5) to establish a uniform munitions controller system.[25]

For the purposes of this book, let us now examine point (3) in greater detail. In a munitions company, the person responsible for production was perhaps the single most important person in the company, and this was a position of great authority and responsibility. Although the Munitions Company Law did not ignore the principles of company law, it amply demonstrated the government's clear intention to set munitions companies free from the control of regulations imposed by both commercial law and decisions usually forced on companies by and at shareholder meetings. Accordingly, when a munitions company did not voluntarily appoint a person responsible for production, the government stepped in and appointed one. When the government judged the person to be inappropriate, the government could likewise remove him. The government even tried to remove company presidents who were felt to have insufficient knowledge of, and experience with, production centers and who had attained their positions merely because they were large shareholders. For presidents who were not shareholders but were judged to have too many outside interests, attempts were made to remove them as well.

When the Munitions Company Law was put in place, the government made it clear that those responsible for production must be full-time company presidents and that nothing else was acceptable. As might be expected, such rulings sparked upper-echelon management changes at some firms. For example, at Toa Fuel, which was designated a munitions company on January 17, 1944, President Keisaburo Hashimoto (who also doubled as chairman) was also the president of Nihon Petroleum and Imperial Oil, and it was thus ruled that he could not be in charge of munitions production at Toa Fuel.[26] In the search for a new person, there were three candidates for the post, including Seiichi Mishima, executive director in charge of office affairs; Nobuhei Nakahara, executive director in charge of technology; and Hashimoto himself. Hashimoto recommended Nakahara and contacted the Fuel Bureau of the government as well as the army and the navy, whose approval was required for designating the person responsible for production at a munitions company.[27] According to Nakahara's diary entry of January 27, 1944, Hashimoto said that the reason he recommended Nakahara, and not the more senior Mishima, was that he considered technology to be a critical field for Toa Fuel and technology was Nakahara's area of expertise.[28] Following through, Hashimoto resigned as president and chairman and Nakahara was subsequently appointed president and given the production responsibility. Besides illustrating the government's emphasis on controlling munitions' productions, from a business standpoint the above example demonstrates how managers, who were capitalists, were forced to draw back from the front line.

Effects of Occupation Policies in the Postwar Period

Much has been written in all sorts of publications about the effects of the dismantling of *zaibatsu* and the purges of top managers from the business world, as well as about reforms pertaining to agricultural land under the occupation-force policies after World War II.[29] In this section, I look at tax reform, an area that has garnered nowhere near as much attention. In November 1945, Allied occupation forces ordered the Japanese government to establish the War Profits Tax and a tax on property, targeted mainly at the very wealthy. In response to this, in January 1946 the Ministry of Finance enacted laws intended to increase both general and individual property taxes, as well as the new Corporate War Profits Tax. Since 1950, a progressive income tax structure, wealth taxes, and inheritance taxes, which were enacted in response to recommendations by a U.S. group established to examine the financial situation in Japan in 1949 and 1950 (the Shoup recommendations), have been the pillars of a fair taxation system in Japan. Wealth taxes, however, were abandoned after two years.[30]

On top of suffering the damage caused by the war and losing their foreign properties, capitalists who had accumulated considerable wealth in the years before the war were nothing less than shocked by occupation-force policies. As for the dismantling of the *zaibatsu*, the stock owned by the *zaibatsu* families and the head offices of the *zaibatsu* were compulsorily transferred to a government agency whose main task was liquidating the holdings. Head offices of the *zaibatsu* (which functioned as holding companies in the days before that term existed) were also shut down. The stock of these firms was not totally confiscated, however, but might well have been since the shares were exchanged for national bonds, which were virtually valueless because of runaway inflation. Furthermore, members of *zaibatsu* families were forced to quit their executive positions. Although many members of *zaibatsu* families were ostensibly only managing the enterprises (a trend that, as I explained earlier, progressed during the war), with the dismantling of the *zaibatsu*, *zaibatsu* families completely lost control of their affiliated companies. Also, needless to say, the controlling families lost control of their head offices because the head offices were shut down. The dismantling of the *zaibatsu* completely deprived the *zaibatsu* families of ownership and management of *zaibatsu* enterprises, ones which they had worked long and hard to establish.

Other occupation policies also dealt severe blows to the capitalists, a large number of whom held important roles in the *zaibatsu* families. We can imagine just how devastating the damage was when we look at the property taxes collected from this class of capitalists in 1946, an amount which was almost the equivalent of 10 percent of Japan's GNP for that year. It is believed that, in one of those years, some 29 percent of property taxes were paid in stock, which also helped lower capitalist stock holdings.[31] Those who had large shareholding stakes were forced to let go of their stock for other reasons as well.

The Dismantling of the Capitalist Layer

Table 3.4 shows a ranking of the final individual income tax returns for the year 1954. A comparison of this ranking with a similar list of final income tax returns for 1942 (table 3.5), which was published in Kojunsha's *Nihon Shinshi Roku (Who's Who in Japan)* in 1944, clearly indicates the decline of Japan's moneyed class. In 1942, the highest rank was occupied by Takakimi Mitsui, head of the Mitsui family. Hikoyata Iwasaki, ranked sixth, was the son of the head of the Iwasaki family, the owner of the Mitsubishi *zaibatsu*. Excluding Genzo Hattori (president of Hattori Tokeiten) and Jingoro Nishikawa (a futon merchant with Shiga Bank connections), all the other taxpayers who paid more than one million yen in income tax on the list were owners of huge *zaibatsu*. In the ranking of final income tax returns for 1954, however, these same individuals are noticeable by their absence. In 1942, those claiming smaller incomes included the owners of both major and minor *zaibatsu*, the titled nobility, major mer-

Table 3.4. Ranking of the Final Income Tax Returns for 1954 (Unit: Yen)

Order	Name	Company	Income
1	Toshio Iue	Sanyo Denki	113,815
2	Konosuke Matsushita	Matsushita Denki Sangyo	95,109
3	Yasuhito Yamaoka	Yanmar Diesel	84,698
4	Seijiro Ueda	Fukuoka Buzen Tanko	75,469
5	Yasuji Hirose	Hirose Kozan	75,360
6	Sazo Idemitsu	Idemitsu Kosan	65,061
7	Nobuo Kondo	Kondo Boseki	51,942
8	Otozo Yamamoto	Nagasaki Tokumasa Tanko	48,524
9	Kiyoshi Nagata	Nihon Gomu	46,371
10	Otoji Taihoya	Kekko Kogyo (Ishikawa)	38,602
11	Tokutaro Nagase	Nagase Sangyo	37,625
12	Nobuhei Nakahara	Toa Nenryo Kogyo	34,461
13	Aiichiro Fujiyama	Nitto Kagaku	33,873
14	Shojiro Ishibashi	Bridgestone	33,635
15	Yonezo Ueda	Fukuoka Hoshu Tanko	33,089
16	Tomizo Uda	Fukuoka Hoshu Tanko	32,965
17	Goro Fukuhara	Nihon Sakusan Jinko Senii	32,169
18	Tameki Morinaga	Nisshin Seito	30,341
19	Junshiro Fukuhara	Fukuhara Keito Boseki	27,727
20	Jinichiro Fukuhara	Fukuhara Keito Boseki	27,655

Source: Shukan Zei no Shirube (Weekly Tax), Vol. 187, March 27, 1955.

Table 3.5. Ranking of the Final Income Tax Returns for 1942 (Unit: Yen)

Order	Name	Income	Order	Name	Income
1	Takakimi Mitsui	4,836,364	17	Takaosa Mitsui	760,680
2	Takaharu Mitsui	2,456,174	18	Takamoto Mitsui	759,813
3	Takahisa Mitsui	2,423,248	19	Sanjiro Katsuhara*	758,916
4	Takanaru Mitsui	2,418,033	20	Takaaki Mitsui	754,097
5	Takahiro Mitsui	2,392,070	21	Koya Iwasaki	661,660
6	Hikoyata Iwasaki	2,151,031	22	Moritatsu Hosokawa	655,068
7	Koyata Iwasaki	1,934,823	23	Takaya Iwasaki	652,970
8	Kishichiro Okura	1,669,831	24	Seijiro Tatsuke	643,877
9	Genzo Hattori	1,332,487	25	Sadakichi Saito**	640,935
10	Hisaya Iwasaki	1,376,487	26	Seiji Kawanishi	634,600
11	Jingoro Nishikawa	1,157,171	27	Takaharu Mitsui	616,703
12	Jujun Furukawa	1,144,953	28	Hanshichi Toyoshima	601,390
13	Jinkichi Terada	874,302	29	Kamesaburo Yamashita	600,869
14	Seitarao Yamaguchi	871,972	30	Jisuke Sugiura	582,538
15	Takamitsu Mitsui	790,694	31	Gonshiro Kubota	574,512
16	Takaatsu Mitsui	771,180	32	Yozaemon Tonomura	555,574

Notes: * Fertilizer merchant in Osaka; ** Tokyo Maruko Manufacturing

Source: Nihon Shinshi Roku (Who's Who in Japan), 47th Edition (Kojunsha, 1944).

chants in Osaka, powerful landlords, owners of larger family enterprises (e.g., Saburonosuke Suzuki of Ajinomoto), and well-known executives who were large shareholders (Heizaemon Hibiya). Their names do not appear in the ranking for 1954, either. The only names that appear in both rankings are those of Aiichiro Fujiyama (58th in 1942 and 13th in 1954) and Sazo Idemitsu (183rd in 1942 and 6th in 1954). People at the top of the rankings for 1954, such as Iue, Matsushita, and Yamaoka, did not appear in the 1942 rankings.

As these tables clearly demonstrate, those who were wealthy before the war were financially devastated by the occupation policies, including the dismantling of the *zaibatsu* and the reform of the tax system. These people could no longer own and manage one or more enterprises by themselves or pursue profits without considering the long-term profitability of their enterprises. The management positions once occupied by these wealthy people—who were also large shareholders—were taken over by salaried managers. Opportunities for salaried managers to become top managers increased and the difficulty of raising capital and labor disputes also encouraged this trend.

Stable Shareholders and Corporate Groups

Although the occupation policies were harsh on the wealthy in postwar Japan, they were not a death blow. There were still capitalists who became large shareholders of large enterprises and pursued profits through the vehicle of high dividends, the rising value of stocks and capital, and stock trading. As table 3.4 shows, the wealthy who built up assets through small and medium-sized coal mining and spinning companies make an appearance in the ranking for 1954 while they are nowhere to be seen in the 1942 list. The shortage of materials after the war, distribution control, inflation, and the black market helped create a favorable environment for the postwar wealthy—who were completely different from the prewar wealthy. It was impossible, however, for these monied people to completely control large enterprises as did their counterparts in the prewar period because of the new tax system and various other factors.

The stock confiscated from the *zaibatsu* families and the head offices of the *zaibatsu* were released into the open market, meaning the stock market. Also, many other companies were issuing new stock because they no longer had munitions compensation and needed more capital to rebuild their companies. New stock was much sought after by the new breed of wealthy people, Japan's postwar nouveau riche.

As could be predicted, the new class of rich businesspeople became large shareholders of large enterprises. However, they were not welcomed by the managers of large enterprises for the following reasons: many of the new shareholders had become rich suddenly, so there was a difference in business and personal orientation, making integration difficult; most of the newly rich did not consider the history and future of the enterprises in which they'd invested and focused on making short-term profits, which made them obstacles for the implementation of rational management policies; and *zaibatsu* enterprises were inexperienced in the detailed workings of the stock market and could not deal with shareholders at general meetings. According to Hideo Edo, conventional managers at large enterprises made an effort to exclude these new shareholders by making enterprises that they managed by their own stock at market under different names.[32] This practice, however, was prohibited by commercial law and, moreover, these managers were unable to continue to collect the money needed to buy them out.[33]

After the occupation was over, regulations on the holding of mutual stock of old *zaibatsu* and limits on the holding of stock of old *zaibatsu* were eased (such changes were promoted by political maneuvering). Within this more relaxed business environment, the companies getting back into the game had their stock held by enterprises that formerly belonged to the same *zaibatsu*, since it seemed a prudent way to go. Requisite capital was provided by the banks, which again belonged to the same *zaibatsu*. In other words, the former *zaibatsu* enterprises became stable shareholders and successfully excluded the new unwelcomed shareholders, who were the unwanted by-products of *zaibatsu* dismantling. The salaried managers who had by now finally become the top managers of former *zaibatsu* enterprises viewed themselves as protecting their management power by having as their stable shareholders those groups of enterprises that formerly belonged to the same *zaibatsu*.[34]

To maintain their status as strong and stable shareholders, groups of enterprises organized informal associations whose members were company presidents. Sumitomo organized its presidents' association in 1951, Mitsubishi in 1954, and Mitsui in 1961. Mitsui's delay was related to the complexity of Mitsui Corporation's revival (amalgamation of a number of companies that have resulted from the sweeping partition of Mitsui Trading coerced by the occupation policies).[35] The presidents' associations functioned as sort of ad hoc representatives' councils of stable shareholders and as forums for the exchange of information and discussion on any number of issues. Such issues might be related to joint investment for national policy concerns (petrochemicals and atomic energy), the provision of aid (financing and reallocation of employees laid off by coal companies), mergers (e.g., the merging of Mitsubishi Chemicals and Mitsubishi Petrochemicals to form the Mitsubishi Chemical Corporation), the sponsorship of events, and the granting of the trademarks of former *zaibatsu*.[36]

Other large enterprises that had once been *zaibatsu* (as well as enterprises that had no *zaibatsu* connections) also wanted to establish stable shareholder corporate groups. They were at a loss as how to do so, since they did not have enough businesses to create the large body of stable shareholders needed.[37] For this reason several corporate groups, in which each corporation within the group acted as a stable shareholder through the holding of mutual stock, were established, with three major banks at their cores. Presidents' associations were also established. These groups included the Fuji

Bank Group (established in 1966 with a presidents' association called the Fuyo Kai) and the Sanwa Bank Group (established in 1967 with a presidents' association called the Sansui Kai). The Daiichi Bank Group was established in 1978 with a presidents' association called Sankin Kai, but its history is slightly different from the others since it was an integration of subgroups of presidents (from both Daiichi Bank Group and the Kangyo Bank) that had taken place as a result of the Daichi Kangyo Bank's establishment in 1971.

The corporate groups mentioned above are different from traditional vertically aligned corporate groups, which usually consist of a parent company and its subsidiaries. These corporate groups, however, featured the mutual holding of stock and presidents' associations. Companies in the groups functioned as mutual shareholders and guaranteed the management rights of salaried managers. These horizontally linked corporate groups played an important role in the development of managerial enterprises in Japan, a role both significant and often unheralded.[38]

The Supremacy of Promoted Salaried Managers

Table 3.6 shows trends in the development of managerial enterprises in Japan from 1930 to 1992. In the table below, data are taken from four separate years that fell within the period mentioned: 1930, 1955, 1975, and 1992. To create this table two new methods were used. First, I gathered data on the presidents of the largest enterprises in key business fields; to do so, I used the key business fields as specified and delineated in the *Kaisha Shiki Ho (Seasonal Company Report)*. As a measure for determining the largest enterprises in each business field, the *amount of paid-up capital* was used for the year 1930 while the *amount of total assets* was used for the other years. As table 3.3 indicates, however, many large enterprises in Japan after the war had chairman/president systems, and in some cases the types of president and chairman were different. In an attempt to avoid confusion, I have included parentheses in the table to show the number of cases where the chairman and president were of a different type. For example, of the 65 enterprises listed in 1992, chairmen of types B or C were the top managers in seven enterprises. Another method employed was to classify salaried managers and owner managers as either full-time or non-full-time managers and to gather data for each category.

Table 3.6. Development of Managerial Enterprises Run by Promoted Salaried Managers in Japan: 1930–1992

Type of President	1930	1955	1975	1992
Category A: Full-timers (1)				
Promoted salaried manager	3 (1)	35 (5)	41 (8)	49 (7)
Founder	8	3	3 (1)	3
Subtotal	11	38	44	52
Category B: Full-timers (2)				
Wander vogel–type salaried manager	4	3 (1)	3	2 (1)
Former bureaucrat	1	0	2 (1)	1 (1)
Founder's family	4	4	8 (1)	6 (1)
Large shareholder	1	0	0	0
Agent of financial institution	0	2	1	1 (1)
Representative of small parent company	0	1	2	0
Heir of salaried manager	0	1	2	3 (1)
Subtotal	10	11	18	13
Category C: Non-full-timers				
Former bureaucrat	5	3	3	0
Founder's family	4	0	0	0
Large shareholder	11	2	1	0
Agent of financial institution	0	1	0	0
Representative of parent company	2	0	0	0
Heir of salaried manager	0	1	0	0
Subtotal	22	7	4	0
Total	43	56	66	65

Sources:

1. Shogyo Koshin Shiyo (Commercial Inquiry Agency), *Nihon Zenkoku Shogaisha Yakuin Roku (Record of Company Directors in Japan),* 1930 Edition.
2. *Diamond Kaisha Shokuin Roku (Diamond Company Employees Record),* 1955, 1975, and 1992, Diamondsha.
3. H. Morikawa, "The Role of Managerial Enterprises in Post-War Japan's Economic Growth, Focus on the 1950s," *Business History* 37, No. 2 (London: Frank Cass, 1995).

Promoted Salaried Managers and Founders

In the above table, I have classified full-time managers into two categories. In category A, I have included promoted salaried managers and company founders (owner/managers). Although it may be problematic to include these two in the same category, these managers share some common characteristics. Notably, both groups have accumulated knowledge and information about the human networks that exist among top, middle, and lower managers, engineers, and on-site operators in all sorts of business areas including production, distribution, and research and development. According to A. D. Chandler, organizational capacity is based on facilities, equipment, and human skills. Human skills are optimized when a network of skilled people is formed. Top managers who understand the fundamental value and workings of human networks are those who have fundamentally grasped the key to the organizational power of enterprises. Which is why, in a nutshell, company founders and promoted salaried managers usually have the best opportunities to help their companies fully realize their potential, since they have either created these kind of networks or have been part of them themselves.

Promoted Salaried Managers and Wander Vogel*–Type Managers*

Salaried managers in category B, however, have generally not had long, arduous experiences in the managerial hierarchies of their enterprises. Therefore, whether they are presently full-time presidents or not (not to mention non-full-time presidents), it is unlikely that they have a thorough understanding of the networks of skilled people mentioned above. This classification, I believe, also applies to other countries. For example, in the United States, where headhunting is common, employees tend to have rather critical assessments of removed salaried managers and other professionals who do not understand the skills networks in their company, or even industry. IBM is one such example. IBM, as is well known, was built by founder Thomas Watson and grew in leaps and bounds during his presidency. Thomas Watson II, CEO, who succeeded his father, was another chief executive firmly rooted in the company's human networks and played a vital role in the company's continuous growth from 1956 to 1970. Following the younger Watson, the next string of IBM's CEOs were promoted salaried managers, including the well-known John Akers. Akers, however, took responsibility for a serious decline in the company's profits and dividends and stepped down in 1993. Akers was replaced by Lou Gerstner, former president of American Express and chairman of RJR Nabisco. IBM employees were shocked that someone from outside the company became chairman, which was not the tradition at the company, and the decision to hire an outsider was, in a way, a refutation of the company's internal human network system.[39]

A Detailed Analysis of Table 3.6

A detailed analysis of table 3.6 helps one understand some of the trends that can be seen in this longitudinal analysis of top-management structures. First, we learn that the percentages of founder-presidents of large companies in major fields were low, but never zero. We can also see that the number of founder-presidents was low. The numbers of and percentages for founder presidents of the largest companies in the major fields in 1930, 1955, 1975, and 1992 were low at eight (19%), three (5%), three (5%), and three (5%), respectively, but were never zero.

Next, we learn that, postwar, the number of salaried managers who had been promoted increased and that full-time presidents were becoming more numerous. In 1930 the number of promoted salaried managers was low at three (7%) but after the war rose to 35 (63%), 41 (62%), and 49 (75%). Full-time presidents (Type 1) also dominated at 26 percent, 68 percent, 67 percent, and 80 percent.

The percentages for full-time presidents (Type 2) were lower than those for full-time presidents (Type 1), at 23 percent, 20 percent, 27 percent, and 20 percent. The primary characteristic of the full-time president (Type 2) category was that they were members of founders' families and *wander vogel*–type managers. The percentages for presidents who were members of founders' families were 9 percent, 7 percent, 12 percent, and 9 percent, while those who were *wander vogel*–type managers amounted to 9 percent, 5 percent, 5 percent, and 3 percent. One of the primary reasons for the low percentages for presidents who were members of founders' families was the decline of family enterprises. The low percentages for *wander vogel*–type managers was because these managers (managers who jumped from one company to another as a way of advancing their careers) were not widely accepted in Japanese society.

If we look at non-full-time managers, we see that the numbers of and percentages for this group were high in 1930 at 22 (51%) but dramatically decreased after the war. The total number of non-full-time presidents was seven (13%) in 1955, four (6%) in 1975, and zero in 1992, figures that show how totally alien the concept of a part-time company president had become in Japan.

If there is one conclusion to be drawn from table 3.6, it is that it clearly shows that, in managerial enterprises after World War II, promoted salaried managers were becoming more numerous, a situation that continues to the present day.

Rapid Economic Growth and Managerial Enterprises

Takeo Kikkawa's Misunderstanding

As table 3.6 shows, during the period of high economic growth after the war, the presidents of the largest companies in Japan's major industries were increasingly men who had risen through the ranks in their companies, or what he has called promoted salaried managers. In keeping with the times, these salaried managers were also becoming increasingly influential and important in both the business world and society at large. This new breed of hard-working managers was conspicuous in terms of their efforts and successes. To say that they helped propel their managerial enterprises and the Japanese economy to new levels of success and expansion would not be overstating the case.

What must not be misunderstood, however, is that managerial enterprises were not the sole propellants of Japan's economic growth. In fact, I have been credited as one of the leading voices of the commonly held view that salaried managers within managerial enterprises helped develop and expand the Japanese economy and I consider this to be an inaccurate interpretation.[40]

The roles played by salaried managers and managerial enterprises are but one strand (although an important one) that runs through the historical process that is the economic development of modern, post-Meiji-restoration Japan. As large Japanese companies in the modern era grew larger and underwent tumultuous changes, the greater the role that salaried managers played in their companies' top management, as the age and its manifestations played off one another to create a new dynamic.[41] Moreover, I am keen to make it clear that I do *not* believe capitalist enterprises or businesses run by capitalist managers were unimportant or an obstruction to the development of the modern Japanese economy, since they did play a role and had an effect on the shape of things to come.

Among the capitalist enterprises, founder enterprises were particularly influential. There are some periods in the modern economic era in which it is abundantly clear that founder enterprises were extremely prominent: right after the Meiji restoration; in the economic rise after the Russo-Japanese War; in the boom period after World War I; in the period of great prosperity for the heavy chemical industry prior to Word War II; and in the period of economic growth after the Second World War.

Looking at some concrete examples, if we compare founder enterprises like Matsushita and Sanyo to the managerial enterprises of Toshiba and Hitachi, we can see the founder enterprises outperforming the others in growth terms. On the contrary, if we change industries and look at the toiletries field, managerial enterprises such as Kao outperform family-run ones like Lion. The founder enterprise, Suntory, is head and shoulders above managerial enterprise rivals in the whiskey business, but when it comes to beer, Suntory is a mere shadow of managerial enterprise firms like Kirin. By bringing up cases like these and others like them, can one really say that founder enterprises were more important to Japan's postwar economic development? I don't think so.

Yet even those who agree with Kikkawa's views must take note of the information presented later in table 3.9. As we can see from this list, the capitalist-run businesses (meaning both founder and family enterprises) and managerial enterprises for which we have data show almost no discernible growth-performance differences in the high-growth postwar period.

What is also important to note about founder enterprises is that even though they may have followed brilliant growth paths, the founders who were largely responsible for their companies' emergence grew old, retired, and passed away. When founders no longer control their companies, their firms can wither and die or be crushed by the competition after founder enterprises lose their guiding lights. Founder enterprises are, by definition, short-lived and they must be transformed into either family enterprises or managerial enterprises. If not, they die. As we will later learn in greater detail, founder enterprises sometimes become family enterprises right away, sometimes they immediately become managerial enterprises, and sometimes they become managerial enterprises after being family run, when management difficulties become too much for the families to handle. Although founder enterprises may shine brightly and attract great attention during their ascendance, in the long term they become subsumed to extended trends that favor managerial enterprises.

To summarize my own views, I stress once again that the role of managerial enterprises in Japan's postwar, high-growth period should not be minimized and I call the reader's attention to tables 3.7, 3.8, and 3.9, which support this view.

A Breakdown of the Advances Made by Large, Leading Enterprises during the High Economic Growth Period

The information contained in tables 3.7 and 3.8 was taken from a book edited by Keichiro Nakagawa and others, called *Kindai Nihon Keieishi no Kiso Chishiki (Fundamental Information on the History of Modern Japanese Business)*, published by Yuhikaku Publishing in 1974. Table 3.7 lists the top 100 mining and manufacturing companies in order of total assets for the latter half of the year 1940 while table 3.8 lists the top 100 for the latter half of 1972. Table 3.9 is a list of companies that do not appear in table 3.7 but are present in table 3.8. The companies in table 3.9 are ones that showed exceptional growth during the postwar economic expansion and are listed by top-management categories.

It should also be noted that the appearance of a company in table 3.8 but not 3.7 does not mean that all such companies were rapidly growing firms. To ensure conformity of data, companies that were dismantled during the Allied occupation, firms that created subsidiaries, and companies that were merged or changed names have been excluded from table 3.9.

Here is some information regarding the companies listed in the tables: Jujo Paper, Honshu Paper, and Oji Paper all appear in table 3.8—companies derived from Oji Paper, which appears alone in position 3 of table 3.7. Kawasaki Seitetsu, which appears in table 3.8, separated from the company Kawasaki Jukogyo (which is in table 3.7, position 13).

Nihon Sekiyu Seisei, listed in table 3.8, is a subsidiary of Nihon Sekiyu, the company listed in position 25 in table 3.7.

Kureha Boseki, in position 40 in table 3.7, was absorbed by Toyo Boseki of table 3.8, as was Nihon Senryo (3.7, position 97) by Sumitomo Kagaku (3.8). Mergers were also a factor: Dai Nihon Boseki (3.7, position 17) merged with Nihon Rayon (3.7, position 93) and appeared in table 3.8 under the company name of Yunichika.

Also of note is the large number of company name changes. Asano Cement (3.7, position 38) became Nihon Cement in table 3.8, Osaka Tekkosho (3.7, position 45) changed its name to Hitachi Zosen, Asahi Benberugu Silk (3.7, position 51) became Asahi Kasei, Nihon Kasei (3.7, position 81) transformed into Mitsubishi Kasei, Kurashiki Kenshoku (3.7, position 77) turned into Kurare, Tama Zosensho (3.7, position 81) changed to Mitsui Zosen, Uraga Senkyo (3.7, position 87) became Sumitomo Jukikai, and, among others,

Table 3.7. Top 100 Mining and Manufacturing Companies in 1940 (in thousands of yen)

Position	Company Name	Total Assets	Position	Company Name	Total Assets
1	*Nihon Seitetsu	1,242,321	31	*Nihon Seikosho	143,143
2	*Mitsubishi Jukogyo	969,491	32	Meiji Seito	140,906
3	*Oji Seishi	562,088	33	*Diesel Jidosha Kogyo	138,595
4	*Hitachi Seisakusho	552,515	34	*Nihon Keikinzoku	136,880
5	*Nihon Kogyo	547,892	35	Dai Nihon Beer	134,133
6	Nihon Chisso Hiryo	540,344	36	Katakura Seishi Boseki	132,809
7	*Kanegafuchi Boseki	434,716	37	Ensuiko Seito	127,908
8	*Tokyo Shibaura Denki	414,761	38	*Asano Cement	123,742
9	*Mitsubishi Kogyo	407,555	39	Nihon Yushi	122,940
10	*Sumitomo Kinzoku Kogyo	380,200	40	*Kureha Boseki	122,124
11	Showa Seikosho	378,961	41	*Nihon Denki	121,831
12	*Nihon Kokan	324,017	42	*Asahi Glass	120,020
13	*Kawasaki Jukogyo	306,616	43	Rasa Kogyo	114,125
14	*Toyo Boseki	284,444	44	Furukawa Kogyo	113,382
15	*Mitsui Kozan	283,604	45	*Osaka Tekkosho	106,032
16	Honkeiko Baitetsu Konsu	280,201	46	Manshu Keikinzoku Seizo	105,277
17	*Dai Nihon Boseki	235,839	47	Nihon Keori	105,187
18	Nihon Soda	234,754	48	*Sumitomo Kogyo	103,064
19	*Kobe Seikosho	222,219	49	*Sumitomo Denki Kogyo	101,484
20	Nissan Kagaku Kogyo	212,353	50	Naigai Wata	101,315
21	*Showa Denko	209,917	51	*Asahi Benberugu Silk	100,153
22	Chosen Chisso Hiryo	206,873	52	Shanghai Seizo Silk	99,991
23	Nihon Suisan	199,028	53	Aichi Tokei Denki	99,339
24	Hokkaido Tanko Kisen	190,487	54	Showa Kogyo	93,315
25	*Nihon Sekiyu	170,791	55	Nichiro Gyogyo	93,201
26	*Mitsubishi Denki	164,994	56	Fuji Gas Boseki	92,761
27	*Furukawa Denki Kogyo	159,964	57	Nisshin Seito	90,504
28	Nihon Koshuha Jukogyo	159,956	58	*Daido Seifun	89,505
29	Dai Nihon Seito	158,706	59	*Toyota Motors	88,635
30	Taiwan Seito	158,186	60	*Sumitomo Kagaku Kogyo	88,099
			61	Nakayama Seikosho	87,154
			62	Riken Jukogyo	86,127
			63	Ishihara Sangyo Kaiun	85,190

(*continued*)

Table 3.7. *(continued)*

Position	Company Name	Total Assets	Position	Company Name	Total Assets
64	*Nihon Kasei Ko-	83,196	82	Showa Sangyo	61,553
	gyo		83	Kawanishi Ko-	60,287
65	*Tokyo Ishikawa	79,446		kuki	
	Jima Zosensho		84	Yuho Boseki	59,725
66	Nisshin Boseki	78,333	85	*Toyo Rayon	57,942
67	Kurashiki Boseki	77,578	86	Ikegai Tekkosho	55,902
68	Nittestu Kogyo	75,828	87	*Uraga Senkyo	55,397
69	*Onoda Cement	74,435	88	Nihon Seifun	54,111
	Seizo		89	Ri Kagaku Kogyo	53,831
70	*Fuji Denki	74,154	90	Nitto Boseki	53,592
	Seizo		91	*Kubota Tekko-	53,293
71	*Nissan Motors	72,774		sho	
72	Nihon Aluminum	71,567	92	*Niigata Tekko-	52,718
73	Fujikoshi Kozai	70,419		sho	
	Kogyo		93	*Nihon Rayon	52,000
74	*Teikoku Jinzo	68,056	94	Nichiman Kogyo	51,848
	Silk		95	Nihon Sharyo	51,375
75	Nanyo Kohatsu	64,871		Seizo	
76	Gunze	64,870	96	*Suzuki Shok-	50,692
77	*Kurashiki Ken-	64,214		uryo Kogyo	
	shoku		97	*Nihon Senryo	49,807
78	Nisso Kogyo	64,158		Seizo	
79	Manmo Keori	63,870	98	Kisha Seizo	49,605
80	Denki Kagaku	63,650	99	Teikoku Seima	49,525
	Kogyo		100	Kawaminami Ko-	48,682
81	*Tama Zosensho	63,191		gyo	

Note: Companies marked with an asterisk are those that also appear in table 3.8.

Source: Kindai Nihon Keieishi no Kiso Chishiki (Fundamental Information on the History of Modern Japanese Business), Keichiro Nakagawa, et al., eds. (Yuhikaku Publishing, 1974): 454.

Suzuki Shokugyo Kogyo (3.7, position 96) later became known as Ajinomoto.

Taking out of the equation companies like the ones mentioned above, there are 51 firms appearing in the top 100 (in table 3.8) for the first time. In that regard, these 51 companies could be considered ones that grew dramatically during Japan's high economic growth period.

By the same token, if we subtract from table 3.7 the companies that merged and changed names, there are 52 companies that do not appear in table 3.8. These companies, in other words, are firms

Table 3.8. Top 100 Mining and Manufacturing Companies in 1972 (in millions of yen)

Position	Company Name	Total Assets	Position	Company Name	Total Assets
1	Shin Nihon Seitetsu	2,113,335	38	Kumagaya Gumi	245,794
2	Mistsubishi Jukogyo	1,648,235	39	Mitsui Toatsu Kagaku	242,485
3	NKK	1,162,308	40	Isuzu Motors	237,961
4	Hitachi Seisakusho	1,036,178	41	Honda Motors	235,641
5	Ishikawajima Harima Jukogyo	982,021	42	Nisshin Seiko	231,649
			43	Fujitsu	221,212
6	Nissan Motors	949,029	44	Asahi Glass	220,615
7	Sumitomo Kinzoku Kogyo	930,197	45	Takeda Yakuhin Kogyo	219,216
8	Tokyo Shibaura Denki	852,999	46	Fujita Kogyo	216,761
			47	Kanebo	213,663
9	Kawasaki Seitetsu	843,838	48	Toyo Boseki	213,425
10	Kobe Seikosho	683,629	49	Mitsubishi Sekiyu	213,186
11	Toyota Motors	634,952	50	Nihon Sekiyu Seisei	206,288
12	Matsushita Denki Sangyo	624,450	51	Mitsubishi Yuka	203,152
			52	Goyo Kensetsu	196,771
13	Mitsubishi Denki	552,315	53	Mitsubishi Kinzoku Kogyo	192,371
14	Kawasaki Jukyogyo	539,279			
15	Hitachi Zosen	529,315	54	Kirin Beer	192,084
16	Toyo Kogyo	513,670	55	Yunichika	188,469
17	Taisei Kensetsu	468,652	56	Fuji Denki Seizo	185,212
18	Kashima Kensetsu	465,321	57	Nihon Kei Kinzoku	182,754
19	Idemitsu Kosan	458,750	58	Sony	179,797
20	Obayashi Gumi	458,277	59	Sanyo Denki	178,046
21	Mitsubishi Kasei Kogyo	429,390	60	Shokusan Jutaku Sogo	177,796
22	Takenaka Komuten	427,944	61	Toa Nenryo Kogyo	175,065
23	Komatsu Seisakusho	397,848	62	Mitsubishi Rayon	173,127
24	Nihon Denki	377,711	63	Jujo Paper	171,205
25	Toray	361,451	64	Hino Jidosha Kogyo	167,911
26	Shimizu Kensetsu	359,785	65	Bridgestone Tire	167,696
27	Sumitomo Kagaku Kogyo	358,924	66	Furukawa Denki Kogyo	161,464
28	Mitsui Zosen	358,002	67	Sanyo Kokusaku Pulp	161,312
29	Asahi Kasei Kogyo	324,882	68	Showa Sekiyu	160,797
30	Nihon Kogyo	324,116	69	Oji Paper	159,628
31	Showa Denko	311,372	70	Sumitomo Denki Kogyo	158,462
32	Sumitomo Jukikai Kogyo	300,047			
			71	Taiyo Gyogyo	155,153
33	Nihon Sekiyu	295,624	72	Kurare	152,704
34	Ube Kosan	292,104	73	Saseho Jukogyo	151,314
35	Maruzen Sekiyu	272,516	74	Mitsui Kinzoku Kogyo	148,684
36	Teijin	271,426	75	Dai Showa Paper	148,437
37	Kubota Tekko	247,969	76	Hazama Gumi	146,746

Table 3.8. (*continued*)

Position	Company Name	Total Assets	Position	Company Name	Total Assets
77	Toda Kensetsu	143,978	88	Honshu Paper	126,607
78	Sumitomo Kinzoku Kozan	143,120	89	Arabia Sekiyu	126,154
			90	Nishimatsu Kensetsu	125,585
79	Sharp	138,936	91	Chiyoda Kako Kensetsu	124,768
80	Onoda Cement	138,196			
81	Fuji Shashin Film	138,060	92	Eidai Sangyo	123,148
82	Mitsui Kensetsu	135,157	93	Fuji Jukogyo	121,890
83	Mitsui Sekiyu Kagaku Kogyo	134,961	94	Nihon Cement	121,486
			95	Nihon Seikosho	119,866
84	Dai Nippon Ink Kagaku Kogyo	133,151	96	Dai Nippon Print	117,399
			97	Suzuki Motors	116,784
85	Daiwa House Kogyo	132,059	98	Matsushita Denko	115,504
86	Daido Seiko	128,903	99	Niigata Tekkosho	114,080
87	Daikyo Sekiyu	127,889	100	Ajinomoto	112,702

Source: Kindai Nihon Keieishi no Kiso Chishiki (Fundamental Information on the History of Modern Japanese Business), Keichiro Nakagawa, et al., eds. (Yuhikaku Publishing, 1974): 456.

that either went bankrupt or could not maintain the pace of the competition in the high-growth period after Japan's defeat in World War II. Here is a breakdown of those companies:

- *Old colonial period businesses*: 12 companies (Showa Seikojo, Honkeiko Baitetsu Konsu, Chosen Chisso Hiryo, Naigai Wata, Nanyo Kohatsu, and others).
- *Textiles*: 8 companies (Katakura Seishi Boseki, Gunze, Nihon Keori, Teikoku Seima, Fuji Gas Boseki, Nisshin Boseki, Nitto Boseki, Kurashiki Boseki).
- *Foodstuffs*: 11 companies (Dai Nihon Seito-Sugar, Taiwan Seito, Meiji Seito, Ensuiko Seito, Nihon Seifun-Flour, Nisshin Seifun, Showa Sangyo, Nihon Suisan, Nichiro Gyogyo, Nihon Yushi, Dai Nihon Beer). (Dai Nihon Beer was broken up and incorporated into the Sapporo and Asahi beer companies, neither of which appears in table 3.8.)
- *Chemicals*: 4 companies (Nihon Chisso Hiryo, Nisso Kogyo, Nissan Kagaku, Denki Kagaku).
- *Heavy industries that boomed owing to war-related munitions sales*: 12 companies (Aichi Tokei Denki, Riken Juko, Kawanishi Kokuki, Kawaminami Kogyo, and others).
- *Mining*: 5 companies (Hokkaido Tanko Kisen, Furukawa Kogyo, Showa Kogyo, and others).

Table 3.9 is a list of the 51 companies that appeared for the first time in table 3.8 (companies that did not merge, or acquire other companies, etc.). Among these companies, managerial enterprises represented the largest group, with 23 such firms included. Having said that, however, these 23 firms total less than half of the total represented by the other types of businesses, which numbered 28.

As we examine this list, it is apparent that of the mining and manufacturing companies who did well during the economic growth years, more than half of them are capitalist enterprises. Although this result appears on initial investigation to be very close to the Kikkawa model, when we consider that almost half of these leading firms were managerial enterprises, we realize that Kikkawa's postulations are not perfect. When all is said and done, all that we can really conclude from looking at the high-growth mining and manufacturing companies of the postwar era is that is that the capitalist enterprises slightly outnumbered the managerial enterprises.

Significance of the Trend toward Domination by Managerial Enterprises

Even if the growth power of capitalist enterprises (particularly founder enterprises) is stronger than that of managerial enterprises, as Dr. Kikkawa has noted, there is a long-term trend for capitalist enterprises (particularly founder enterprises) to become managerial enterprises and to grow more than capitalist enterprises. How did this contribute to Japan's rapid economic growth?

First, managerial enterprises, particularly managerial enterprises with promoted salaried managers, generally had access to much more first-hand information about actual working environments or working situations (which we might term "work sites") than did capitalist enterprises. Founder enterprises, which were capitalist enterprises, also possessed a great deal of information about work sites, but they were fewer in number than managerial enterprises (particularly managerial enterprises with promoted salaried managers). It was this practical use of information and knowledge gained from work-site experience that managerial enterprises used to make their particular and significant contribution to the country's rapid economic growth.

Second, management strategy that stressed managerial enterprises rather than the payment of large dividends to shareholders also contributed to rapid economic growth. In founder enterprises and family enterprises, capitalists (founders and their families)

Table 3.9. Mining and Manufacturing Companies Appearing on Top 100 List for the First Time in 1972 (Total: 51 companies, ranking is in terms of total company assets)

Managerial Enterprise (23)	Founder Enterprise (12)	Family Enterprise (11)	Major Stockholder–Controlled Enterprise (4)	Subsidiaries (1)
Taisei Kensetsu	Matsushita Denki Sangyo	Toyo Kogyo (Matsuda/Mazda)	Ube Kosan	Matsushita Denko
Komatsu Seisakusho	Idemitsu Kosan	Kashima Kensetsu	Shokusan Jutaku Sogo	
Maruzen Sekiyu	Honda Motors	Obayashi Gumi	Arabia Sekiyu	
Mitsui Toatsu Kagaku	Sony	Takenaka Komuten	Dai Nihon Insatsu	
Nisshin Seiko	Sanyo Denki	Shimizu		
Fujitsu	Bridgestone Tire	Kumagaya Gumi		
Mitsubishi Sekiyu	Toda Kensetsu	Takeda Yakuhin Kogyo		
Mitsubishi Yuka	Sharp	Fujita Kogyo		
Kirin Beer	Dai Nippon Ink Kagaku Kogyo	Goyo Kensetsu		
Toa Nenryo Kogyo (Tonen)	Daiwa House Kogyo	Taiyo Gyogyo		
Mitsubishi Rayon	Eidai Sangyo	Dai Showa Paper		
Hino Jidosha Kogyo	Suzuki Motors			
Sanyo Kokusaku Pulp				
Showa Seikyu				
Saseho Jukyogyo				
Hazama Gumi				
Fuji Shashin Film				
Mitsui Kensetsu				
Mitsui Sekiyu Kagaku Kogyo				
Daikyo Sekiyu				
Chiyoda Kako Kensetsu				
Fuji Heavy Industries				
Nishimatsu Kensetsu				

Source: Kindai Nihon Keieishi no Kiso Chishiki (Fundamental Information on the History of Modern Japanese Business), Keichiro Nakagawa, et al., eds. (Yuhikaku Publishing, 1974): 454–456.

strive to maintain their wealth and lifestyle, which tends to have a negative impact on management resources, a necessary ingredient if enterprises are to grow.

Third, as I discussed earlier, not only founders and their families but salaried managers as well may diminish the effectiveness of management if they rest on their laurels. However, if an enterprise has mechanisms for shifting personnel either around or out, top managers who fail to perform can be replaced. Managerial enterprises have the most effective, built-in, personnel renewal systems—systems that capitalist enterprises, particularly founder enterprises, are usually without. Given the above point, the possibility of more elastic response to the failure of top management, I feel confident in postulating that the supremacy of managerial enterprises was an important factor in the rapid economic growth of postwar Japan.

Personnel Renewal Systems

Given that enterprises are constantly striving to grow, that all leaders age (no matter how good they are), and that many companies fail to keep pace with the times, all organizations—enterprises or otherwise—must have a built-in renewal system for their leaders. Many enterprises have rules to limit the terms of their presidents and have age limits for their managers because they understand the need for such mechanisms to renew personnel. Unfortunately, many enterprises do not implement such systems because they do not appreciate their importance. I am not simply referring to the matter of aging. Even when the top managers are young, if they become complacent because of success and are surrounded by "yes" men, morale within the company and the desire of employees to innovate inevitably decline. When the top managers are old, problems related to aging must also be factored in.

I think we often erroneously believe that the natural abilities of leaders that help their enterprises succeed last forever. Among founder enterprises, family enterprises, and managerial enterprises, managerial enterprises are the most likely to establish renewal systems for their top managers because the top managers are evaluated both by the families who are the owners and by their employees.

Why Have Founder Enterprises Received So Much Praise?

Why do many researchers, including Dr. Kikkawa, conclude that founder enterprises experience greater growth than managerial enterprises? One of the reasons is the mystique that surrounds entrepreneurs, who are often founders of companies. These entrepreneurs, or capitalist managers, are perceived as investing their assets to establish and grow businesses, and as taking a great deal of risk and being innovative. Salaried managers, however, are thought to focus on their salary and job security, and to be more conservative. Other reasons include the tendency of successful founders to boast about their experiences and write autobiographies and reports of various types, which have served as useful references for studies on the history of management in Japan. Salaried managers, however, tend to be less self-centered and to write little about themselves. And even when they do write such reports, they rarely have a heroic tone to them and do not create strong impressions.

Managerial Enterprises and Corporate Groups

It might strike some as strange that salaried managers owning little or no stock in their enterprises can rise to become top managers. It's possibly even stranger that they can become all-powerful in these enterprises. Both A. D. Chandler and I have explained the phenomenon from the perspective of the development of managerial hierarchies, especially the multiple layers of salaried managers. Both Chandler and I have emphasized that the development of these hierarchies is a more important factor than the deconcentration of stock.

Takeo Kikkawa has a different view. He states that such a general perspective cannot explain how salaried managers obtained control of top management of large enterprises after the war. He also states that it cannot be explained, except by the mutual holding of stock among large enterprises, which was common in six primary corporate groups (Mitsui, Mitsubishi, Sumitomo, Fuji, Sanwa, and Daiichi Kangin). The mutual holding of stock among large enterprises was a distinctive characteristic of the Japanese economy after the war. Under this system, the power of salaried managers of large enterprises within a corporate group was guaranteed.[43] Although I am quite critical of Kikkawa's views on the growing power of capitalist enterprises, I agree with his explanation regarding the power of salaried managers from the perspective of the mutual holding of stock. I would add that the issue of managerial enterprises becoming the dominant type of large enterprise after the war cannot be discussed without considering the growth of corporate groups mentioned above. However, the growth of corporate groups is one factor to reinforce the development of managerial enterprises. Without the fundamental factor, the growth of managerial hierarchies, the development of managerial enterprises in Japan cannot be understood from the perspective of world history.

Another important issue revolves around what supports the salaried managers of large enterprises that do not belong to those corporate groups and are not capitalist enterprises, such as Sony, Seibu, and Matsushita. These enterprises include Shinittetsu, Nisseki, Asahi Kasei, Asahi Beer, and Tokyu. Does Dr. Kikkawa explain the existence of these managerial enterprises from the perspective of support by the main banks? In corporate groups, enterprises do support each other for their mutual benefit, but banks do *not* support managerial enterprises to protect the benefits of salaried managers. Rather, they support them when the management of these enterprises is stable. When capitalist enterprises have the same management and financial conditions, banks support them as well. If the management and financial conditions of a managerial enterprise deteriorate, banks do not hesitate to request a change in top management. The banks may even assign capitalist managers if the enterprise cannot replace its top people with other salaried managers.

Hereditary Salaried Managers in Japan

Table 3.6 showed that promoted salaried managers gained power by becoming the top managers of large enterprises and that non-full-time capitalist managers in large enterprises disappeared. Promoted salaried managers are prosperous in Japan. Recently, however, the Japanese economy, led by the managerial enterprises, has faced a number of difficulties, which I will discuss later in chapter 5. Here, I would like to raise some issues related to table 3.6. Some full-time salaried managers who are hereditary presidents are listed in the column of full-time presidents (Category B: Full-timers 2). The number of such presidents has recently been increasing and reached three in 1992. The three presidents are Kunio Anzai of Tokyo Gas, Hiroshi Kawakami of Yamaha, and Yoshitoshi Kitajima of Dai Nippon Printing.

Apart from the issue of whether hereditary presidencies are good or profitable, it is understandable that the top managers of founder enterprises and family enterprises strive to hand over their presidencies to their descendants. It's not understandable, however, for salaried managers to strive to hand over their positions to members of their families because they or their ancestors did not establish the enterprises for which they work. Salaried managers own little or none of the stock in their companies. They are appointed to their jobs by their superiors simply because they have the requisite skills, which is why it's unreasonable for them to hand over power in their companies to their descendants. Top salaried managers who have handed over their companies to their descendants feel a sense of ownership of their companies—and have worked in an atmosphere that tacitly encouraged this. In managerial enterprises there should be no inheriting of power, however. Salaried managers are not restrained by capital or family connections and are appointed to their positions because of their management skills and nothing more.

Hiroshi Anzai, who is now chairman of Tokyo Gas, was promoted to director in the Materials and Equipment Department in November 1946, when he was 44 years old. He worked hard to secure raw materials and other supplies for Tokyo Gas, and a year after was promoted to executive director. He became vice president after seven years with the company and then president in November 1967. In 1972 he became chairman, and Katsutoshi Tsuru was appointed president. In 1976 Takeo Murakami—called the emperor of Tokyo Gas—became president, but he died in 1981. After Murakami, Hiroshi Watanabe, a brother-in-law (Anzai's wife's brother) of Chairman Anzai became president. During Watanabe's presidency, Kunio—Anzai's second son—was promoted from managing director to executive director, a most unusual personnel appointment.[44] This was not the end of things. At a meeting of shareholders held in June 1988, Chairman Anzai demanded of President Watanabe that Kunio be appointed president and that Watanabe be appointed advisor. Watanabe was hesitant and Kunio declined, saying, "This is too much for me at this time." Chairman Anzai, who was then 87 years old, told Watanabe that he lacked courage. In the end Anzai and Watanabe came to a compromise and agreed that Kunio be appointed vice president. Two vice presidents were then transferred to and appointed chairmen of affiliated companies.[45] In April 1989 Hiroshi Anzai died, Kunio became president, and Hiroshi Watanabe became chairman.

Hereditary Salaried Managers in the United States

Although there are not many hereditary salaried managers in the United States, they do exist. Let's look at the example of RCA (Radio

Corporation of America). In 1919 RCA was established as a joint venture by GE and Westinghouse, but it later became independent because in its original form it contravened antitrust laws. David Sarnoff, at age 39, was appointed president of the new RCA. Sarnoff was a promoted salaried manager and was CEO until 1970. Highly regarded as a manager, Sarnoff has been called the "father of radio and TV." Four years prior to his retirement, however, David appointed his son Robert, 48, as president. Rumors suggested that David had misused his power to appoint his son president. The Sarnoff family owned less than 1 percent of RCA stock at the time. Sarnoff's decision to appoint his son was thus severely criticized as the elder Sarnoff was a salaried chairman and his actions were contrary to business practices in the United States. Upon his father's retirement Robert became chairman at the age of 52 and subsequently carried out some questionable actions, such as entering and withdrawing from the computer industry. In 1975, after five years as chairman, RCA's directors removed Robert from his post.[46]

The Study of Management History and Long-Term Trends

Taking a long-term view (over a period of 100 years or more), it seems obvious that managerial enterprises have overwhelmed capitalist enterprises and become dominant in Japan's capitalist economy. To look at history in longer chunks is to look at trends, an obviously fundamental method of studying history, a method that also applies to the study of management history. In management history, it is, of course, possible to look at the trends and histories of large leading enterprises, such as Sony and Honda, over shorter periods of time, perhaps 10 or 20 years. Studies based on shorter time spans, however, have also been done in the area of corporate strategies, primarily by Ikujiro Nonaka, Takayuki Itami, Akihiro Okumura, and Tadao Kagono.

Although I'm convinced that studies in management history and management often overlap, there is an area in which there is little duplication, an area that only researchers of management history can satisfactorily deal with—studies of the management of enterprises that cover periods of 50 years, 100 years, or longer. While researchers of both management and management history can examine the establishment, innovations, and successes of Sony and Honda, for example, studies covering these companies over 50 years—from their establishment to the present—or studies covering 120 years of the history of Mitsubishi, say, or 320 years of the history of Mitsui, can only be conducted by management historians. Needless to say, it is impossible for any management researcher to study every detail in the entire history of a company that has been in operation for 50 years, 100 years, or even longer. But what management historians *can* do is examine the management of these companies from a long-term perspective. It's when this kind of research takes place that management researchers become management historians. When researchers of management do this, they essentially become researchers of management history.

The same principles apply to the examination of enterprises in the broader sense, such as the rise and fall of capitalist enterprises and managerial enterprises. As emphasized earlier, it's essentially meaningless to discuss the superiority and inferiority of one type of enterprise over a short period of time. The essence of our work is the examination of how managerial enterprises gained supremacy over capitalist enterprises over the long haul.

CHAPTER FOUR

Family Enterprises in Japan Today

Overview

Redefining Family Enterprises

In chapter 1, the definition of the term "family enterprise" was broadened. The broader definition includes companies where the founder (after retiring or dying) has left his company to his family, who then cooperates with salaried managers in the running of the business. Other definitions in chapter 1 include families who run their businesses themselves, as well as families who don't run their businesses but hold substantial management responsibilities, such as employing and dismissing salaried managers from outside the family. Yet despite the apparent clarity of the above definition, in order to carry out more in-depth, objective research, I believe it's necessary to have a definition based on quantifiable criteria.

The first thing to consider in a more rigorous classification process is that if we use the term family enterprise in a broad sense (as most people do) the number would grow unwieldy. Moreover, the proportion of family businesses among small- to medium-sized firms is extremely high. Suffice it to say, then, that an analysis of this scale would require resources that go beyond the limits of this book. The focus of our study, therefore, will be confined to large-scale family enterprises. Let us now think about the meaning of large-scale businesses in the context of family enterprises. By large, we refer not only to companies with a large capital base or high sales turnover, but also to companies that, in addition to the above characteristics, have multilayer organizations. In these kinds of enterprises, even though the founders' families may employ teams of salaried managers to help them run their businesses—and even though family members may not control every aspect and level of their business from middle-management level downward—family members still hold the top-management positions and should be considered as running the family business.

Moreover, in the Japanese joint-stock company (*Kabushiki Kaisha*) system, whereby top-management structure and decision making revolve around directors' meetings, the number of directors is likely to increase to unwieldy levels. Thus, new hierarchies are created within the top-management structure and bring an accompanying set of organizational problems. Another feature of family enterprises run by the families of the founders is that some relatives often want to be more than figureheads who attend directors' meetings. Commonly, the goal of such family managers is to take on an active role as CEO, president, or chairman. In other words, they want to *lead* the company, not sit passively by while nonfamily managers run the show.

Yet despite this desire on the part of family members to run their companies, there is a question of competency. Although these relatives may assume the lofty position of chairman or vice-chairman, there's usually still debate in the corporate corridors about whether these high-level posting are just perks or are true reflections of management ability. Although salaried managers might grumble that the position of "advisor" (*sodan yaku*) is a better and more realistic one for such high-level family managers, these situations differ from company to company and can be handled by organizations only on that basis.

To come to some final, strictly defined criteria about what constitutes a true family enterprise is a difficult task, one made harder by the sheer volume and variety of companies that fit into one category or another. In order to escape the inherent vagaries of classifying organizations by subjective categories, the only viable method I have found is to collect massive amounts of objective data and assess it quantitatively.

D. F. Channon has described three conditions whereby an enterprise can be described as a family enterprise: first, that the CEO of the company is a family member; second, that the family has run the business for at least 60 years; and third, that the family or its trust interests hold at least five percent of voting stock. Channon contends that all three of these conditions must exist for a company to be called a family enterprise, and his view could be called an uncompromising one. His viewpoint seems even more rigid particularly in the context of postwar Japan, when the proportion of institutional stockholders in Japanese joint-stock companies was extremely high. Even though families' direct or trust interests may have been less than Channon's required 5 percent, family members were still extremely influential in the direction of company business.[1]

The same issue can be looked at from another perspective. According to the February 26, 1979, issue of the magazine *Nikkei Business*, the proportion of shares issued to directors of Japanese companies (as of March 1978) averaged 2.0 percent, a figure lower than that of family enterprises. In order to achieve a clearer picture of what Japanese family enterprises really are, I have taken into account the two disparate opinions described above, as well as the factors discussed earlier in this chapter concerning the term family enterprise. Listed below are the conditions that this book uses to define present-day, large-scale, family enterprises in Japan:

1. Companies listed in the First Section of the Tokyo Stock Exchange whose total assets were valued at 30 billion yen or more as of 1978.
2. Companies equivalent in stature to the ones described in condition (1), above, but which are not listed on the Tokyo Stock Exchange.
3. Companies whose founder has either died or retired from a high-ranking position such as chairman or president (emeritus positions are included among retirement).
4. Companies whose family representatives continued in positions of either chairman or president.
5. Companies whose founder's families and family trust interests hold 10 percent or more of the company's overall voting stock.

For the purpose of this study, I decided to combine conditions (3) to (5), in order to reevaluate the criteria for what constitutes large-scale family enterprise, and I came up with these new conditions:

6. When families and family trust interests hold neither the position of chairman nor president but still control 10 percent or more of the company's overall voting stock.
7. When families and family trust interests control less than 10 percent of the company's overall voting stock but still hold positions of either chairman or president.

Table 4.1 lists the large-scale, family enterprises that, as of 1978, met the criteria described above. In order to show the changes in stockholding and management roles that occurred over time in these enterprises, data have been given first for the year 1978, as stated, and then for the year 1993. It should be noted, however, that for the 1978 data, two companies (Ina Seito and Daimaru) have been listed as exceptions since they don't meet the conditions for minimum 10 percent stockholding or have family members holding chairman or president roles (although family members were vice presidents). These exceptions were allowed since, in both cases, the vice presidents were promoted to presidents in or before 1993 and were therefore included in this table. One further exception, Nintendo, has been included for different reasons. Although Nintendo had total assets of only 13 billion yen in 1978 (although the founding families did hold 13% of stock), it has been added because of the company's recent importance and explosive growth (including total assets valued at 600 billion yen as of 1993).

Concerning the unlisted companies (companies not listed on the Japanese stock exchange) included in table 4.1, all eight were documented as having total assets of 30 billion yen or more.

Table 4.1: Considerations and Conclusions

Table 4.1 lists a total of 100 large-scale family enterprises with total assets of 30 billion yen or more. Of the 100, 92 were companies listed on the stock exchange and 8 were nonlisted companies, which have been included because of their relative importance in the Japanese business world. Forty-four of the companies had family investments totaling 10 percent or more of the total shares as of 1978, and 48 companies had family investments representing less than 10 percent of the total shares.

As a general rule, data of this kind need to be analyzed within a strictly defined framework, but by doing so there is a real danger of losing some of the substance provided by the overview that the data provide. A good example would be companies where the founder has retired from the position of chairman or president (e.g., Bridgestone or Matsushita). A strict framework-based analysis would categorize these companies as family enterprises, but the mere absence of a job title does not mean that these important company figures no longer directly exert a powerful influence over the organizations they founded. Conversely, an overly strict analysis

Table 4.1. Changes in Family's Investment Ratios and Managerial Positions of Large-Scale Family Enterprises (1978–1993)

	1978		1993	
Company Name	Ratio of Family Stock Holdings (%)	Positions Held by Family Members	Ratio of Family Stock Holdings (%)	Positions Held by Family Members
Kashima Kensetsu	10.0	Chairman, Vice Chairman, President	3.2	Chairman, Vice Chairman
Obayashi Gumi	12.6	President, Auditor	12.0	Chairman, Vice President
Shimizu Kensetsu	19.2	Sr. Director	16.6	
Toda Kensetsu	37.4	Chairman, President, Vice President, Sr. Director x 2	27.8	Chairman, Vice Chairman, President
Fujita Kogyo (Fujita)	10.6	President	4.5	President, Vice President
Zenitaka Gumi	53.3	President, Vice President	50.0	Chairman/President
Matsumura Gumi	29.5	President, Exec. Director,	26.2	Chairman
Misawa Homes	17.3	President	8.8	President
Taiyo Gyogyo (Maruha)	19.4	President, Vice President, Exec. Director	19.0	President
Ezaki Glico	14.1	Chairman	12.4	President, Director
Fujiya	17.9	Chairman, President, Sr. Director x 2	6.2	President, Vice President
Kikkoman	13.0	Chairman, President, Vice President, Sr. Director, Director	10.6	President, Vice President, Sr. Director, Exec. Director, Director/Advisor
Kyupi	35.7	Chairman	22.5	Chairman
Yamazaki Seipan	10.5	(Owner), President, Director, Auditor	14.9	President, Director
SB Shokuhin	28.0	Chairman, President, Vice President x 2	18.9	Chairman, President
House Shokuhin	32.7	President, Auditor	20.4	Director
Omikenshi	21.6	President, Vice President, Auditor	23.3	Chairman, Vice Chairman
Daishowa Seishi	12.7	President, Vice President, Sr. Director, Director x 3	22.2	Chairman, President, Vice President, Sr. Director, Exec. Director

(*continued*)

Table 4.1. *(continued)*

	1978		1993	
Company Name	Ratio of Family Stock Holdings (%)	Positions Held by Family Members	Ratio of Family Stock Holdings (%)	Positions Held by Family Members
Taisho Seiyaku	49.7	Chairman, Vice Chairman, President, Sr. Director	33.5	Chairman, President
Dai Nippon Ink Kagaku	26.2	President	15.7	President, Director
Bridgestone Tire (Bridgestone)	30.2	Chairman, Sr. Director	20.3	Chairman Emeritus
Maruichi Kokan	19.7	Chairman, President, Auditor	16.9	Chairman, President, Sr. Director
Tokyo Seitetsu	38.9	Chairman, President, Sr. Director	26.0	President, Director
Nakayama Seikosho	19.1	Director	13.7	Director
Sanoyasu Senkyo	17.3	President, Director	(Sanoyasu Hishino Meisho) 5.3	Director/Advisor
Casio Keisanki	29.1	Chairman, President, Sr. Director x 2, Exec. Director	7.8	Chairman, President, Vice President
Nintendo	13.1	President	10.9	President
Tadano Tekkosho (Tadano)	24.5	President, Vice President, Director x 2	4.8	Chairman, President, Vice President
Fuji Tech	21.1	President, Vice President, Sr. Director	10.0	Chairman, President, Vice President
Hattori Tokeiten (Hattori Seiko)	34.7	President, Vice President, Director	33.6	Chairman
Dantani Industries	27.6	President, Vice President, Exec. Director, Director	14.6	Chairman, President, Director/Advisor
Kokuyo	26.4	President, Vice President, Exec. Director, Director	11.0	Chairman, President, Sr. Director, Exec. Director
Mizuno	36.6	President, Exec. Director, Director	20.2	Chairman, President
Iwatani Sangyo	17.8	President, Vice President	10.8	Chairman, Director

(continued)

Table 4.1. *(continued)*

Company Name	1978 Ratio of Family Stock Holdings (%)	1978 Positions Held by Family Members	1993 Ratio of Family Stock Holdings (%)	1993 Positions Held by Family Members
Nagase Sangyo	20.8	President, Vice President, Sr. Director	7.1	Chairman, President
Descente	18.2	President, Sr. Director	3.8	
Matsuya	10.3	President, Director/Advisor	3.4	President, Exec. Director
Kotobukiya	28.6	President, Director	19.3	Sr. Director, Sr. Advisor
Ito Yokado	25.2	President	15.5	Exec. Director, Director/Advisor
Sankyu Unyu Kiko(Sankyu)	10.4	President, Vice President	3.6	President
Seino Unyu	30.2	President, Vice President, Sr. Director, Exec. Director	17.8	Chairman, President, Sr. Director, Exec. Director
Yamatane Shoken	19.5	Chairman, President	21.9	
Seibu Tetsudo	22.9	President, Director x 2	48.7	Chairman, Director
Suruga Ginko	10.2	Bank President, Vice President of bank	15.0	Chairman, bank President, Vice President of bank
Satoh Kogyo	6.1	Chairman, President, Vice President, Sr. Director, Auditor	5.1	Chairman, President, Vice President
Tobishima Kensetsu	x	President, Vice President, Exec. Director	14.5	President
Okumura Gumi	x	Chairman, President	x	Chairman, President, Vice President, Exec. Director
Magara Kensetsu	9.4	President, Vice President, Auditor	5.0	President, Sr. Director
Asanuma Gumi	3.0	Chairman, President, Vice President, Sr. Director, Auditor	x	President, Vice President x 2, Sr. Director
Ajinomoto	3.4	Chairman, Exec. Director, Auditor x 2	x	Chairman, Auditor

(continued)

Table 4.1. *(continued)*

Company Name	1978 Ratio of Family Stock Holdings (%)	1978 Positions Held by Family Members	1993 Ratio of Family Stock Holdings (%)	1993 Positions Held by Family Members
Morinaga Seika	x	President, Director x 2	x	President, Sr. Director
Kagome	6.7	Chairman, Sr. Director, Exec. Director, Director, Auditor	4.4	President, Director, Auditor
Nisshin Shokuhin	6.5	President, Director	6.7	Chairman, President
Fukusuke	6.5	President, Director	2.7	President, Sr. Director
Lion Hamigaki (Lion)	3.5	Chairman, President	x	President
Ishihara Sangyo	3.4	President	1.6	Chairman
Ina Seito (INAX)	x	Vice President, Sr. Director, Auditor (Director/Advisor)	1.5	President
Takeda Yakuhin Kogyo	6.1	Chairman, Vice President, Director	2.0	President, Director
Shionogi Seiyaku	2.8	Chairman	x	President, Sr. Director
Banyu Seiyaku	4.5	President, Sr. Director	(Merck-affiliate) x	Chairman, Sr. Director, Exec. Director
Amada	7.4	President, Exec. Director, Director/Advisor	3.2	Chairman Emeritus, Vice Chairman
Ryobi	4.7	President, Sr. Director, Exec. Director	2.6	President, Sr. Director
Ebara Seisakusho	3.2	President	x	
Iseki Noki	x	President, Auditor	x	Auditor
Tateishi Denki (Omron)	8.6	President, Vice President, Sr. Director, Exec. Director	x	Chairman, Vice Chairman, President, Director
Yokokawa Denki Seisakusho	x	President	x	Chairman Emeritus
Matsushita Denki Sangyo	6.6	Chairman, Director/Advisor, Auditor	3.5	Chairman, Sr. Director
Sanyo Denki	x	President, Director	x	Chairman, Director
Hokushin Denki Seisakusho	8.3	President, Exec. Director	x	

(continued)

Table 4.1. (*continued*)

Company Name	1978 Ratio of Family Stock Holdings (%)	1978 Positions Held by Family Members	1993 Ratio of Family Stock Holdings (%)	1993 Positions Held by Family Members
Yuasa Denchi (YUASA)	7.3	President, Sr. Director	7.1	Chairman, President
Yasukawa Denki Seisakusho	x	Chairman, President	x	Chairman Emeritus, Exec. Director
Akai Denki	7.3	President, Sr. Director	2.6	
Toyota Jidosha Kogyo (Toyota Jidosha)	x	President, Vice President,	x	Chairman, President, Chairman Emeritus
Suzuki Jidosha Kogyo (Suzuki)	x	Chairman, President	x	President
Nihon Oil Seal Kogyo (NOK)	5.0	Chairman, Vice President	5.2	Chairman, President
Kawai Gakki Seisakusho	3.7	President, Director	5.1	Chairman, President
Katoh Seisakusho	5.1	Chairman, President, Sr. Director, Auditor	4.0	President, Sr. Director
Namura Senzosho	4.2	President	x	President, Auditor
Minolta Cameras	x	President, Exec. Director, Director	x	Chairman, Exec. Director
Asahi Kogaku Kogyo	8.3	President, Exec. Director	5.6	President, Exec. Director
Citizen Tokei	3.0	President	x	
Daimaru	x	Vice President	x	President
Matsuzakaya	x	Chairman, President	x	Chairman Emeritus
Takashimaya	x	Chairman, President, Vice President	3.3	Sr. Director
Isetan	5.2	President, Exec. Director	x	Chairman Emeritus
Nagasakiya	7.3	President	4.3	
Marui	2.6	President, Exec. Director	x	President, Vice President, Director
Ichida	2.3	President, Exec. Director x 2, Auditor	x	Chairman, President
Uchida Yoko	6.3	President	2.0	President, Auditor
Inahata Sangyo	2.5	President, Director/Advisor	2.0	President, Vice President

(*continued*)

Table 4.1. *(continued)*

Company Name	1978 Ratio of Family Stock Holdings (%)	1978 Positions Held by Family Members	1993 Ratio of Family Stock Holdings (%)	1993 Positions Held by Family Members
Shochiku	x	President	3.4	Sr. Director
Dai Tokyo Kasai Kaijo	3.7	President	x	
Konoike Gumi	27.0	Chairman, President, Vice President, Director	26.0	Chairman, President
Takenaka Komuten	45.0	President, Exec. Director, Auditor	47.0	Chairman, President
Idemitsu Kosan	75.0	President, Vice President, Director, Proprietor, Director/Advisor	77.9	Chairman, President, Sr. Director
Yanmar Diesel	68.0	President, Director	68.9	President, Director
Suntory	95.0	President, Vice President, Exec. Director x 2	89.0	Chairman, Vice Chairman, President, Vice President
Otsuka Seiyaku	23.0	Chairman, President, Auditor	25.4	Chairman, President, Vice President, Exec. Director
Seibu Hyakkaten	(data unavailable)	Chairman	70.4.	Vice President (data unavailable for Saison)
Kokubu	(data unavailable)	President, Vice President, Sr. Director, Director	85.0	President, Auditor

Notes:

1. Companies listed are ones where the major portion of investment has come from either the founder family or family trust. It should be noted, however, that the resources (see Note 2, below) from which the above list was drawn only record stock controlled by eight to ten of the largest stockholders so that the actual shareholding ratio is probably much higher.
2. Data on Japanese listed companies were taken from the 1979 (Collection 1) and 1994 (Collection 1) collections of the Jojo Kaisha Ban (Listed Companies Edition) of the *Kaisha Shiki Ho (Seasonal Company Report)*, published by Toyo Keizai Shinhosha. Data for unlisted companies were taken from Diamondsha's 1979 Hijojo Kaisha Ban (Unlisted Companies Edition) of *Diamondo Kaisha Yoran (Diamond's Guide to Companies)* and also from Toyo Keizai Shinhosha's 1994 Mijojo Kaisha Ban (Unlisted Companies Edition) of *Kaisha Shiki Ho (Seasonal Company Report)*.
3. Companies are listed in order by: listed companies with over 10 percent of shares controlled by family and family interests; listed companies with fewer than 10 percent of shares controlled by family and family interests; unlisted companies.

might include as family enterprises companies whose relatives of the founder's family might hold the position of chairman or president but actually don't hold the true reins of power. In these cases, the salaried managers are the true top management, and common sense dictates that these kinds of companies be defined as managerial enterprises. There is no doubt that these individual cases are important and require attention. But it is equally, or even more, important to understand that many significant insights can be gained by ignoring some of the more unusual cases in order to take in the overall picture.

I have rounded off the number of companies to an even 100 in order to evaluate what changes took place in terms of family investment ratios and top-management positions in the 15 years from 1978 to 1993. First, let us look at changes in the family investment ratio (as described in Note 1 of table 4.1, these figures may not represent the true family-owned proportion). From 1978 to 1993, there was an increase in the ratio of family investment in 13 companies, a decrease in 67 companies, and data were unavailable for 18 firms. Unavailable data took two forms: in some cases, investment-ratio information was unavailable for both 1978 and 1993, and in others there were no data for either the former year or the latter, making comparison impossible. The companies with unavailable data for 1993 were all listed companies, but it should be noted that for the companies listed in the 1994 edition of the *Kaisha Shiki Ho (Seasonal Company Report)* the number of major stockholders had increased at the same time. Moreover, this dispersal of shares to more stockholders meant that the proportion of overall family holdings dropped.

Suffice it to say that, as far as family stockholding ratio is concerned, family control is on the decline. The next question concerns family influence in terms of top-management positions in the various family enterprises. The next phase of our study tabulates changes in the number of top-management positions combined with changes in who held what positions in the period 1978 to 1993. The results show that in 32 companies, relatives of the founder families expanded their management influence through the number and level of top-management appointments. In 54 companies there was a decline in the role that families played in the highest echelons of their businesses. In 14 companies there was no change. Although the decline in family influence through top-management positions was not as significant as it was in relation to family investment ratio, it is clear that during the 15 years from 1978 to 1993, family control was on the wane.

Of particular interest is the fact that in 1978 there were only four companies that did not have a relative of the founder family as both chairman and president (Shimizu Kensetsu, Nakayama Seikosho, Ina Seito, Daimaru). By 1993, however, the number of companies with similar chief executive situations had increased to 24. This figure succinctly tells the tale of the decline of family influence as firms changed from family enterprises to managerial enterprises.

The 24 companies described above are:

Shimizu Kensetsu	Yokokawa Denki
House Shokuhin	Hokushin Denki
Bridgestone	Yasukawa Denki
Nakayama Seikosho	Akai Denki
Sanoyasu Senkyo	Citizen Tokei
Descente	Matsuzakaya
Kotobukiya	Takashimaya
Ito Yokado	Isetan
Yamatane Shoken	Nagasakiya
Amada	Shochiku
Ebara Seisakusho	Dai Tokyo Kasai Kaijo
Iseki Noki	Seibu Hyakkaten

INAX (Ina Seito) and Daimaru were two companies that had no family members as either chairman or president as of 1978. But in both cases, relatives of the founder family who had been vice president were later promoted to president. For the record, the INAX president was Teruzo Ina, and Shotaro Shimomura became Daimaru's president.

Table 4.1 also does not list some companies that could not be regarded as family enterprises in 1978 and 1993. Of course, if the companies in question had been managerial enterprises from the start, they would not have appeared at all in table 4.1. There are also some companies that could not be considered family enterprises since they were still run by their founders, such as Daiei, Wacol, and Kyocera. Also of note are companies not included in the listing that, as of 1978, were still run by their founders but that later became managerial enterprises.

An excellent example of the type of company described in the previous paragraph is Sharp. Sharp's origins can be traced back to

Tokuji Hayakawa, who founded the company Hayakawa Denki Seisakusho (Hayakawa Electrical Manufacturing). When Hayakawa's company changed its name to Sharp in 1970, Hayakawa took the post of chairman: He died nine years later in 1979, and until that time his business was rightly considered a founder enterprise. At the time of Hayakawa's accession to the post of chairman of Sharp, he entrusted the position of president to Akira Saeki, a nonfamily member, and family succession did not occur. Saeki's association with Hayakawa began when he joined Hayakawa Kinzoku Kogyou Kenkyusho (Hayakawa Metalworks Research Center) in 1931. This loyal, long-time employee, who shared no blood ties with Hayakawa, later became Hayakawa's right-hand man and headed company operations as a salaried manager. Saeki continued as president even after Hayakawa's death and held the position for the lengthy tenure of 15 years and nine months, until he retired in 1986. Saeki then became chairman (the Sharp president at this time was Haruo Tsuji) for one year, and from 1987 on he held the position of company advisor.

Honda is another company that moved directly from being a founder enterprise to a managerial enterprise without any of the top-management positions being held by members of the founder's family. As of 1978, however, the founder of Honda, the well-known Soichiro Honda, was neither chairman nor president and held no position higher than director. As might be expected, though, Honda's influence was substantial and though limits were placed on the charismatic Honda by Takeo Fujisawa, the company founder still wielded plenty of authority. In 1978 Honda was a company that could have been called both a founder enterprise *and* a managerial enterprise. Unlike Sharp, as of 1993 there had been no clearly announced change in Soichiro Honda's status.

The "Total Blockade-Type" Family Enterprise

Why Go Unlisted?

Of the 100 large-scale, family enterprises recorded in table 4.1, the real eye-catchers are the eight companies unlisted on the Japanese stock exchange. The first notable aspect of these firms is that the ratio of stock held by family interests is very high. Moreover, the number of family members holding top-management posts, and the level of these posts, is also very high. Two questions must now be asked: are these the reasons family enterprises of this sort choose not to be listed on the open stock market? And if these are not the reasons, what are?

Let us now try to answer the questions posited above by looking in more detail at some specific company examples: Kokudo (part of the Seibu Group), Suntory, and Idemitsu. Of the three companies cited, Kokudo is the only one excluded from table 4.1, the reason being that data related to Kokudo were unavailable, even from information published about unlisted companies. This lack of available information is an excellent indicator of the "blockade" mentality that exists within Kokudo and companies like it.

Before discussing other companies and their reasons for not publicly listing their stock, it is worth noting that Seibu Department Stores (Saison Group) would have been an interesting addition to this analysis. Seibu has not been included here for two reasons: the listing of stock in companies in the Saison Group is not the most important issue pertaining to this group; and the subject of Saison will be addressed later. Instead now let's turn our attention to other companies, starting with Idemitsu.

Sazo Idemitsu's Refusal to Go Public

Put simply, the refusal of a company to go public means that its owners want their company to be 100 percent private, and for it to remain that way. It's easy to understand why company founders—who have staked their lives and livelihoods on their companies—don't want to hand over the reins to anyone else. Sazo Idemitsu, the founder of the company that bears his name, completely agrees with this line of thought, a position he has made abundantly clear.

Idemitsu has put his beliefs this way: "My management of Idemitsu is like a test tube of the idea of respect for human power: by looking into this tube you can readily see how to treat and respect employees." In Idemitsu's view, going public and taking capital from outsiders is a sure way to crack that test tube into fragments that may never be glued together again. "If you get capital from outside investors, although *some* of them may understand what you're trying to do, by the same token, *some* of them may not. Odds are that the test tube will be muddied, and I don't want that."[2] As the founder of his company, Idemitsu had his own way of running things, and it is this right to act as he sees fit that he wants to protect. Idemitsu also has this to say about public shareholding:

> By going public, capital assets accrued by the company at great effort flow out of the company in the form of dividend. When that happens, people like me are reduced to just earning a share of the profits and, for the first time I'll have private property which will become capital and I'll suddenly become just one of the shareholders, just like everyone else. Also, the confrontation between employee and management is also sure to become an issue. Depending on how you look at it, it's also possible that everything I've believed in over the last 40 years will go out the window and that Idemitsu as a company could be corrupted forever.[3]

Since, as owner, Idemitsu is already receiving a share of his company's profits, his view that going public transforms him from company founder into a mere shareholder who just receives a percentage of profits is a slightly skewed one. Regardless of whether his company's shares are offered publicly or not, the fact remains that he is already receiving a percentage of the profits generated by his company. Having said that, however, Idemitsu is not selfish with his shares. In a unique program, he distributes one-third of the company's shares to an employee association, called the Shoju Kai (Shoju Group), which then uses the stock for retirement packages and to assist in other employee social welfare programs.

Looking beyond founder Idemitsu's somewhat idiosyncratic reasoning, at the core of his reluctance to open his company to public stock trading was the fear that outside investors and their capital would come between the Idemitsu family and their employees. Idemitsu's individualistic views about capital investment were most likely formed when he was young. After the Russo-Japanese War and during World War I, the prevailing attitude was that money was all-powerful and all-important. This is an attitude that Sazo Idemitsu hated and one that was integral in forming his later opposition to the public trading of his company's stock. One can see and understand how his phobia of public trading was born, and he is sometimes the most articulate advocate of his hard-won philosophy. Another reason for his seemingly well-founded paranoia was the attempt by one of Idemitsu's sworn enemies to invest in his company and seize control.

After the Second World War, the stock market in Japan experienced tumultuous change. The unprecedented participation in the market by the general public led to many founder enterprises and family enterprises opening up to public trading. Although these companies for the most part managed to go public while still protecting their treasured family interests, Idemitsu was totally unable to comprehend their willingness to bet the family firm.

Despite Idemitsu's strongly held views, companies need capital to operate. If this money does not come from outside investors, in almost all cases the only resort is the bank. Relying on banks, however, is tantamount to relying on outside investors. Through the vehicle of interest payments, banks acquire indirect right to company assets and interfere in how the company is run. Idemitsu has stated, however, that there is a significant difference between banks and outside investors:

> Since banks invest money they collect from the general public, they are very responsible in where they put their money. When the banks looked at our business, they were fair but careful. We addressed their concerns equally responsibly and were able to answer their questions through our actions and attitude towards business. We decided that by working with banks, we were helping the general public make a profit. This went hand in hand with our goals of having society and business work together in harmony.[4]

In Idemitsu's mind, banks and outside investors were different entities. While he could work with banks, he avoided other outside investors like a financial plague.

Although at first glance it may seem otherwise, Idemitsu's ruminations on banks are not a refutation of his anti-investment philosophy. Instead, he is merely reflecting on the harsh realities of his business experiences and on services rendered to him by his banks. Idemitsu faced severe financing problems a number of times. Although he had any number of offers for outside financial help, his fear of losing management control was even stronger than the threat of economic ruin. In his hours of need, the banks were his ally. As long as he was able to make his interests payments, difficult as that may have been, the banks did not interfere with the running of his business. The banks instead took on a useful support role, serving as business monitor and providing Idemitsu with information and advice. Economic theory to the contrary, in Idemitsu's mind banks and outside investors were clearly cut from different cloth.

Despite his individualistic and outspoken views, Idemitsu was hardly alone in experiencing financial hardships. Many other company founders underwent similar management tribulations. One of the common difficulties of founder enterprises is the procuring of capital needed for business expansion, a predicament that sent many to the well of public stock offerings. Although many of the companies that went public managed to retain family control, losing management authority to outsiders was a constant, nagging worry.

The Logic of Founder Families

Sazo Idemitsu was a business figure whose unique views set him apart from ordinary businessmen. Yet it was not only his personality and philosophy that differentiated him from companies that chose not to take the alternative of public stock offerings. Born in 1885, he founded the Idemitsu company in 1911 and, like most people and organizations, was a product and representative of his times. It is background more than personality that must be taken into account when noting the difference between Idemitsu's company and other nonlisted businesses. Like Idemitsu, other company founders were influenced by their times, but in those instances, the era is later. The period leading up to World War II was one when capitalists grew richer and company founders grew more fearful. This new breed of investors was casting their profit-jaundiced eyes about looking for new companies in which to invest and to control. It was this dog-eat-dog environment that made companies tread carefully and fear going public.

There is a problem in probing the reasons modern family enterprises do not list their shares on the open market: Are these the same as in the case of Sazo Idemitsu? In getting back to the Idemitsu clan, the heirs to the Idemitsu empire (Sazo's eldest son, Shosuke, as chairman; Sazo's two nephews, Yuji as president, Akira as senior director, brother-in-law Masayu Yamato as director/advisor) did not share the founder's passionate aversion to the open stock market, and in this respect they are somewhat representative of the modern generation of top management that runs family enterprises in Japan.

Although many family enterprises, like the modern Idemitsu's, have a more positive attitude toward the stock market, their companies remain unlisted. The modern attitude is that most investors these days, both domestic and foreign, have neither the inclination nor the ability to come in and start running companies on their own as soon as they acquire stock leverage. Despite this relaxation in attitude, however, family enterprises still tend not to jump in headfirst and go public without first taking steps to protect family control and interests.

Regardless of the behind-the-scenes maneuvering that may go on to protect family interests, the data in table 4.1 reveal that a large number of family enterprises that have opened their shares to the public no longer have family members as CEOs. Looking at the situation from an objective standpoint, it is hard to argue against the fact that, when family enterprises go public, there is a justifiable fear that families will lose some measure of control.

As we will see later, however, although many families do lose the CEO post after going public, the cause is not necessarily linked to the actual event of going public but more often is due to some business failure on the part of the family top management. Proof that a top-management problem is a common cause for losing the position of CEO is provided by the fact that the same event occurs even in companies that have not publicly listed their stocks. Saison (Seibu Department Stores) is one example that typifies how nonpublic family enterprises can forfeit the company's top-management post for reasons other than public stockholding. The conclusion, then, is that although some family enterprises *do* lose control of their company's top-management position because of going public, this happens only in a small number of cases.

The puzzle as to why modern unlisted family enterprises continue to stay private remains unsolved. As we have seen, the threat of being taken over by power-hungry raiders is nothing like what it was before the war. Also, private companies stand to make large capital gains by going public and by becoming equity financed. Moreover, they have the opportunity of gaining capital to finance company expansion. Why then do these family companies fight what would seem to be an obvious course of business action?

One major reason privately held family companies refuse to go public, even when missing out on financial opportunities, is a reluctance by the families to let outsiders into their inner circle. The "us" versus "them" mentality is still pervasive in some private organizations, and this fear of corporate culture clash is a large one. By inviting in individual or corporate investors, the host company must protect the new investors' assets as well as maximize profit. Yet for many family enterprises, the quest for profit and expansion is a secondary goal. Instead, these companies are more interested in developing new research and promoting employee welfare than in growing the bottom line. These two essentially conflicting corporate objectives are at the source of potential culture clash on the corporate scale. As may be expected, some family enterprises are quite happy with the way things are and they have no desire to overturn what has taken so much time and effort to build.

For family enterprises, where stability is highly valued, the burden of loan interest and repayment is a small one compared to the problems associated with public shareholder meetings and the constant worry and political intrigue concerning the actions and intentions of the company's outside shareholders. The number of family enterprises that choose not to go public with their stock for these reasons is not small. A good example of one such company is the Hayashibara Company of Okayama, west of Osaka. The company started life as a producer of starch syrup and then developed into a technologically advanced firm well known as a high-quality manufacturer of biochemical products. Through its production of maltose (a major ingredient for intravenous solutions) and sucrose, and its ability to mass-produce Interferon, Hayashibara acquired a well-deserved reputation as a top-class manufacturer of bio-related products.

Credit for growing the company beyond its starch syrup origins goes to Ichiro Hayashibara III. After his sudden death in 1961, the position of company president landed on the young shoulders of Ken Hayashibara, then 19 and still a student in the law faculty of Keio University. As of this writing, the still-young Hayashibara remains at the company helm and his company's ascension into the position as a bio-tech leader is usually attributed to him. Ken Hayashibara is, by all standards, a dynamic individual who has a unique vision for his company and a gift for top management. In his effort to stop the brain drain of Okayama's talented native sons and daughters, he introduced numerous innovations such as flex-time and he has also refused many overtures into the business circle. As a top manager, Hayashibara is known as a rugged individualist who sticks to his guns· and, more important, his vision. "By turning our company into a catchment area for all the region's talent, I can help achieve my number one goal, which is to keep the company going as long as possible. If you want to put it in a more extreme way, increasing profit is purely the secondary objective. Because I want to funnel as much of our profit as I can back to the employees, it's essentially impossible for us to grow very much more."[5]

Hayashibara's individualistic repudiation of growth as the be-all, end-all goal of corporate life runs counter to what many would consider business common sense. But it is equally obvious that he strongly believes that continuation of his management philosophy and practices is dependent on protecting the company from potential invasions by an alien corporate culture that going public might bring. As Sazo Idemitsu and Ken Hayashibara demonstrate, for family enterprises with unique business philosophies and an unwavering determination to travel along their own clearly marked paths, the reasons to avoid public stock listings seem clear.

Another reason family enterprises avoid publicly listing their stock is tax related. To minimize enterprise tax and inheritance tax, these businesses reveal as little about their financial situation as possible. The best example in this category of family enterprises is Kokudo, the parent company of the Seibu Group.

Kokudo and Its Closed Holdings

Kokudo is another example of a family enterprise. When Kokudo was led by President Yoshiaki Tsutsumi (who later became chairman in July 1995), 40 percent of its stock was under Tsutumi's control. At the same time it was the stockholding company of the Seibu Railways Group (capitalized at 100 million yen). As a controlling interest in a number of the Tsutsumi companies, Kokudo held 48.7 percent of the Seibu Railways stock, and 100 percent of the Prince Hotels and the Seibu Lions, to name just a few of the firms in the family's portfolio. To complicate things even further, Seibu Railways also held a 100 percent share in its subsidiary company, Seibu Fudosan (Seibu Real Estate) and a 48.2 percent share of the publicly traded Izu Hakone Railways, as well as a 50/50 share with Kokudo in the jointly controlled unlisted company Seibu Kensetsu (Seibu Construction).

Japanese antitrust monopoly laws prevent company incorporation when the main purpose is the holding of stock in other companies. For this reason, Kokudo also ran its own, nonstockholding-related business activities. These activities were centered around resort-related businesses and included, among others, real-estate ventures, ski resorts, golf courses, and hotels. Since all of these enterprises were subsidiaries, in one form or another, of the Seibu Railways Company, it is easy to conclude that these companies were formed for the dual purpose of generating business and meeting the antimonopoly requirements set out by law.

Although Kokudo is a company unlisted on the stock exchange, it goes one step beyond that classification by avoiding even the slightest mention in the unlisted companies section of the regularly published *Kaisha Shiki Ho (Seasonal Report)*. Very little, if any, information is available about Kokudo's inner workings, a solid indicator of just how closely the Tsutumi clan plays its cards. The lack of available information about Kokudo's financial results is surprising unto itself and, of what little information is available about Kokudo, most of it has been uncovered through the efforts and work of one individual, Yasunori Tateishi.[6] According to Tateishi's investigations, at the end of the March 1994 fiscal period, although Kokudo showed an operating profit of 10.2 billion yen and a non-sales based earnings of 3.5 billion yen, it appears that the company paid little or no corporate taxes on these princely sums (and, even if Kokudo paid taxes, stockholders reportedly received a rebate on the dividend withholding tax, indicative of just how little tax was paid, if at all). As in many countries, Japanese companies are not required to pay taxes when their consolidated losses exceed their earnings, meaning that the companies are in what is called a minus-earnings situation.

The most common reason for large losses in Japan is high interest payments and, in Kokudo's case, this certainly holds true. According to the same March 1994 financial data, Kokudo had outstanding loans amounting to a total of 281.1 billion yen with interest payments on these loans totaling 13.1 billion yen. It is perhaps no coincidence to find that Kokudo's total earnings of 13.7 billion yen are almost identical to the 13.1 billion in interest payments. Also interesting to note is that the proportion of sales profits versus the real profits at Kokudo is relatively low indeed. This ratio can be explained by the fact that in Japanese joint-stock companies, dividends the company earns from other companies may not be treated as profits and fall into the additional income category.

Tateishi's research helps explain how Kokudo has managed, despite its ownership of large real estate operations and huge sales and non-sales-related income, to avoid heavy corporate taxation over a number of years. Tateishi also concludes that the methods described for minimizing corporate taxation would probably apply to inheritance tax issues as well. According to Tateishi, remaining as a private, unlisted company is one method companies like Kokudo use for minimizing the corporate tax burden (with another method being strong connections between top executives like Tsutsumi and conservative politicians).

The above observations effectively summarize our look at Yasunori Tateishi's research into Kokudo and it has chosen to remain a privately listed company. If we take Tateishi's research findings as fact, however, the next question we must tackle is whether Kokudo's reasons for staying out of public shareholding also apply to a number of other, private, family-run companies. Looking at the same problem from a slightly different angle, a loan officer from one of Japan's major banks made several comments that appeared in Tateishi's report, which should be examined in light of what we have already learned about unlisted, owner-run companies and why they don't go public. "Certainly, there's a lot about Kokudo [based on quotes from a separate source concerning Kokudo's tax reviews] that we don't know, but that's hardly unusual with owner-run companies that aren't listed on the stock exchange. But on the other hand, you also have to realize they're still able to borrow that much from the banks and that says something in itself."[7]

From this author's perspective, however, the above view is slightly hard to swallow. To add fact to opinion, let's now compare data from the Tateishi report to 1995 tax-related data published in the year-end Mijojo Kaisha Ban (Unlisted Companies Edition) of the *Kaisha Shiki Ho (Seasonal Company Report)* concerning Kokudo, Idemitsu, and Suntory (data for Kokudo and Idemitsu were as of March 1994, while for Suntory, data were as of December 1993). As we have seen, the cumulative amount of Kokudo's total loans was 281.1 billion yen while for Suntory the figure was 390.8 billion yen. For Idemitsu the number was a staggering 1.433 trillion yen! As if this weren't enough, total loans for the entire Idemitsu group were reported to be over 2 trillion yen. The mind boggles at these vast sums, which make, unbelievably, the Kokudo figures seem relatively small. The Idemitsu numbers are, to say the least, huge and therefore the company's interest payments are likely also enormous. But we must also note that for the period in question, Idemitsu's reported earnings were 22.8 billion yen while Suntory's were 11.6 billion yen. By contrast, Kokudo reportedly earned less than 100 million yen in what is essentially the same time frame, which is why the issue of corporate taxation levels is a key one when discussing Kokudo. But keeping within our frame of reference—why companies remain private—it is clear that in the case of Idemitsu and Suntory, their status as private companies has not played a particularly significant role for tax minimization purposes.

When looking at Idemitsu's net profits of 1.23 billion yen, when compared with Suntory's 4.28 billion yen, the difference is significant and indicates that Idemitsu probably paid far more in corporate tax. Unlike Kokudo, Idemitsu seems far less concerned with tax minimization and the company's relative honesty in terms of profit declaration implies that the company's and family's reasons for staying private have less to do with tax issues than with other concerns. Although both Idemitsu and Kokudo are family enterprises that chose not to go public, in both cases their reasons for doing so are unique and, as such, should not be used to draw conclusions about other family enterprises.

The Possibilities for Remaining Unlisted

Regardless of why family enterprises tenaciously refrain from going public, it's now time to examine the future prospects for such companies. Also, how likely is it that these kinds of firms will be able to remain unlisted and for how long? Finally, in their attempt to remain private, what effects will this policy have on their companies? My personal view is that there are definite limits on a family enterprise's ability to remain private, although it should be pointed out that this view is not based on a strictly objective analysis. Objective data concerning the future do not, of course, exist and instead we are reduced to conjecture, speculation, and prediction.

Nonetheless, the first reason for predicting that family enterprises should find it increasingly difficult to remain private is Japan's taxation system. In particular, pressure from inheritance tax laws may make it very hard indeed to avoid going public, despite aversions to doing so by the families and companies. First, the traditional method of avoiding inheritance tax—through real estate ventures and the purchase of art objects—most probably has its limits.

Second, methods of obtaining working and investment capital from banks are probably limited. The financial world has reached an era of low interest rates and all indications are that this era is to be a long one. In this business climate, it's highly unlikely that, unlike in the good old days, banks will be willing to tie up their long-term loan capital in ordinary businesses.

The third reason concerns changing employer-employee relations. As can be expected, employees may feel unhappy whenever the company family is selfishly controlling stocks and profits. Moreover, even in companies where there are employee stock distribution plans, many employees feel these plans may be in place more for taxation camouflage than for good will, and it is also doubtful whether such plans, irrespective of motive, can be continued indefinitely.

To summarize, no matter how much a family desires to keep its company out of the stock market, mere desire cannot compete with the hard fiscal realities of today's business world. For many unlisted family enterprises, the crossroads are near.

Ways in Which Companies Find, Develop, and Keep Staff

Recruiting Talent from the Family Ranks

No matter what kind of business, it is absolutely imperative that the people occupying top-management positions be the most capable and talented possible. Although this concept is a terribly important one, it can be simply stated: companies desperately need the best management they can get. In the tough modern business climate, second best means second rate, and a company's survival may well hinge on the ability of its top management.

In the case of family enterprises, it is not enough to maintain the company's status quo. Like all companies, many family enterprises also seek growth, but to grow while dealing with the difficulties associated with running a family enterprise is particularly difficult and requires top management that can handle long-term adversity. Not everyone is suited to the role of top management, particularly in enterprises where the job also entails protecting the company's identity as a family enterprise. The problem is compounded, of course, by the fact that the top-quality, top-management team must be chosen from the founder family and—making things even more difficult—usually from the main branch of the family. The task is a challenging one.

Let us now look at two founder families and their unique methods for choosing top-management teams to run and protect their businesses. Kikkoman is our first example. The family enterprise, Kikkoman, was originally financed by eight families and their rules for selecting the necessary top-management personnel from among those eight families are extremely interesting. Our second example, Kashima Kensetsu (hereafter Kashima Construction), is unusual because its founding family was dominated by a female lineage and choosing successors to their top-management team to preserve the family enterprise involved many hardships.

The Succession of Management Talent at Kikkoman

The origins of Kikkoman date back to December 1917, when 10 soy sauce producers joined together to form a company called Noda Shoyu K.K., which later became Kikkoman. The 10 soy sauce producers included the Horikiri family of Nagareyama and the Ishikawa family of Kitakatsushika's Matsufuseryo, and these two families were joined to the other eight businesses through various family ties, although their family lines were different. Six of the families shared the name Mogi, and the other two members were the Hyozaemon Takanashi family and the Chobei Nakano family. The structure of the eight-family cooperative organization was a complex one consisting of relatives and sons marrying into the families, but at the same time it was well organized with the rules governing property and assets written down to minimize confusion and misunderstandings.[8]

What should be stressed here is that the Noda/Kikkoman top-management team, though assembled from members of the clan, was chosen based on mutually agreed standards of merit related to ability, attitude, personality, and educational background. Managers were not selected purely because certain individuals happened to represent one branch of the family or another. An indication of this system's success is that, at last report, the same methods are still in use. Another aspect of the Noda/Kikkoman system established early on was the practice of selecting top-management candidates while they were still young. These chosen clan members then worked their way up through an established set of positions and promotions until they reached their predetermined role in the organization. This system, whereby top-management candidates were selected early on and who then had to work their way up through the management ranks, was tremendously successful in reducing destructive competition within the large family group and could be a considered a model of its kind.[9]

For a better understanding of the Noda/Kikkoman succession system in actual practice, a summary has been included below in table 4.2.

Even as late as the end of World War II, the Noda Soy Sauce Company had never had a salaried manager at the level of director

Table 4.2. The History of Noda/Kikkoman's Top Management

Chairmen	Presidents (Numbers indicate succession order)	Vice Presidents	Senior Directors	Executive Directors (Numbers indicates director's ranking)	Directors
	1 Shichirouemon Mogi VI 1917 (aged 57)–29 Studied chemistry under Saburo Utsunomiya			1 Shichizaemon Mogi XI 2 Saheiji Mogi IX (Tokyo Kosho-commercial college)	
	2 Shichizaemon Mogi XI 1929 (aged 51)–43			1 Saheiji Mogi XIX 2 Eisaburo Nakano (Keio U.)	
Shichizaemon Mogi XI	3 Saheiji Mogi IX 1943 (aged 52)–46			1 Eisaburo Nakano	
	4 Eisaburo Nakano 1946 (aged 59)–58			1 Fusagoro Mogi V (Keio U.) 2 Keisaburo Mogi II (Tokyo Shodai, *Tokyo Commercial U.)* 3 Heizaemon Takanashi XXIX (Kyoto Imperial U., Law)	
	5 Fusagoro Mogi V 1958 (aged 65)–62			1 Keisaburo Mogi II 2 Heizaemon Takanashi XXIX	

(*continued*)

Table 4.2. *(continued)*

Chairmen	Presidents (Numbers indicate succession order)	Vice Presidents	Senior Directors	Executive Directors (Numbers indicates director's ranking)	Directors
	6 Keisaburo Mogi II 1962 (aged 63)–74	Heizaemon Takanashi XXIX	Shichizaemon Mogi XII (Tokyo Imperial U., Economics)	1 Saheiji Mogi X (Tokyo Imperial U., Economics)	
Keisaburo Mogi II	7 Saheiji Mogi X 1974 (aged 60)–80	Katsumi Mogi (Adopted heir through marriage of Junsaburo VII of the Shichirouemon line, Keio U.)		Yokotsuka, Todate, 1 Kozaburo Nakano (adopted son through marriage, Keio U.) Murai, Negishi	
	8 Katsumi Mogi 1980 (aged 65)–87	Kozaburo Nakano 1983–87		1 Kozaburo Nakano, Yokotsuka, Todate, Murai, Negishi, Iguchi, Minegishi 2 Tomosaburo Mogi (2nd son of Keisaburo, Keio U., Columbia U.), Yoshida 3 Shinichiro Takanashi (later to become Heizaemon XXX , Musashi U.), Itoh, Masuda, Karube	Keisaburo Mogi II 1980–82 (Advisor)

(continued)

	9 Kozaburo Nakano 1987 (aged 69)–95	Tomosaburo Mogi 1994–95	Minegishi 1990–93 Tomosaburo Mogi 1990–94 Heizaemon Takanashi 1994–	1 Tomosaburo Mogi 2 Shinichiro Takanashi (Heizaemon), Minegishi, Karube, Itoh, Masuda, Yoshida, Fukushima, Suzuki 3 Kensaburo Mogi (Keisaburo's third son & Shichizaemon's adopted heir by marriage, Hitotsubashi U., Harvard U.), Ono, Sugiyama, Ishii, Enokido	Katsumi Mogi 1987–94 (Advisor)
	10 Tomosaburo Mogi 1995 (aged 60)–		Heizaemon Takanashi XXX, Yoshida	Suzuki 1 Kensaburo Mogi, Ishii, Enokido, Nagasawa, Komuro	

Sources: Noda Shoyu—Kikkoman Shashi (Noda Soy Sauce/Kikkoman Company historical records), *Jinji Koshin Roku (The Directory of Personnel), Kaisha Shiki Ho (The Company Seasonal Report).*

or higher. Considering the relative lateness of the era, this was perhaps an unusual situation. Having said that, however, Noda's rather exclusive board of directors was not totally closed to outsiders, since a representative from the Kawasaki financial group who had invested in Noda was a member of the board, along with several other nonfamily members. A salaried manager was finally appointed to the board after the war, but it was not until the reign of Keisaburo II as chairman and Saheiji X as president that a salaried manager achieved a level equivalent or higher than executive director.

From that time on, the ascension of salaried managers increased dramatically. In 1990 Kyusaburo Minegishi was appointed as a senior director, as was Tomosaburo Mogi, but he retired without having risen beyond that position. Minegishi's younger successor, Sadao Yoshida, also appears to have hit a family glass ceiling, however, since at this writing he remains a senior director.

There are also eye-catching examples of top-management roles allocated to members of the clan after they retired from the company presidency. Keisaburo II was awarded the positions of both chairman and company advisor, and Katsumi Mogi, who served seven years as the firm's eighth president, was appointed as company advisor, a role he held also for seven years. At this point we are forced to wonder if the clan practice of appointing top-management hopefuls to positions like executive director with an eye to future promotions has gone slightly out of favor. Or has it? As of February 1995, Kozaburo Nakano was Kikkoman's president, Tomosaburo Mogi was vice president, Heizaemon Takanashi was senior director, and Kensaburo Mogi was executive director, each one taken from the ranks of the clan that originally helped form the company. Things were not to remain completely stable, however, as Nakano, Kikkoman's president, suddenly died in February and, on February 6th, Tomosaburo Mogi succeeded him as the tenth president in the company's history. Each one of the positions of senior director and executive director also remained in the clan's possession. Among the regular directors, as in the past, the names of clan members do not make an appearance.

Have there been any significant changes in the rules and practices of how the family-run Kikkoman secures and appoints their company management? Have revolutionary measures commenced during Tomosaburo's tenure? Whether they have or not remains to be seen, but what *is* clear is that the Kikkoman family enterprise is in a period of flux.

Securing Talent at Kashima Construction

Securing staff and management in a family enterprise with a purely female lineage has traditionally presented an unusual and interesting set of management issues in Japan. Kashima Construction (formally called the Kashima Group) is a particularly good representative of this kind of enterprise. By looking at the family tree in figure 4.1, we can conclude, however, that calling the Kashima Group a purely female family company is not strictly accurate. If we look at the family lineage descending from Kashima's founder, Iwazo Kashima, we can see right away that there was a male heir, Ryuzo Kashima, and that the family was not from the start purely female.

Ryuzo lived in the Tabata area of Tokyo, which in the late Taisho era was inhabited by artists and men of letters, and he used his wealth to become a leading patron of the arts. More can be read of Ryuzo's role as art patron in Tomie Kondo's *Tabata Bunshi Mura (Tabata Literary Village)*, and we learn from this book that Ryuzo was born in 1880, the eldest son of Iwazo Kashima.[10]

Tracing the family line back further, Iwazo's father was Iwakichi Kashima, who started in the construction industry in Edo in 1840. After the opening of the ports, Iwakichi made his way to Yokohama and took part there in the construction of the English *Ichibankan* building and other foreign merchant offices. Despite Iwazo's interest in foreign trade, he dutifully assisted his father in helping build the western-style buildings of the time, and on his father's retirement in 1873, the family business was left in the younger Kashima's hands.

It was around this time that Iwazo started making important personal and business connections, including those with the railway company head, Masaru Inoue, Eiichi Shibusawa, and the Dai Ichi National Bank. From this point on, Iwazo started receiving contracts from various government groups. Seizing his chance, Iwazo took this opportunity to officially establish the Kashima Group and his business interests moved mainly into railway-related contracting.[11]

The year 1876 saw the birth of Iwazo's eldest daughter Itoko, and four years later Ryuzo was born. As was common at that time, expectations were that Ryuzo, as the eldest son, would inherit the family name and business, but that was not to be. The role of family and business successor fell instead to that of Itoko's husband, Seiichi Kasai. After graduating from the civil engineering

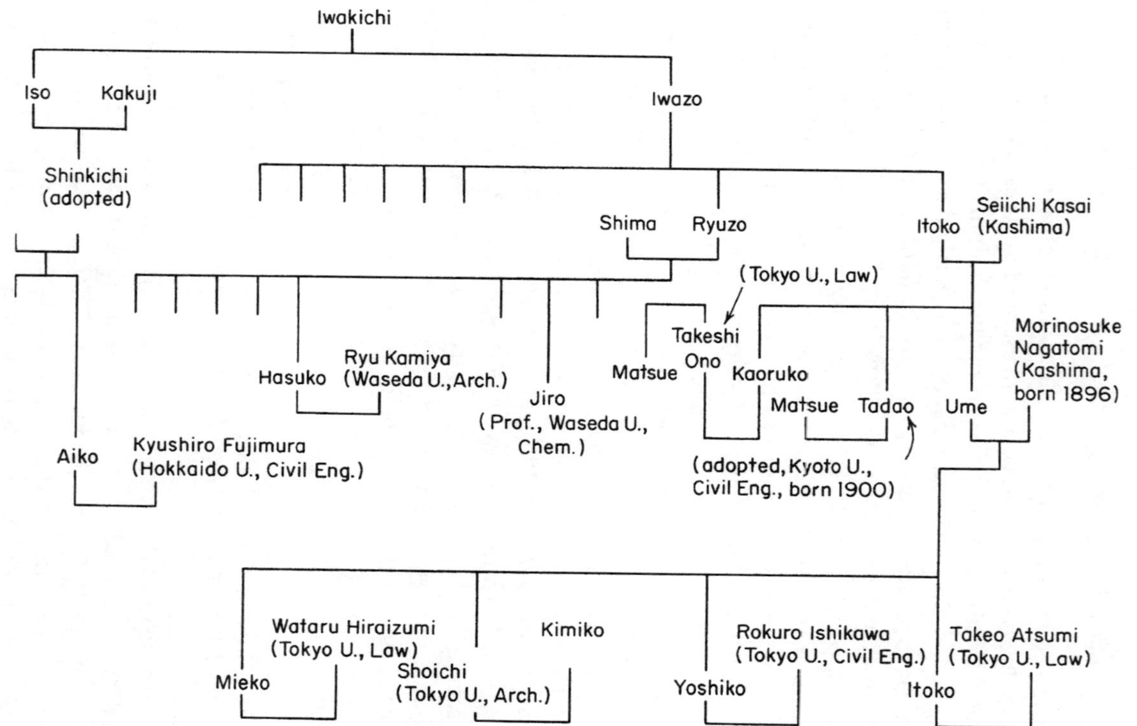

Figure 4.1. The Kashima Family Tree

faculty of Tokyo Imperial University (which later became Tokyo University), Kasai married Itoko on the condition that he would be adopted into the family through this marriage and that he would inherit the family name and business. Why then did Ryuzo shy away from his natural inheritance? Author Tomie Kondo puts it this way:

> While Ryuzo was a student at the First High School, he liked playing around too much and he failed twice. Ryuzo enrolled in Scotland's Glasgow University where he managed to graduate from the naval architecture program there. Just as he was about to return home, the Russo-Japanese war broke out and Ryuzo's parents, worried that he would be drafted, instructed him to stay overseas. Ryuzo followed his parents' instructions and before returning home he traveled in the States and Australia.

The truth is, however, that Ryuzo did not graduate from the First High School, but neither did he drop out. That he graduated with a naval architecture degree from Glasgow (he attended from 1900 to 1904) is a fact, though, and we also know that after returning to Japan he found work in the Kawasaki Shipyards. On the recommendation of Seiichi, his new older brother, Ryuzo then came to work for the Kashima Group.[13]

As author Kondo points out, although Ryuzo was given the positions of trustee and director, he was not a natural leader with leadership abilities. After receiving his inheritance, Ryuzo lived his life as he wanted and devoted himself to his hobbies, not the family business. One of Ryuzo's compatriots from Tabata, the writer Ryunosuke Akutagawa, had this to say about Ryuzo: "Because he spent his youth in the west, the sound of a *shamisen* or the sight of a Japanese lantern in front of a theater did nothing for Ryuzo. But as soon as he saw a lampshade or anything else western, that's when he would get in the party mood."

> The range of Ryuzo's hobbies and interests was incredibly wide: calligraphy, seal-engraving, the chanting of Noh texts, traditional Japanese dance, *nagauta* music, *tokiwazu* and *utawaza* ballads, *kyogen* (farcical Noh plays), tennis, and skating. He moved to the Tabata area in Meiji 45 (1912). . . . There were children all over the place. He had eight boys and one girl and he was always adding extensions to the house as soon as they had another child. The house was the sort of house you'd expect from a family that

> ran a construction business and he was very enthusiastic about building and design. The house also had a lawn and, very unusually for that time, there was also a concrete tennis court.[14]

Ryuzo was also well known for using his private income to help support a variety of writers and artists who lived in Tabata at that time. He particularly enjoyed sponsoring gatherings through an organization he founded called the *Dokan Kai* (Dokan Circle), where he could eat, drink, and enjoy lively conversation with his friends among Tabata's artistic set.[15] The emergence of art patrons from within a family enterprise is hardly an unusual phenomenon and Ryuzo seemed like a modern version of the characters in Thomas Mann's book *Buddenbrooks*.

The marriage between Seiichi and Itoko Kashima produced two daughters, Ume and Kaoruko, but no male heirs. Seiichi was made head of the Kashima Group on Iwazo's passing in 1912 when Ume was still only nine years old, and we can hazard the guess that the couple was very concerned about young Ume's future marriage partner since the family succession would fall upon the yet unknown heir through adoption by marriage.

In 1922, Seiichi met the diplomat Morinosuke Nagatomi while taking an inspection tour to Europe and America. Nagatomi was born in Tatsuno, Hyogo Prefecture, to a wealthy family, and for this reason he had no need to be adopted into the Kashima family. But Seiichi and Itoko were so enamored of Morinosuke that they managed to persuade him to join the family. Morinosuke wed Ume in 1927, becoming the family heir and acquiring the name Morinosuke Kashima.

In the Kashima family, adoption was a common method employed to secure family succession. Although adoptions usually came about through marriage, this was not always the case. In 1926, around the same time that Morinosuke took the Kashima family name, Tadao Yoshii, who was four years younger than Morinosuke and a graduate from Kyoto University in civil engineering, entered the family and the family company. To complicate matters further, Matsue, the younger sister of Takeshi Ono (the husband of Kaoruko, Ume's younger sister), was married to Tadao. The reason for this complex combination of adoption and intermarriage was probably that the family was worried that Morinosuke's diplomat's position and political ambitions would prevent him from running the Kashima Group's business. The fact that Tadao was brought into the family at a time when Morinosuke hadn't yet started working for the Kashima Group could hardly have been a coincidence, and it is probably safe to say that Tadao was being groomed as an understudy.

As expected, Morinosuke resigned from the Foreign Ministry in 1930 and ran for election in the House of Representatives. Unexpectedly, however, Morinosuke lost. He then devoted his energies to writing a history of international diplomacy, and in 1934 he also received a doctorate in law. With his political urges temporarily stifled by his election defeat and his academic ambitions fulfilled, Morinosuke at last turned to the business world. He officially joined the Kashima Group in 1936 as a director and in 1938 he was made president, with Seiichi becoming chairman. Morinosuke obviously did not have his heart set on succeeding to the family business because in 1942 he ran again for the House of Representatives. Although he lost again, in 1942–43 he occupied a political post as head of the Investigation Division of the *Taisei Yokusan Kai*.

During the Second World War, Morinosuke served the dual role of president of the Kashima Group and head of the *Taisei Yokusan Kai* Investigative Division, but his political life suffered another setback after the war when the occupation authorities prohibited him from holding public office from 1946 to 1951. It was during that time, in 1947, that Seiichi died. Seiichi's passing, however, had no effect on Morinosuke's political leanings. As soon as his political ban was lifted, Morinosuke leaped back into the fray and he was at last successful. In 1953, he was elected to the Upper House and continued to hold his seat there for 18 years, even serving as a minister of state during that time. As many had suspected for a long time, Morinosuke never felt truly at home in the family business and these suspicions were finally and irrevocably confirmed.

Yet despite the failure of Morinosuke to live up to the family succession hopes, this case does point out some of the strengths inherent to family enterprises in general and to female-lineage families in particular. First, before the war and while his health permitted, Seiichi as chairman was able to help Morinosuke, and to cover for him when his interests were elsewhere.

Of the children born to Morinosuke and Ume, three were daughters but only one was a son. The son, Shoichi, was born in 1930 and was still only 15 when the war ended. Taking Shoichi's young age into account along with the family's business needs, Morinosuke and Ume saw to it that their two eldest daughters brought husbands into the family fold. Their eldest, Itoko, married Takeo Atsumi and their next daughter, Yoshiko, wed Rokuro Ishikawa.

Itoko and Atsumi were married in 1948, when Atsumi was 29, while Yoshiko and Ishikawa were wed in 1953 when Ishikawa was 28 years of age. This was a time when the family was scrambling to seek order out of the chaos presented by Morinosuke's political commitments, the uncertainty of the postwar era, Chairman Seiichi's passing, and Shoichi's youth. From all appearances, the entrance of Atsumi and Ishikawa into Kashima Construction (which had undergone a name change in 1947) family was a blessing. After graduating from the Law Department of Tokyo University, Atsumi became a bureaucrat with M.I.T.I. while Ishikawa had become a national railways man after graduating in civil engineering, also from the University of Tokyo. That both men were talented seemed to bode well for the family and its business.[16]

Despite the promise of their new sons-in-law, it must have seemed to the family and other interested parties that the succession gap had still to be definitively filled, what with Morinosuke's continuing ban from politics, Seiichi's death, and young Shoichi still a student at Todai, as Tokyo University is often called. In an attempt to fill the family management void, Atsumi entered the Kashima firm as an executive director in 1951, the same year that Morinosuke's ban on holding public office was lifted. Ishikawa entered the company as a director four years later, in 1955. In the interim, the management gap was temporarily filled, according to the records, by the adopted son of Itoko's uncle Kakuji, Shinkichi, who served as de facto president. Also filling the ranks of Kashima's top management was Takeshi Ono, husband of Kaoruko, who became an executive director in 1942, rising to vice president in 1951. Other individuals with family connections worked as well. These individuals included Tadao, the adopted son of Seiichi, Ryuzo's son-in-law, Ryu Kamiya (a graduate of Waseda's architecture faculty), and Shinkichi's son-in-law, Kyushiro Fujimura (a graduate in civil engineering from Hokkaido University). Thanks to their efforts, the management crisis at Kashima was not allowed to overcome the company.[17]

The following period was an eventful one for the Kashima family and the Kashima company: Morinosuke re-embarked on his political career, which included 18 years (1953–1971) as a member of the upper house and even a two-month stretch as a minister of state; Kashima Construction went public (1961) and the company built Japan's first-ever skyscraper (1968)—to name just a few milestones in this remarkable time for both family and company. Yet despite the burdens such events must have placed on Chairman Morinosuke and President Ume, thanks to the solid family ties they had helped create, they weathered the storm smoothly.

As mentioned earlier, Ono became vice president in 1951, and he was soon followed first by Atsumi in 1956 and then Ishikawa in 1959, essentially forming the nucleus of Kashima's management. Shoichi had also grown, graduating from Tokyo University in 1953 and joining the company immediately as a director at the tender age of 23. He became vice president in 1959.

By looking at table 4.3, we can get a clearer picture of the Kashima management structure in 1959. The chairman and president positions were held by Morinosuke and Ume, respectively, with four family members as vice presidents (plus one salaried manager). At the same time, Tadao and Kamiya and one salaried manager were senior directors, with Fujimura and eleven salaried managers as executive directors. Closing out the ranks were nine salaried managers as regular directors.

As table 4.3 shows, the strong family presence in Kashima's top management of this period is self-evident. Equally obvious is the fact that such a presence was unlikely to continue and a changing of the guard was inevitable. By 1995, of the 53 people at director level or higher, only three Kashima family members remained: Ishikawa as chairman emeritus, Shoichi as director/advisor, and Naoki Atsumi (Takeo's eldest son) as a director. By this time, the shift in Kashima Construction from a family enterprise to a managerial enterprise seemed to be almost certain.

Failed Succession and Crises in Family Enterprises

We must now ask the question: for founder and family enterprises, what is the single most important element for protecting and ensuring the survival of the business? Although this question is a central one, the answer is simple: identifying and empowering family members to succeed to the running of the business. If the goal is merely to place family members in figurehead roles for succession purposes, then of course it's not necessary to find talented business minds to fill the open spots. The one thing that *is* absolutely necessary, however, is that someone, anyone, from the family step in when needed.

For most family enterprises, the custom has been for the oldest succeeding male member of the family to follow as head of the

Table 4.3. Changes to the Board of Directors at Kashima Construction (at the end of March of each year)

	Chairmen	Vice Chairmen	Presidents	Vice Presidents	Senior Directors	Executive Directors	Directors	Advisors
1959	Morinosuke		Ume	Ono, Atsumi, Ishikawa, Shoichi, SM1	Tadao, Kamiya, SM1	Fujimura, SM11	SM9	
1966	Morinosuke	Ume	Atsumi	Ono, Ishikawa, Shoichi, SM1 (Prof. Mutoh)	Kamiya, Hiraizumi, SM5	SM11	SM9	
1975	(Morinosuke died in Dec. 75) Ume	Ono	Atsumi	Ishikawa, Shoichi, Kamiya,	SM11	SM14	SM17	
1978	Atsumi	Shoichi	Ishikawa	Kamiya, SM5	SM7	SM17	SM14	Ume
1983	Atsumi	Shoichi	Ishikawa	SM6	SM10	SM8	SM19	Maeda (SM)
1984	Ishikawa		Shoichi	SM4	SM9	SM14	SM15	Atsumi, Maeda
1988	Ishikawa	SM2	Shoichi	SM7	SM9	SM10	SM16	Atsumi
1990	Ishikawa	Shoichi	Akira Miyazaki (SM—Appointment of former govt. official)	SM12	SM6	SM11	SM19	Atsumi
1993	Ishikawa	Shoichi	Miyazaki	SM10	SM10	SM16	SM16	Atsumi
1995	Ishikawa (Emeritus)	Miyazaki		SM8	SM9	SM17	SM15, Naoki Atsumi	Shoichi

Note: SM stands for Salaried Manager

Source: Kaisha Shiki Ho *(Company Seasonal Report).*

family business. As simple as it may sound, the issue of family succession is indeed difficult—as well as delicate—and many family enterprises, regardless of their line of business, face perplexing problems in successfully handling it.

The Case of the Kawasaki Family

If we were to search for a representative example of a family enterprise that collapsed owing to its inability to find a successor from within the family, we would probably do well to look at the Shozo Kawasaki family in the period that bridged the Meiji and Taisho periods.[18]

Shozo Kawasaki, as many may know, founded the company known as Kawasaki Zosensho (Shipbuilding), later to be divided and called Kawasaki Juko (Heavy Industries) and Kawasaki Seitetsu (Steel). In 1885, the Kawasaki family was visited by misfortune when their second and third sons both fell victim to illness and died shortly after one another. Compounding these terrible circumstances was the fact that their eldest son had already died and the second son had become the heir. Taking quick action the following year, Shozo adopted an infant boy named Shoji and in 1892 he married his daughter Chika to a man named Yoshitaro, who was Shozo's nephew, son of his younger sister. Although Shozo initially had great expectations for Yoshitaro, who was sent to the United States to study, he gradually began to have serious misgivings about Yoshitaro as successor and decided not to adopt him as a registered son.

In 1896, Shozo listed Kawasaki Shipbuilding as a joint stock company and retired from its management. By this time, Shozo had also decided not to appoint Yoshitaro as successor but instead planned for Shoji, still only 10 years old, to be groomed to take over the reins. In the interim, Shozo appointed as president Kojiro Matsukata, the third son of one of Shozo's backers, Masayoshi Matsukata. In Shozo's mind, however, it was very clear that Matsukata was merely a substitute player brought into the game until young Shoji was ready to step in and take over.

But, as we all know, even the best-laid plans go awry and Shozo's designs proved the truth of this adage. After entering Keio University, young Shoji decided to study literature instead of pursuing business interests. Shozo was so bitterly disappointed that he disinherited his adopted son in 1905. Reacting quickly to his latest setback, Shozo once more turned to Yoshitaro and adopted him as heir and successor the following year. Despite his newly elevated status, however, Yoshitaro lacked the ability to replace Kojiro Matsukata as president. Whether it was relieving him of his misery or striking the final blow of his tragic destiny, in 1912 Shozo became ill and died, at last reunited with his predeceased sons.

The result of these tragic circumstances was that, on the retirement of Shozo, Kawasaki Shipbuilding was unable to make the transition from a founder enterprise to a family enterprise for the fundamental reason that a suitable successor could not be found. After Shozo's death the Kawasaki family moved into real estate and other businesses unrelated to Kawasaki Shipbuilding. When new stock was issued in the company founded by Shozo, the family chose not to increase their holdings. Instead, Kojiro Matsukata and his immediate family seized the opportunity to upgrade their stock holdings in Kawasaki Shipbuilding and the company effectively became the property of the president and his clan. Whether comfort to the memory of Shozo or not, the Kawasaki example of failing to make it as a family enterprise through the inability to find a suitable successor from within is hardly unusual and is the downfall of many a family enterprise.

The Case of the Mikimoto Family

There is another case of a family enterprise that suffered so much because it was unable to find a successor to take over the family business. This case involves the king of the pearl industry, Kokichi Mikimoto.[19]

Mikimoto's business successes can be traced back to the Shima Peninsula, where in 1893 he managed to produce a semicircular cultured pearl. Following up on this initial triumph, in 1905 he developed a perfectly circular cultured pearl. Mikimoto became such a success both in Japan and abroad that he even became known as the king of the pearl industry and his family became, as a matter of course, one of the richest in Japan. But as is often the case, wealth alone did not bring happiness. Kokichi's beloved wife, Ume, who had also helped tremendously on the business side of things, passed away leaving Kokichi alone with their only son, Ryuzo, who was 3 years old at the time. As an indication of Kokichi's affection for his late wife, he failed to remarry and instead devoted his energies to Ryuzo's education.

Ryuzo and his education became his father's raison d'être. Kokichi selected his son's educational path with great care, plotting out an elite route through schools and subjects that would cumulate in Ryuzo's entrance into the First High School and then Kyoto University's department of literature. Under the tutelage of a famous Marxist scholar, Hajime Kawakami, it was decided that Ryuzo's research subject would be the work of Englishman John Ruskin, which Ryuzo delved into with great enthusiasm. Once again, Kokichi's heart was broken as Ryuzo defied his father to marry (and have two children) while still a student. Ryuzo then compounded things by failing to graduate from Kyoto.

As if this weren't enough of a betrayal of Kokichi's wishes, Ryuzo then began to spend his father's money, first by amassing a collection of Ruskin's works and then by opening four coffee shops that had Ruskin themes. After Ryuzo fell into debt from usury over this profligate spending, Kokichi was forced to have his son declared quasi-incompetent so that he could no longer deplete what remained of the family's wealth. Kokichi's actions were not out of anger but instead were a product of paternal love. After rescuing Ryuzo from financial disaster, Kokichi bought back Ryuzo's prized Ruskin collection and returned it once again to his son. As an interesting aside, the Ruskin collection eventually transformed into an organization that, to this day, is one of Mikimoto's primary stockholders.

Looking back on these events, Kokichi managed to save his relationship with his son. But it is very clear that, in doing so, he lost his only chance at finding a successor from within his immediate family. Having given up on Ryuzo, Kokichi then turned to his eldest grandson, Yoshitaka, born in 1918. Once again Kokichi hoped that a savior was in sight and that his grandson would follow in his grandfather's professional footsteps. Recalling his failed educational experiences with Ryuzo, Kokichi attempted to stop young Yoshitaka from attending university. But Yoshitaka was apparently as strong-willed as his father, for he was accepted into Keio University. Unlike his father, however, Yoshitaka graduated from Keio and then went to work for his grandfather. Yoshitaka's education was not strictly formal, however, since around this time his grandfather began almost desperately passing on his knowledge about how to run people and an organization.

This teamwork between grandfather and grandson seemed to work, because in 1949 they jointly opened the Mikimoto Shinju Kaisha (Pearl Company) and the Mikimoto Shinju Ten (Pearl Store). The former was founded as a limited liability company specializing in pearl culturing, and the wholesale business ran with Kokichi as president. The Pearl Store was a retail outlet, established as a joint stock company with Yoshitaka as president. What is truly amazing about this event is that at the time these new companies were being formed, Kokichi was 91 years old and still performing his duties as company president. Some say that Kokichi had lived only for this day, but in truth he survived another five years before passing away at age 96. It's also been said that the men who found companies cannot die until they have found and trained a successor and turned their founder enterprise into a family enterprise. In Kokichi's case, it would almost seemed to have been true.[20]

Unlike Shozo Kawasaki, Kokichi Mikimoto was able to find and appoint a successor, even though the succession skipped a generation, and to turn his company into what I define as a family enterprise. According to the data available at the time of this writing, Mikimoto K.K. is a private company unlisted on the stock exchange and is capitalized at an estimated 480 million yen. Its major stockholder is, as previously mentioned, the Ruskin Collection, which holds 14.9 percent of the company's shares and, as such, can be considered to be a Mikimoto family enterprise. On the management front, Yoshitaka became chairman in 1969 and Yoshitaka's brother-in-law, Toshio Honma, served as president until his death. Taking over as president was Katsutoki Sugita, who came from the Mitsubishi Bank. Replacing him was Toyohiko Kasuga, son-in-law of Yoshitaka's younger sister, Sachiko. Yet, the jury is still out about whether or not the Mikimoto company can continue as a family enterprise, particularly since the death of Yoshitaka in January of 1996.

The Transformation into a Managerial Enterprise—and Back Again

The Weaknesses of Family Enterprises

As mentioned earlier, the people who found and build new businesses from the grassroots level up are special people. It goes without saying that they are not perfect people, either. But even taking into account the egocentric and conceited natures of some company founders, the truth is that to start and grow a successful company takes talent—one thing all company founders share. One of the greatest business ironies, however, is that the greater the founder, the more likely it is that the successor to this family enterprise will not be as good. Following in the founder's footsteps is undeniably a hard act.

Although the transition from founder to successor in most cases leads to a decline in a company's top-management capabilities, there is a variety of possible scenarios. One of these scenarios is that the founder recognizes at an early stage that the named successor is not up to the task and brings in a salaried manager. This scenario is a perfect example of a founder enterprise being immediately transformed into a managerial enterprise without the more usual transition to a family enterprise. Another scenario is that the founder hands over power to the family, but it soon becomes apparent that the decision is an ill-fated one because the top-management representative of this new family enterprise is incapable of improving company performance. Thus, salaried managers are brought in. In this scenario, the transition is from a family enterprise to a managerial one.

There is one more scenario that should be mentioned, one which shows that the transition from founder enterprise to family enterprise to managerial enterprise is not necessarily a one-way street. In some cases, families or founders may turn over their companies to salaried managers but then later decide—for one reason or another—that they want the company back. In some cases this may not be possible, but in others it most definitely is. This so-called counterrevolution is an intriguing process that bears more scrutiny as we examine what happens when companies move toward becoming managerial enterprises.

Bridgestone and the Ishibashi Family

The Establishment of the Bridgestone Tire Company. This is the story of two brothers, Tokujiro Ishibashi, who was born in 1886, and Shojiro, born three years later. Another brother, Shinichi, was born in 1907, but he does not figure prominently in the story I am about to tell.

Tokujiro and brother Shojiro got their start in the *tabi* business in Kurume (Japanese-style socks designed to be worn with thong shoes or sometimes as shoes themselves). In 1918 they transformed their business to a joint-stock company called Japan Tabi K.K., capitalized at 300,000 yen. As coincidence would have it, in 1917 another *tabi* company called Tsuchiya Tabi (an unlimited partnership capitalized at 500,000 yen and now known as Tsukiboshi

Gomu) started up in Kurume. The Ishibashi brothers were more successful by virtue of their innovative idea of placing rubber bottoms on their *tabi*. This product was produced in 1922 under the name of Asahi Jika Tabi. The brothers were so successful that, for a time, all Japanese *tabi* seemed to be Asahi Jika *tabi*. The brothers then moved on to large-scale production and sales of rubber boots. They even expanded to the point of exporting their products and establishing overseas production centers. Although it was the height of the depression, the brothers' company made substantial profits: 900,000 yen in 1927, 720,000 yen the following year, and 920,000 yen the year after. They no longer had rivals and seemed to have risen above the competition and the difficult economic times.[21]

With expansion as the goal, Shojiro Ishibashi made the decision to use some of their company's accumulated profits to move into tire manufacturing. Although the timing of this decision is uncertain, it was probably around 1928 since an order was placed by the Ishibashi company for a tire-making machine in April 1929.[22] The decision to enter the tire business was not taken lightly. It was based on Shojiro's thorough understanding that the largest area of business for European and North American rubber companies at that time was the relatively new field of tire production. Another aspect of Shojiro's interest in the tire business was not purely financial. He was very nationalistic and hoped to reduce tire imports into Japan. Moreover, the idea of becoming merely a domestic agent or representative of a large multinational held no interest for him; he wanted to do it himself.

Yet Shojiro had some catching up to do with his competition. Dunlop Far East had already set up its Japanese head office and automobile tire production facility in Kobe and had gone into production as early as 1913. Also, in 1917, the Furukawa Group had set up a company called Yokohama Gomu Seizo K.K. (Yokohama Rubber Manufacturing Ltd.), a joint venture with the American company, Goodrich. By 1921 this new example of international business cooperation was up and running and producing a variety of corded tires on a significant scale. Things were not all rosy for this new enterprise, however, as its Yokohama factory was destroyed in the Great Kanto Earthquake of 1923. Plans were made to rebuild the factory, which opened in October 1930, and the company went full steam ahead into tire production to meet the demand of the booming passenger-car market.

Other players also attempted to get into the burgeoning field of passenger-car tire production. The Morimura *zaibatsu*'s Tokyo rubber factory started producing tires, as did Naigai Rubber of Kobe, but neither was able to take full advantage of the opportunities of the new marketplace. So, the enterprising Shojiro Ishibashi essentially faced two major outside rivals: Dunlop, and the revitalized Yokohama Rubber.

Another hurdle facing Shojiro, however, was that he had an internal obstacle: his older brother, Tokujiro (president of Japan Tabi), was dead set against Shojiro's plans. Tokujiro believed that entering a new and dangerous business field when their other company was doing so well was nothing short of foolhardy and that there was no need to expend the time, effort, and money on such a plan. Tokujiro also had allies in his technical people and their customer base. The Mitsui company, one of the brothers' largest clients, also believed such diversification was foolish. Shojiro, however, ignored these warnings. His mind was made up, and as far as he was concerned it was all systems go. In February 1930, just as their tire production facility was being built, Shojiro replaced his brother as president of the Japan Tabi Company. Adding to his list of titles, Shojiro became president of the Bridgestone Tire Company when it was incorporated in March 1931.[23] It is also of interest to note how the new company arrived at its name. Ishibashi, the brothers' family name, can be translated into English as "stone bridge." Reverse the order and you have the name Bridgestone.

The establishment of this new company, despite serious opposition, is just one example of Shojiro's dynamism. He was reputed to be a thoroughly unique character, and the success of the Japan Tabi Company is also generally attributed to his skills and talent. Bridgestone Tire was initially capitalized at 1 million yen (half in paid-up capital), with Shojiro putting up two-thirds of the cash and Tokujiro the rest. The Japan Tabi Company was capitalized at that time at 5 million yen in fully paid capital and all stock was controlled by the Ishibashi family.

The Breakup of the Ishibashi Family Enterprise. In the storm surrounding the Allied occupation's dismantling of the large-scale Japanese *zaibatsu* after the war, the Ishibashi family sustained damage, as their operations were considered to be in violation of antitrust and similar laws. On February 20, 1947, the brothers complied with the imposed regulations and broke up their organization into independent units. Specifically, this action consisted of 213,330 shares of Bridgestone stock owned by Tokujiro and Shinichi being transferred to Shojiro who, in turn, gave 185,788 shares of Japan Rubber (formerly Japan Tabi, the name of which had been in changed in April 1937) to his brothers. Also, Shojiro was forced to resign the presidency of Japan Rubber. After this breakup, the two companies drifted apart to such a degree that it is almost hard to believe that they were once part of the same family business. As of 1951, the only connection the two companies had with one another was when Bridgestone completed a new building and Japan Rubber moved into the building as Bridgestone's tenant. Japan Rubber also changed names once again, and they are now known as the Asahi Corporation.

Although we know about Japan Rubber's last name change, since they have remained a private operation, little is known about the state of their business. On the other hand, from 1953 on Bridgestone experienced tremendous growth. In the domestic tire market, Bridgestone managed to capture over a 60 percent share and also moved into the production and marketing of bicycles and products for industrial use. This rise in Bridgestone's fortunes led to an increasingly wide gap between the personal fortunes of Shojiro's family and those of his two brothers. The sibling rivalry finally came to an end in 1958 when Tokujiro passed away, succeeded by his eldest son, Yoshio, who, on his father's death, changed his first name to Tokujiro and also assumed the role as head of the family. As for Shinichi, he became the president of Japan Rubber and then moved up to the position of chairman. It is also interesting to note that after Tokujiro's death, houses and country homes in Kurume and Karuizawa formerly owned by Tokujiro and Shinichi were bought either by Shojiro himself or by the Bridgestone company.

Going Public and Changes in Top Management. In May 1961 the Bridgestone Tire Company owned by the Ishibashi family finally put their stocks on the open market. The reason for the public stock offering was the company's dire need for capital for rapid expansion and investment in plant facilities. The amounts needed were so large that the Ishibashi's were unable to finance everything through private means and the money had to be found elsewhere. Although the company could probably have been aided by the banks, it made more sense in the company's long-term financial picture to increase their overall capital.

Let's now look at the period of high economic growth after World War II in greater detail. As discussed earlier, large companies had created a hierarchical business structure that allowed them to create skill-based networks—networks of workers who knew of each other through professional, educational, and even personal contacts, and who might even work in different fields. Building on this, these same companies began to utilize these networks by promoting competent, salaried managers who were able to manage this process more efficiently. Moreover, company founders were able to take their subordinates along with them and, by joining together, could take on risks and responsibilities that overcame most, if not all, of the challenges thrown their way, largely by creating and controlling their own skill networks more effectively. Any examination of the facts and case studies during this high-growth era and the founder enterprises who labored within it makes it abundantly clear that these men and their firms played significant roles. Just to list the names of these founders and their companies should be enough to understand their impact: Matsushita, Honda, Sanyo, Sharp, Sony, Daiei, to name just a few.

Founder Enterprises and Managerial Enterprises

The next argument to arise out of this discussion concerning managerial enterprises and founder enterprises is which played a greater role in the high-growth economic development of Japan in the post–World War II period? One side of this argument is put forth by Takeo Kikkawa, who says that "In the processes that led to Japan's economic development after the war, it would not be overreaching to say that capitalist enterprises (meaning founder enterprises) had a greater impact on a wider range of industries than did that of managerial enterprises."[42] Although Kikkawa represents one side of the debate, the grounds on which he bases these views are, I believe, somewhat unclear.

My own position in this debate is that, without objective data to verify one side of the argument or the other regarding which group was more responsible for stimulating Japan's high economic growth, it is impossible to come to a definitive conclusion. What views I do have about the relative management strength of family enterprises versus managerial enterprises have already been discussed in the previous chapter and I continue to stand by those opinions.

The family's decision to go public also reflected nonfinancial factors. There had been some criticism of large corporations being held by a single family, and there were also company morale benefits to be had by becoming a publicly held company. The stock issue raised 2.5 billion yen on the 50 million shares made available. Of these shares, about 0.21 million shares valued at 160 yen a share were made available to employees. Goodyear Japan received 1 million shares while banks, investment firms, and insurance companies got an additional 3 million shares. Later, 5 million shares were sold on the Tokyo and Osaka stock markets at a price of 330 yen per share. Of the total stock, about 10 million shares, which represented about 20 percent of the total stock, were put on the open market. Later, more shares were released in a number of other, smaller public offerings with the result that the Ishibashi family's portion decreased even further. In 1984 the company also changed its name, simplifying it from Bridgestone Tire to just Bridgestone. In 1995, at the time this book was being written in Japanese, Bridgestone was capitalized at approximately 80 billion yen and it is estimated that the Ishibashi family and relations controlled about 30 percent of the company's stock.

In February 1963, about two years after the company went public, Shojiro retired from the post of president and became the company's chairman. He was replaced by his oldest son, Kanichiro, who moved up from being vice president to take over the number-one spot at the relatively young age of 43. At the time of these top-management changes, Shojiro was a robust 74 years old and the reason for his move was unrelated to his age. Instead, Shojiro wanted to ensure Kanichiro's ascension while he was still powerful enough to do so; and even though Shojiro was now in the chairman's seat, he was still at the core of the company's top management.

The next move in top management occurred in May 1973 when Shojiro announced his retirement as chairman. He was replaced once again by Kanichiro and the newly appointed president was Shigemichi Shibamoto, who had been previously brought in as a salaried manager to take up the position of vice president during Kanichiro's reign as president. Although this change in leadership took place a mere four months before the oil shock hit Japan, the reasons for the change were unrelated to the oil crisis.

Shojiro's retirement as chairman and move to the essentially honorary position of director/advisor at age 84 was for health reasons; two or three years after he left the presidency he was diagnosed with Parkinson's disease. Shojiro suffered another blow, in that his son Kanichiro became company chairman after only 10 years as the company's president. In his place, a salaried manager with no blood connection to the Ishibashi family was appointed president. The question, however, about why Kanichiro was moved out to be replaced by a nonfamily member has never been fully answered. I have arrived at my own educated guess, however, which is described below.

My theory is that Kanichiro was shuffled out of the president's hot seat and into the more comfortable chairman's position because Shojiro had come to the conclusion that Kanichiro was just not up to the task of running the company effectively. The problem stemmed from Kanichiro's personality, which was noble minded to the degree that he often had trouble understanding the harsh realities of society. Worse, he was reportedly so unable to understand others who were less high minded than himself that his ability to communicate was a real problem. Kanichiro was undoubtedly a warm and good-natured person who, if anything, became even more so as he got older. But whether Kanichiro's personality was suited to the often difficult role of top manager was a serious issue. Despite fierce competition, the family patriarch Shojiro had taken his company to the top of its field in both Japan and overseas through the force of his character. Shojiro seemed to feel that his son was somehow lacking the drive and strength needed to keep the company growing. This is not to mean, however, that Kanichiro's role as chairman was a meaningless one. He was still an Ishibashi and, as such, he was expected to be the chief family watchdog among the company's top management.

Let us now move on to the question of why Shigemichi Shibamoto was chosen to replace Kanichiro as Bridgestone president. Shibamoto was a graduate of the economics department of Tokyo University. He joined the company now known as Bridgestone, first serving in a number of sales-related positions. His experience was extensive and he brought to the company a broad range of internal experience that was rewarded when he became a director of the company in 1947 and an executive director two years later. Shibamoto later held the posts of senior director and vice president before ascending to the presidency, as mentioned earlier. At the time of his appointment as president, Shibamoto was 64 years old, and it's a good guess that Shibamoto's age and experience were key factors in Shojiro Ishibashi's decision to hand him the job.

Yet despite Shibamoto's sparkling qualifications, it was not all smooth sailing to the top spot in the firm, mainly because a large number of Ishibashi's relatives remained on the company's board of directors. Besides Kanichiro, Shojiro's son-in-law (Shuichi Narumo) was a vice president, Shojiro's nephew Kenichiro Hirakawa was an executive director, as was Koichiro Ishii, husband to Shojiro's fourth daughter. As might be imagined, there were certain parties who thought it only natural that the next president of the company should come from within this group, particularly since Narumo, Hirakawa, and Ishii were all full-time employees of the company and experienced managers with plenty of seniority at Bridgestone. After graduating from Tokyo University, Narumo had spent nine years at Mitsubishi Bank and been in the navy while Hirakawa and Ishii joined the family business directly after university (Ishii graduating from Keio and Hirakawa leaving Akron University in the States before finishing). It's possible that age played a factor in the decision to make Shibamoto president, since his 64 years would have been considered more appropriate that Hirakawa's 56, Narumo's 53, and—in particular—Ishii's tender 40. Discounting the age issue, it is somewhat perplexing that Narumo was not chosen to succeed Kanichiro. Although he might have been considered a touch too young, when considering Narumo's experience (including a directorship since 1958) and the confidence shown him by his staff and other employees, he should have been an outstanding candidate indeed.

So why then did Shojiro Ishibashi choose to go outside the family and deny his own daughter's husband the chance of leading the family company? One answer is possibly health related. A short two and a half years after Shibamoto was given the top job, Narumo died at the surprisingly young age of 55. Although this might well explain Shojiro's reticence in appointing his son-in-law as CEO, there is one other possible reason. In many respects, Shojiro was a self-made man and, as such, he may not have cared at all about whether or not his bloodline continued on in his company's management suite. In both his career at Japan Tabi and at Bridgestone, there's evidence that Shojiro never placed much value on family ties. If you look at how he parted with his brother on entering the tire business; if you examine how the gap in family wealth grew increasingly wider; if you imagine how he engineered his son's removal from the company's presidency after only 10 years, it becomes clear that family was not the force that drove Shojiro Ishibashi. In fact, it's highly possible that Shojiro may have believed that water was thicker than blood and thought that an overconcern with family succession might be detrimental instead of beneficial to the businesses he had worked so hard to create. Like another unique Japanese business pioneer, Soichiro Honda, Shojiro Ishibashi was a rugged individualist—and he stayed that way to the end.

Shojiro Ishibashi passed away in September 1976. Kanichiro moved on to become director/chairman emeritus in 1985, and a succession of salaried managers became president in turn. Shibamoto's reign as president ended in March 1981, when he was replaced by a man named Kunio Hattori who, in turn, retired early in 1985. Following Hattori as president was Akira Ieiri, who continued in that position until 1993. As for other Ishibashi family members, Hirakawa retired as senior director in 1978, as did Ishii in 1979, although Ishii then moved over to become president of Bridgestone Cycle. At the time this book was written, the only family board member of Bridgestone is Kanichiro in the role of chairman emeritus, although he could also still be considered the owner of the company.

The Increase in Influence of Kanichiro Ishibashi. In the two or three years before this book was finished, it was felt by many that the winds of change had come to the top management of the Bridgestone Company, and that these changes were the result of the increased influence of the chairman emeritus, Kanichiro Ishibashi. Despite Ishibashi's comeback, however, it should not be interpreted that the company was moving back to being a family enterprise after its period as a managerial enterprise.

The purchase of Firestone by Bridgestone in March 1988 is cited as an example of Ishibashi's renewed imprint on the company. As competition for the world automobile tire market became an increasingly pitched battle among Bridgestone, America's Goodyear, and France's Michelin, Bridgestone eyed Firestone's American factories and distribution network. As a first step, Bridgestone purchased Firestone's truck and bus radial tire plant in Tennessee in 1982, rebuilding the factory and improving labor relations to the point where the company was brimming with newfound confidence.

In early 1988, the intense competition in the tire industry heated up even further when the Pirelli Tire Company of Italy made a takeover bid for Firestone. After learning that Pirelli's bid was backed by Michelin, Ieiri and the rest of Bridgestone's management team concluded that an offensive strategy was the best defense and decided to put in an offer for Firestone's stock. Knowing that Pirelli had an offer on the table, price per share was a critical issue. The decision finally came down to the Bridgestone president Ieiri, whose bid of $80 per share won the day. Bridgestone ended up purchasing 96.4 percent of Firestone's stock, which totaled 33.15 million shares. As can be imagined, the purchase was a huge one. Bridgestone's bill for Firestone was $2.65 billion in 1988 dollars.

Bridgestone's outlay didn't end there, however. In the same year, the company decided to modernize a slew of Firestone's factories and invested another $1.5 billion to do so. Also, in 1991, in order to reduce the burden of Firestone's long-term debts, Bridgestone pumped in another $1.4 million. In the three years since the purchase of Firestone, Bridgestone's total bill came to a staggering $5.5 billion. As of August 1995, the Bridgestone company was capitalized at 80.9 billion yen.

In taking on board this huge external investment, the pressure on Bridgestone's finances had become enormous and was the impetus for Kanichiro's rejuvenated role as the opinion leader in Bridgestone's boardroom. Since Ishibashi had agreed to the buyout of Firestone from the beginning, he had no axe to grind on this particular issue with company president Ieiri or the other top-level salaried managers. Despite this, Ishibashi was justifiably concerned about the company's worsening financial picture, labor issues, and the slow pace of renovation of Firestone's aging factories.

In 1993, Ieiri had reached the end of his agreed-upon term as president and he was replaced by Yoichiro Kaizaki. This changing of the guard meant that the Bridgestone board would become considerably younger, and this is also believed to be another reason that Kanichiro's voice in company affairs was growing increasingly influential. Yet for all of Kanichiro's renewed stature there was no movement for the company to return to being a family enterprise or for Kanichiro's eldest son, Kan Ishibashi (who was the company's auditor), to become CEO.[24]

Matsushita Electric and the Matsushita Family

The Family Misfortune of Konosuke Matsushita. The tribulations of Konosuke Matsushita's youth are well known: he was forced to leave his rather ordinary elementary school in the fourth grade and was then apprenticed to an electrical manufacturer in Osaka. Matsushita left the Osaka Dento company at age 23 and, using his severance pay and whatever other funds he could scrape together, began manufacturing electrical sockets, starting with a mere 100 yen to his fledgling company's name. March 7, 1918, is an important day in the history of Japanese business, because on this day Matsushita Denki Kigu Seisakusho (the Matsushita Electric Appliances Manufacturing Company) was officially established.[25]

That Matsushita Electric grew from such humble beginnings to its current size and level of prestige is nothing short of a miracle. Moreover, no matter how much praise has been lavished upon Konosuke Matsushita as the company's founder, innovator, and leader, it is probably insufficient. Yet despite Matsushita's prodigious skills and feats as company founder, his ill-starred family life would plague him—notably that there was no successor of his own blood to take over and run the company as a family enterprise. It is true, however, that after establishing his company, Matsushita did have plenty of help from his relatives. The first person of note to help run the socket manufacturing business was Toshio Iue, brother of Matsushita's wife, Mumeno. Others who would help included his nephew Takeo Kameyama, Tetsujiro Nakao (the husband of Mumeno's sister), and Iue's two younger brothers. When the company became a full-fledged *kabushiki kaisha* (joint-stock company) in 1935, these relatives all became company directors.[26]

Yet despite the apparent support of his extended family, it's still valid to say that as far as family was concerned, Matsushita was not a lucky man. Although Konosuke and Mumeno had a son and a daughter, their son died just before his first birthday. Also, although Matsushita received ample support from relatives, as we have seen, this help was almost exclusively from Mumeno's side of the family, the reason being that the Matsushita side of the clan, Konosuke included, was cursed with ill health. Konosuke had lost both his father and mother at a relatively early age and had also lost two brothers and a sister while he was still in primary school. His two remaining older sisters also died young, leaving Konosuke behind just after he had established his company.

Matsushita's misfortune's did not end there, for the postwar Allied occupation forces designated him and his family as a *zaibatsu* and the company had restrictions placed on its stockholding and stockholders. Moreover, in a related action, the directors of the company were purged and banned from holding public office, which coincided with Toshio Iue's leaving the Matsushita company to go out on his own and form a company that became Sanyo

Electric. To make matters worse, if imaginable, Iue took his two brothers and other relatives with him.

Konosuke and His Adopted Heir, Masaharu. In 1940 the only daughter of Konosuke and Mumeno, Sachiko, married Masaharu Hirata, who was brought into the family as an adopted son by marriage. Hirata was a graduate of Tokyo University's law department and was the grandson of Tosuke Hirata, a high-ranking bureaucrat during the Meiji period who had even achieved the rank of Count. Thus, Masaharu was the second son of a count, and his education (he had also graduated from the elite Tokyo High School) and background were so different from his father-in-law's that they almost belonged to two different worlds.

In 1944 Konosuke appointed Masaharu as the company's auditor, which built on his five years' experience working with the Mitsui Bank, where he had been employed until his marriage. Masaharu had no working experience outside banking, and on entering the innovative corporate culture of Matsushita Electric he found himself in a very different and unfamiliar world. Although Konosuke had had frequent sessions with Masaharu about life at Matsushita even before Masaharu's marriage, the lessons were all theory and very different from hands-on learning. Even though Masaharu's experience was essentially second-hand and he was, businesswise, still wet behind the years, Konosuke took the plunge and appointed him as the company auditor four years after joining the family.

We can only speculate that Konosuke appointed Masaharu as auditor with the hope that he would quickly gain top-management experience, knowing that he'd be there to support Konosuke if the need arose. Also likely is that the departure of the Iues to Sanyo left a big management void that Konosuke was eager to fill. Masaharu's ascension up the Matsushita ladder was rapid. In 1948 he became a director and in September of the following year he was made vice president. As for the other key members of Konosuke's top-management team at this time (Kotaro Takahashi as senior director and Tsuyoji Fujio as executive director), most were nonfamily salaried managers who had worked their way up from within company ranks.

Family members, although few, were not totally excluded, however. Members of Mumeno's family who held various positions in the organization included Tetsujiro Nakao (Mumeno's brother-in-law), who served at various times as auditor, executive director, and senior director, and Shoji Niwa, the second husband of Masaharu's younger sister, brought into the company by Konosuke's, probably more from family obligation than professional necessity.

Masaharu's climb to the top of Matsushita reached its pinnacle when he became president in January 1961. The other members of the management team at this time were Konosuke as chairman, Kotaro Takahashi as vice president, Nakao as senior director, and Tanimura, Nishinomiya, Ogawa—all salaried managers—as executive directors. But, as the saying goes, it's tough at the top and Masaharu must have found it difficult. For the true power at Matsushita still lay, natural as it may have been, with the man whose name the company bore. Moreover, Konosuke was surrounded by loyal supporters who were likely unhappy about the arrival of the new kid on the block.

A well-known event in the history of the Matsushita company is the "Atami Meeting" of July 1964. There had been a bad slump in the sales of home electrical products and Matsushita too had been badly hit, with its sales division and distributors wallowing in red ink. The poor results, combined with other frustrations on the part of the dealers (who were mainly railing against products being forced on them, an obsession with profit, the company's bureaucracy, and the slow pace of new product development), meant that fuses were short and Atami was where the explosion would happen. The meeting, or conference, was titled "A Japan-Wide, Informal Gathering of the Presidents of Domestic Sales Outlets" and was attended by some 170 company presidents. Although the meeting was scheduled to last two days, the scale and volume of criticism hurtling Matsushita's way was so volatile that the meeting was extended an extra day.

The barrage was finally stopped by Chairman Konosuke, who accepted the criticism, apologized profoundly, and pledged that remedies would be found for the dealers' problems. Konosuke's first step came one month later, when he appointed himself head of the sales division and set about reorganizing how sales were made at Matsushita. Whether or not it can be attributed to Konosuke's actions, only two years later (in 1966), Matsushita registered its best first-quarter results ever. Possibly even more important, the sales division and the dealers were successful as well—poor results were at last behind them.

The Atami Meeting became an important part of the Konosuke Matsushita legend and a model for later chief executives as to how to conduct themselves and their business. If we look at the Atami Meeting from a different angle, we see that, although Konosuke gained points through his actions, adopted son Masaharu was put into a highly unenviable position. When Matsushita made his famous apology, he completely ignored Masaharu who was, after all, the company president. Also, Konosuke confessed to all manner of crimes without attempting to defend his company, his staff, or, most poignantly, his adopted son. What must have been even more grating to Masaharu was that his father practiced what he preached and revitalized and reorganized the sales department. The higher Konosuke's star rose, the further Masaharu's plummeted.[27]

The real problem, of course, was that Masaharu was and always had been company president in name only. The power, as we've seen, lay elsewhere. The Atami Meeting was surely salt in the wound, because it is one thing to be a figurehead and another to have this fact trumpeted to your customers and associates alike. Even in 1973, when Konosuke retired as chairman and became an advisor for health reasons, even when Kotaro Takahashi became chairman, even when in 1977 Masaharu himself became chairman with Toshihiko Yamashita as president, for Masaharu nothing had really changed.

Changes at Matsushita during the Yamashita Era. Putting aside Masaharu's position and situation, the Matsushita company entered a new era when Toshihiko Yamashita took over as president and change began happening in small though important increments. First, Yamashita was finally able to keep Konosuke (who was company advisor at this time) and his autocratic manner in check. Next, he was slowly able to put Konosuke's loyal band of supporters on the management team out to pasture. And finally, he was able to successfully move the company from being a family enterprise into being a managerial one.

That Toshihiko Yamashita was able to jump directly from being a regular director (as opposed to senior or executive director) into the president's chair caused such a sensation that this event was labeled the "Yamashita leap." The general view of why this happened is that Konosuke wanted to inject some youth into Matsushita's top-management team. But Yasunori Tateishi, a historian specializing in the history of the Matsushita company, has a different view. Tateishi believed that the appointment of Yamashita was actually engineered by Masaharu as a way of preventing Konosuke from returning as CEO.[28] Not being a specialist on this particular company, I'm hard-pressed to say which theory is correct, although both are certainly plausible.

Regardless of why these events occurred, the commonly held view was still that, as long as Konosuke Matsushita remained active and healthy, the question of who was president was irrelevant. The Matsushita Electric Company was Konosuke Matsushita's company, and his alone. Although Yamashita gave Konosuke the respect he deserved, the truth is that much of it was probably lip-service, since Yamashita was working behind the scenes simultaneously to undermine the deification of Konosuke and to lessen his influence on the company. Konosuke scoffed at computers and multimedia as mere flavors of the month and believed that an overemphasis in these areas would be detrimental to the firm's health. As a measure of his skill, Yamashita was successfully able to contain the senior Matsushita's views and limit the damage they caused.

The relationship between Yamashita and Konosuke during the later years of Yamashita's presidency was marked by friction. More than once Konosuke let slip that he thought Yamashita was "going overboard" and that he was far from happy with his latest CEO.[29] That Konosuke was complaining about Yamashita is probably a measure of just how successful the Yamashita revolution had become. Probably much to Konosuke's relief, Yamashita retired as president in February 1986 and was appointed director/advisor. Let's now take a look at the Matsushita board shortly before Yamashita stepped down as president. Masaharu held the chairman's post with Yamashita as president, backed up by three vice presidents—Akira Harada, Shunkichi Kisaka, and Akio Tanii. There were four senior directors (Yoshio Asada, Ken Abe, Shigeru Hayakawa, and Mitsuo Nakai), three executive directors (Takashi Yamazaki, Toshio Nakao, and Shoji Sakuma), and 12 regular directors. Rounding up the stable, of course, was Konosuke Matsushita as director/advisor. What's interesting about this lineup was how much it had chanced since the time when Yamashita was still a lowly director. Of the 25 members of the Yamashita Board (for lack of a better term), there were only six from the time when Yamashita had been at the bottom of the pecking order. If anyone was looking for proof that Matsushita's top management had experienced a youth revolution, here it was.

Another indicator of Yamashita's political skills is that his replacement as president was Akio Tanii, who had risen through the ranks along with Yamashita. Another event in 1986 underlined Yamashita's aggressiveness: at this time, Chairman Masaharu was endeavoring to have his 41-year-old eldest son, Masayuki, elected to the board. Yamashita's response? "It's too soon. And the next stockholders' meeting is too soon. And the one after that is also too soon." But Yamashita was not the only one who could attempt power plays and, after all, it was not *his* name on the company letterhead. Masaharu, despite Yamashita's objection, continued to push hard to get Masayuki onto the board and with Konosuke's backup, he succeeded. Yamashita's response this time? "This may be all well and good, but I'll have you know that the thought of young Masayuki one day becoming president of this company is something that has never, not once, crossed my mind."[30]

Matsushita after the Death of Konosuke. Regardless of the result, it was clear that one of Toshihiko Yamashita's primary goals was to turn the Matsushita company into a full-fledged managerial enterprise. Three years after Yamashita stepped down, several events occurred to make it more likely that Matsushita's period as a family enterprise would finally end. First, the legendary Konosuke Matsushita died. And, next, Masaharu was either unwilling or unable to fill the leadership gap occasioned by his adopted father's death. The route to becoming a managerial enterprise was now clear.

The company's new structure, however, did not prevent misfortune. In the first instance, at the height of the bubble economy in the spring of 1992, one of Matsushita's subsidiaries, National Lease, was found to have forged savings account statements with the Toyo Trust Company and to have made fraudulent credit claims. In another monumental event for Matsushita, two years earlier the company had shocked the world by buying the American entertainment giant, MCA. Whatever arguments could be made defending the purchase (arguing that it would lead Matsushita into the brave new world of multimedia), the price was a staggering $6.2 billion in 1990 dollars. As it turned out, the only thing as huge as the price would be the burden this purchase imposed on the new owners.

In order to take responsibility for the National Lease scandal, Matsushita's president, Tanii, resigned and made way for another promoted salaried manager, Yoichi Morishita. That this appointment—particularly in light of the reasons behind it—went to another salaried manager who had no Matsushita bloodlines was another indicator that the company was on its way to erasing its recent past as a family enterprise, although Masaharu was still continuing to make his presence felt as best he could. Previously, Masaharu had been particularly vocal on issues relating to the acquisition of MCA and Matsushita's moves into the field of multimedia. Masaharu had also continued to successfully push the career of his son, Masayuki, who was promoted to executive director in 1990 and then senior director in 1992. Also, Masaharu began to promote the idea that the company was in danger of breaking up into constituent parts and needed greater unity at its center; in other words, he was pushing son Masayuki for the company's top job and was, for all intents and purposes, saying that a return of the Matsushita family to prominence was just what the company needed.[31]

The Shimizu Family and Shimizu Construction

We now return to the discussion of founder's families trying to wrest back company control from the salaried managers who had been so instrumental in the formation of managerial enterprise. Although this idea of counterrevolution is often brought up by founder's families and is a concept to which they're sympathetic, it is usually more of a theory than something actually put into practice. If ever such battles are to be waged, the odds are stacked strongly against the families; after all, a small group of vested-interest insiders competing against a hardened group of professionals backed by foot soldiers in the form of the company employees is not a good position in which to be. And, as if this effort wasn't difficult enough, when a company is based on a network of core competencies and is multileveled in its organizational structure too, the castle walls become that much higher to scale and that more impenetrable to breach. Once a company has become a managerial enterprise, it is usually on a one-way street and the founder's families usually have to lump it. It is worth keeping in mind, however, that the relationship between founder families and salaried managers is by no means a constant one. Instead, depending on the how conditions and situations change, the relationship fluctuates in relation to those changes, and the Shimizu Construction Company is an excellent case in point.[32]

The Relationship between the Shimizu Group and the Shimizu Family. The start of the Shimizu empire can be traced back to 1804, when its founder, Kisuke Shimizu, was working as a carpenter in the Kanda district of Edo, as Tokyo used to be called. Kisuke had acquired a reputation as a skilled builder of important buildings such as shrines, temples, and structures erected for various feudal lords.

Kisuke had a number of apprentices working under him, and one of those lucky apprentices, Kisuke's favorite, Seishichi Fujisawa, was given the opportunity to marry Kisuke's daughter, Yasu, and be adopted into the family.

While working on the construction of the port at Yokohama, Kisuke died and Seishichi took over both the family and the family name, becoming Kisuke II. Kisuke II had been handed an opportunity—one on which he capitalized by becoming a major force in the construction business in Tokyo and Yokohama. After restoration of the Meiji Emperor, Kisuke II became heavily involved in the building of foreign embassies in Tokyo and grew to be a leader in his field. The Tsukiji Hotel Mansion and the Mitsui Bank buildings are considered to be some of his most representative works.

Kisuke II followed in his adopted father's footsteps by adopting the husband (Mannosuke Murata) of his eldest daughter, Mume. In 1881, the elder Kisuke died and, again following tradition, the adopted son, now Mannosuke Shimizu, took over as head of the family. Six years later, Mannosuke himself was to die suddenly and his eldest son, 8-year-old Kisaburo, became the fourth head of this branch of the family and had his name changed to Mannosuke. At this time, with the company needing a father figure, a well-known man named Eiichi Shibusawa stepped in and became the family's advisor. Shibusawa was the president of the Dai Ichi National Bank, and in recognition of the help he had given to the Shimizu family over the years, his role was formalized. Mannosuke IV had support from others as well. Shimizu's general manager and the cousin of the widow, Mume, Rinnosuke Hara, also helped raise the youngster, as did a family boarder, Teikichi Ono, a graduate of Tokyo University's civil engineering faculty.

Ono then married Mannosuke III's daughter, Take, and the young couple left home to start a new branch of the family. Despite all the support he received over the years, Mannosuke IV was a sickly individual and the major responsibilities for running the family company fell to Teikichi (who had become a Shimizu) and Rinnosuke. As the family expanded, another branch of the family was set up by Kazuo Irie, the husband of Mannosuke III's second daughter, Shitsu. As a way of managing the extended family's housekeeping and business affairs, the family advisor Shibusawa suggested in 1892 that formal family meetings be set up. These meetings were conducted as family-only events until 1900, when they were changed to include family advisor Shibusawa and the company's general manager.

The structure of the Shimizu family and company continued on in the manner described above, and the result was a weakening of family influence. As more family branches were created and more outside advisors and professional managers were brought into even the most innermost family circles, it seems obvious that the roots of the Shimizu organization as a family enterprise were already in danger. Things escalated even further when technical people (mainly Todai graduates) began entering the company in droves and some of the more senior ones even started attending official family meetings. Although it is a chicken-and-egg situation, one of the unique aspects of the Shimizu style was that many of the adopted sons were university graduates, which was unusual for that time. But with so many bright young Tokyo University graduates around, perhaps it is no wonder.

In 1915, a limited partnership was set up linking all branches of the Shimizu clan. The company was called, appropriately, the Shimizu Group (Gumi) and was capitalized at 1 million yen. Here is a breakdown of each family branch's investment and status in the group:

Mannosuke Shimizu IV (main family)	¥450,000 (limited liability)
Teikichi Shimizu (branch family)	¥250,000 (unlimited liability)
Kazuo Shimizu (branch family)	¥150,000 (unlimited liability)
Yonosuke Shimizu (branch family)	¥150,000 (limited liability)

Teikichi was appointed leader and manager of the group, with Kazuo and Yonosuke sharing the role of second-in-command. As a quick aside about Yonosuke, he created the third branch of the family after marrying Mannosuke III's third daughter, Toku.

Teikichi Shimizu's Hegemony and the Graduate Technicians. One of the key elements in understanding the Shimizu situation is realizing that even before the family established its limited partnership they were effectively operating as a hegemony under Teikichi's direction. Moreover, Teikichi's influence reached new levels in terms of both his official and his behind-the-scene roles after the company's general manager, Hara, died in 1912. Although Teikichi's stamp was printed on the company in a number of ways, perhaps one of his most significant legacies was in the number of university graduate technical people he brought into the company after the end of World War I; in the period from 1919 to 1926, 99 such individuals were brought into the firm.[33]

In the meantime, Mannosuke IV continued to suffer from ill health and, as a result, failed to marry and produce an heir. His mother, Mume, then got her wish for a family successor by having Mannosuke IV adopt Teikichi's third son, Yasuo, who was to succeed as the fifth head of the main trunk of the Shimizu clan when Mannosuke IV died in 1929. The Shimizu Group became a full-fledged ***kabushiki kaisha***, or joint-stock corporation, in 1937 with the first president being, of course, Teikichi. The first chairman was the latest head of the main family, Yasuo.

Yasuo had graduated in 1923 from Waseda University with a degree in political economics; technical matters were not his specialty. When his natural father, Teikichi, retired as president in 1940, Yasuo became the firm's second president. At the same time, the two uncles who had been vice presidents retired and were replaced by Teikichi's eldest son, Toshio (Yasuo's older brother), and the eldest son of Kazuo (who had been one of the vice presidents), who was named Masao.

Although the core of Shimizu Construction's new top-management team was from the family, none of the new members could match the retired Teikichi's business and management skills. This shortfall in top-management ability was made up for by the extremely competent salaried managers brought in by Teikichi. Thanks mainly to the efforts of these individuals, the company grew by leaps and bounds during and after the Second World War, even expanding overseas.

All was not good, however, in the aftermath of Japan's defeat in World War II. The company, like many others, had to rebuild and, in doing so, required the help and cooperation of the company's employees, suppliers, and customers. The result of this cooperation was that, as of 1948, the Shimizu family's stock holdings had fallen to less than 30 percent. When shares were split in 1960 during the company's first stock market listing, the percentage of family holdings dropped even further, this time to around 25 percent. As the family's holdings dropped, so did the family's influence on the business. In order to deal with an increase in the number of board members and the diversification of the business, in 1960 (the year the company first listed its stock) an executive directors' meeting was held for the first time. Attending the meeting were Yasuo (president); Masao, Tokuzo Ozasa, Choji Tominaga (vice presidents); Seiichi Yoshikawa (senior director); and five executive directors. In 1943, Yasuo's older brother, Toshio, died, followed by Teikichi, who died at a ripe old age in 1948. As always, time moves on.

The Transformation to a Managerial Enterprise. In September 1966, Yasuo, the president of Shimizu, also died and major management changes occurred as a result. Masao Shimizu went from being vice president to chairman, and Seiichi Yoshikawa was appointed as the new president, a jump up from his former position as senior director. This was a major event since it was the first time in the history of the company that a nonfamily member had held the top job in the company. The blows to the family were felt at other levels as well. Of the five senior directors, one of whom was Kiichi Noji, only one, Tsunetaka Sakano (Yasuo's son-in-law), was related to the Shimizus. Worse, all nine executive directors were salaried managers. The Shimizu presence in the company's top-management ranks was a mere shadow of what it once was. The next year, Noji became vice president and the transformation to a managerial enterprise was effectively complete.

Noji graduated from Tokyo University's faculty of engineering in 1931, specializing in architecture. Among the insider technical group, there were great hopes for Noji when he joined the company, and early on he seemed destined for great things. In May 1972 Yoshikawa moved up to chairman from president and was succeeded as CEO by Noji. The predictions of his rise to the top had come true. But as salaried managers like Noji rose higher, the Shimizu family influence sunk lower. Masao, who had been the prime representative of the family as chairman, was now just a director/advisor.

The next set of changes happened nine years later, in 1981. Noji became chairman, Tsunetaka Sakano became vice chairman, and the new president was Teruzo Yoshino, backed up by four vice presidents (Goto, Kinoshita, Nakagawa, and Saji). Yasuo's eldest son Mitsuaki had also risen in the company but, at that time, still did not have voting rights. The only other board representative from the founder family was Sakano. After Yasuo Shimizu's death, the next three presidents—Yoshikawa, Noji, and Yoshino—all had something in common beside their position as president: they were graduates of Todai's engineering faculty and had technical backgrounds. In other words, Teikichi's legacy was still the driving force in the company. His policy of hiring technical people from the universities and building a diversified network of skilled associates had served the company well, and was a major reason for the company's continued success—even if as a managerial enterprise—and a symbol of Teikichi's foresight and vision.

Despite the decline in the Shimizu family's presence in the company's top-management ranks, the family was still consulted and not ignored. As mentioned, Mitsuaki had joined the company after the death of his father (after graduating from Keio and a longish stint at the Dai Ichi Bank) and had risen as high as senior director (even though he had no voting rights). Mitsuaki's role meant that a representative of the main branch of the Shimizu family still had a part to play in the Shimizu top-management structure.

Unfortunately, Mitsuaki had to take a demotion to regular director in 1983 after the media reported a scandal in the family. He later returned to his position as executive director and also became president of Shimizu Jisho, a company in which Shimizu Construction is the leading stockholder. As for other Shimizu family members, younger brother Yasuaki holds a management position in the sales division of Shimizu, although he is not a board member. The former vice chairman, Sakano, was at last report a director/advisor of the company. The former president and chairman of Shimizu, Teruzo Yoshino, was forced to resign in 1993 because of a corruption scandal, although the president at that time, Harusuke Imamura, was able to keep his post.

The question of whether any member of the Shimizu family will rise to become president essentially can't be answered. Managing the huge network of technical people and systems is a task of such magnitude that I doubt anyone in the family has the ability to do so. In the final analysis, however, no one knows what the future will bring. Whether a change in the relationship between the family and salaried managers—or in any of a number of areas—can lead to a new era and new developments or not depends on the human resources within the family.

The Divisions within Family Enterprises

Fate and Family Feuding

In the previous section we discussed and analyzed the pluses and minuses of various aspects of the family enterprises of the Bridgestone and Matsushita Electric companies. Both companies achieved high levels of long-term growth and excellent profitability, as well as commanding market shares, as leaders in their respective industries. Moreover, both companies had relatively simple family structures that probably contributed to their success.

As you will recall, Bridgestone's origins can be traced back to the two Ishibashi brothers (later to be joined by another brother) who built up their business starting out as *tabi* manufacturers. The brothers were later to separate, however, for a number of reasons. First, there was the desire to go into the new field of passenger-car tires while at the same time remaining in the *tabi* business. Second, the sibling enterprise was broken up further owing to the postwar occupation forces' anti-*zaibatsu* law; in retrospect, this was probably perfect timing for the tire and *tabi* businesses to go their separate ways. Not only did the businesses separate, but the brothers also grew more and more distant. As the businesses of Tokujiro, Shinichi (who were closely aligned), and Shojiro Ishibashi grew further apart, so did their wealth and their families.

On Shojiro's side, another reason for the lack of internal competition within the Bridgestone family business empire was that Shojiro had only one son, hence there was no sibling rivalry. This son, Kanichiro, had only to contend with the husbands of his four sisters, and even when views differed, the in-laws did not have the pull of true siblings.

Much was the same within the Matsushita family, for they also suffered the wrath of the anti-*zaibatsu* law and probably also indirectly benefited from this enforced diversification at a propitious time. The split that then occurred between the Konosuke Matsushita and Toshio Iue families meant that each group was free to go its own way, thus preventing damaging rivalries that might have sprung up later when Matsushita grew so quickly. Iue and his brothers' leaving Matsushita to create Sanyo Electric was, in hindsight, probably the best thing that could have happened to either side. The break was clean.

Having said that, although there are no public records outlining the rivalry between Matsushita and Sanyo (and the families behind them), common sense dictates that competition must have existed. After all, the companies were competing for the same dealers, the same customers, and the same talented employees—which even includes the distribution of assets and wealth when Sanyo was created. But competition between business rivals is never as intense as it is between flesh and blood. Civil wars are always the most bitter and tragic wars, and it seems that Iue's departure may have averted civil war.

More family feuding was prevented because Konosuke had only one son and one daughter, with the boy dying at an early age. Since Konosuke also had no surviving siblings, this is another area in which interfamily squabbles were avoided. Although Konosuke suffered great misfortune because of the early deaths of many of his relatives, it might have helped his career by allowing him to focus on growing the business instead of on family politics. As you will remember, Konosuke did bring Masaharu, his adopted son through marriage, into the business. But in terms of natural ability and power within the organization, Masaharu was incapable of competing with his adopted father and, as a result, the two seemed to avoid serious conflict.

The two cases we have just reexamined show how relatively simple family structures can help prevent counterproductive family feuds. But, as we can all guess, this is not always the case. There are lots of founder families in which bitter infighting is or has been the order of the day. Some, indeed, may say that blood feuds in family enterprises are more the norm than the exception and may well represent the destinies of most family enterprises.

Let's now take a look at the cases of the Hattori Seiko and Matsuzakaya companies.

The Hattori Seiko Extended Family

The founder of the Hattori watch empire, Kintaro Hattori, began his career by opening up his own timepiece shop in 1881. Seizing every opportunity that came his way, this Japanese business visionary soon moved into wholesaling, direct and tradinghouse importing, and independent manufacturing. Hattori started making his own timepieces in 1892 by building a small, experimental production facility. The next year he geared up and built a true factory in Honjo Yanagishima and named the organization Seiko.[34]

The Hattori Tokei Ten (Timepiece Store) became a full-fledged ***kabushiki kaisha*** in 1917, with the founder, Kintaro Hattori, keeping 98 percent of the stock for himself. When Hattori died in 1934, the company was capitalized at 10 million yen in paid-up capital and was owned by the Hattori family. Kintaro had three boys (Genzo, Shoji, and Takesaburo) and, at the behest of their father, all were employed at the Hattori store. After Kintaro died, the eldest son, Genzo, inherited his father's assets and became the second president in the company's history. Genzo held this post until 1946, when he became chairman and was replaced by Shoji, Kintaro's second son.

Around this time, the Hattori family and the Hattori business became complex. There were discussions in the family about who had the right to run the business. During this period a number of family offshoot companies were formed, complicating the picture even further. In 1937 the Hattori family established another company call Dai Ni Seiko, or Number 2 Seiko. The purpose of this company was to build the organization's new head office and factory in the Kamedo area of Tokyo and to take over all of Seiko's watch production responsibilities. Also the company was by now working under wartime conditions and was obligated to produce munitions. The move to create a second company was to free this new enterprise for producing watches and clocks. The then-president, Genzo, is credited for what proved to be a wise business move, which freed the new organization from military responsibilities. It remains unclear, however, whether Genzo's intention at that time was to go into the mass production of watches.

In 1942, Dai Ni Seiko expanded again, establishing a new company called Yamato Industries in Suwa, Nagano Prefecture. The main objective in creating this company was to use shared facilities to escape air raid damage, but in 1944 Dai Ni established its own plant in Suwa and left the jointly run premises. In 1959 the Suwa factory and Yamato industries went independent, with the new enterprise being called Suwa Seiko.

In 1970, the Hattori Timepiece Store established the Seiko Company as a wholly owned but independently operated subsidiary and officially changed its name to Hattori Seiko in 1973. In the same year, they also changed the Dai Ni Seiko Company into Seiko Denshi Kogyo (Electronic Industries), and in 1985 the parent company merged Suwa Seiko with a company called Shinshu Seiki (established by Suwa Seiko in 1961), forming the Seiko Epson Company, of which you will read more later.[35]

The situation gets even more complex. First, there's Hattori Seiko. Under this company is the wholly owned subsidiary, Seiko. Then there's Seiko Electronics Industries (wholly owned by the Hattori family). And finally there's Seiko Epson, the company born from the Dai Ni Seiko. To try to clarify things, the Hattori Seiko Company and Seiko were both owned by the main branch of the Hattori family, with 9.4 percent of the Hattori Seiko stock owned by the head of the family, Reijiro Hattori, and his nephew, Junichi. These Hattoris also owned 23.6 percent through a series of holding companies called Sanko Kigyo, Kyobashi Kigyo, and Aoyama Kigyo. One unusual aspect of these holdings is that Seiko Electronics (formerly Dai Ni Seiko) was owned by a different branch of the family, although the main family also established this firm. When Dai Ni Seiko was established, one of founder Kintaro's sons, Shoji, became the head of the new company and received a large portion of the company's stock.[36] It also appears that Shoji received more stock in Suwa Seiko (antecedent of Seiko Epson) when that company was established.

Reijiro, son of Genzo, and the successor to the main branch of the Hattori family, became chairman of Seiko Electronics and Seiko Epson but, interestingly, had no stock and therefore no voting rights in these two companies. Until he died suddenly in 1978, Ichiro (son of Shoji) was president of the same two firms. His death was followed shortly by that of Kentaro (a former professor at Keio University), eldest son of Genzo. These deaths added to the complexity of the Seiko family's tangled blood and business relationships.

Within the Seiko group, Shoji is often credited as the most able businessman of founder Kintaro's three sons. The most famous example of his business acumen is when Shoji geared up his company to produce electronic timers and sign boards for the 1964 Tokyo Olympics, gaining the contract, accolades, and new recognition as an international businessman. For his Olympic bid, Shoji succeeded in getting his project teams to come up with a number of key innovations: the production of quartz watches, new integrated circuit technology, and advanced liquid crystal displays. These innovations rocked the industry, putting Seiko at the front of the class and Shoji's name in the pantheon of revolutionary Japanese business leaders. Shoji was also, it appeared, a skilled backroom player, as evidenced by the speed with which he acquired stock when Dai Ni Seiko and Suwa Seiko went independent. It is also possible, however, that Shoji acquired the stock because he and Genzo had irreconcilable differences and decided to go their own ways.

The case of the Hattori family enterprise is unusual in the context of family enterprise for two reasons. First, the second son was better at business than the eldest. Second, the branch family outgrew the main family and acquired significant ownership in the main family's subsidiary companies instead of the other way round, which is far more common. In order to understand the degree of conflict within the Hattori family and the Seiko group, all one has to do is look at the policy and products coming from each of the group's three production centers. There was no common strategy within the group and each acted independently in a way that can only be described as monumentally inefficient and a gross waste of resources. Even though outside competition was fierce and market share invaluable, each group separately produced the same types of main and peripheral components for the computer and other industries: timing mechanisms, electronics, liquid crystal displays, integrated circuits, personal computers, printers, and more. That these organizations were actually all part of one family enterprise is nothing short of incredible.[37]

Despite the varied manufacturing programs, the heart of the Seiko business empire had always been timepieces, but the lack of family synergy even interfered in this key area. Many insiders in the Seiko empire blame the lack of coordination among member companies of the Seiko group for allowing companies like Casio and Citizen, as well as Swiss timepiece manufacturers, to eat away at their markets.

The question naturally arises as to what the major protagonists were doing at this time. Yasuo (younger brother of the late Ichiro) became vice chairman of Epson, which was not unexpected. More interestingly, Junichi (son of Kentaro and grandson of Genzo), who had worked in Seiko Electronics for many years, suddenly was promoted to senior director in June 1994, skipping a customary stint as executive director. Some believe this management jump was an attempt to reconcile the main and branch Hattori families and to return some rationality to the group's wasteful, uncooperative practices. It had long been the wish of Ichiro and many of the salaried managers inside Seiko that the group's individual companies work more closely with one another. It seemed that Junichi had a shot at making this happen.

In June 1995, things began to move in the right direction. First, Hattori Seiko took over the unified development, manufacture, and selling of all timepieces. Directors from Seiko Electronics and Epson even moved over to Hattori to ensure that the new spirit of cooperation was implemented smoothly. Two of the key members of this team were Itoh, the president of Seiko Electronics, and Yasugawa, the Epson president. Both were salaried managers who were company veterans, and they are credited with convincing Reijiro, Hattori's chairman, to encourage group and family synergy in order to cut down on investment waste and to make the group more competitive.[38]

These top-management insiders decided that increasing market share in the key timepiece market was the only course of action for the Seiko group. Whether or not this has been achieved with computers and liquid crystal displays is still up in the air, but the new joint-business approach to clocks and watches seems bound to pay off. Although these reforms were backed by some parts of the Hattori family, many believe that credit for breaking the stranglehold on cooperation imposed by the family enterprise structure should go to the top salaried managers within the various group organizations.

The Case of Matsuzakaya

Although internal family strife can negatively influence company development, there are also cases where the effect is indiscernible in terms of company results. In this sort of situation, however, there is often a fundamental shift away from being a family enterprise to being a managerial enterprise. Such is the case with Matsuzakaya.

The origins of the Matsuzakaya business empire can be traced back as far as 1611, when founder Sukemichi Itoh ran a dry goods store in central Nagoya called Matsuzakaya. Matsuzakaya's 400 years of history make for an interesting case study. Included among Itoh's descendants were Sukemoto II and his successor, Jirozaemon, who ran a number of businesses centered around, among others, clothing and money changing. Although these businesses were largely small scale, they expanded to a number of regional locations and built their *zaibatsu*-style organization in this way.[39]

These two main business lines were embodied by the Matsuzakaya Department Store (which got its official name in 1925), representing the family's clothing and dry goods interests, and the Itoh Bank, which had grown from the money-changing and money-lending businesses. In June 1941, because of wartime circumstances and stipulations, the Itoh Bank was merged with the Aichi Bank and the Nagoya Bank and was reborn as the still-extant Tokai Bank. In one respect, this timing was fortuitous because it saved the bank from the Allied occupation's policy of dismantling *zaibatsu*. Therefore, the only remaining company that can be traced back to Jirozaemon Itoh is the Matsuzakaya Department Store.

Let us now move to a description of some of the personalities and positions of recent key players in the Matsuzakaya clan. In 1933, Jirozaemon XVI Sukeshige became president of Matsuzakaya, leaving two younger brothers to, as it were, mind the shop. The two brothers were named Senjiro and Suzusaburo. Suzusaburo was of a very aggressive nature but was also a student of economics, having graduated in this subject from both Keio University and England's London University. These two factors led Suzusaburo to have very definite opinions about the running of Matsuzakaya from a relatively early age. In 1957, Suzusaburo was appointed vice president and when his older brother, Jirozaemon, was to retire in 1967, Suzusaburo grabbed the post, pleading that Jirozaemon's oldest son, Yotaro, was still too young for such an important job.

Despite Suzusaburo's aggressiveness, Jirozaemon XVI was no pushover and he continued to retain the position of CEO along with his chairmanship. Jirozaemon was supported in this arrangement by his vice president, Sasabe, and senior director, Watanabe, who had held their posts since 1948 and 1954, respectively. After graduating in law from Tokyo University, Sasabe had been employed by the Bank of Japan, Itoh Bank, and Tokai Bank (as a director) before entering Matsuzakaya. Watanabe, on the other hand, had been at Sumitomo Bank prior to joining Matsuzakaya. Moreover, both were relations of the Itoh family. However opposed these three were to Suzusaburo's power plays, they were neither able to stop Suzusaburo from becoming president nor able to get him to step down once he got there.

One of the tasks Suzusaburo undertook was to move the company's planning department and head office from Nagoya to Tokyo. Jirozaemon was opposed to the Tokyo move and the splitting up of the business, complaining that the heritage of the company was at stake. A battle ensued between the two brothers. The shift to Tokyo succeeded in creating Nagoya and Tokyo factions within the organization, and the company's management was sharply criticized by both the company's union and the Nagoya region's business community. Sasabe and Watanabe tried to unsuccessfully diffuse the situation and were forced to resign as a result. The conflict then only grew worse.

It was at this juncture that another family member joined the fray. Kunio Miki was the brother-in-law of both Suzusaburo and Jirozaemon and had held the position of executive director at the Bank of Tokyo before entering Matsuzakaya as a vice president in 1971. Miki also tried to quell the feuding but he failed, too. He was essentially put out to pasture as a mere advisor in 1976. In 1980, a coup d'état rocked the company. Before the coup, the top management at Matsuzakaya had been Jirozaemon as chairman and Suzusaburo as president with three vice presidents (Yotaro, Masao Suzuki, and Kazuo Kano). Suzuki was considered to be a particularly able man, well liked by the employees, who had worked his way up through the ranks since joining Matsuzakaya in 1936 after graduating from Okazaki Business Hi-School.

It was Suzuki, at the bidding of Jirozaemon, who was finally able to cut Suzusaburo's legs from under him as Suzusaburo was shifted from president to director/advisor. The new president was Yotaro, with Suzuki remaining as vice president. In 1985, Suzuki became chairman of Matsuzakaya, and with the death of Jirozaemon XVI (who had passed away at the end of 1984) Suzuki became watchdog, looking out for the new, young president, Yotaro (Jirozaemon's son) who became the Jirozaemon XVII. The watchdog moved quickly and, in the same year, Suzuki arranged for the latest Jirozaemon to be bumped up to chairman, a step which had the approval of the company's union, the company's banks, and the local business community. Jirozaemon XVII went looking for support to the chairman of the Tokai Bank, complaining that he'd only been brought in as a figurehead. Miyake, the Tokai Bank chairman, was unsympathetic, however, and told Jirozaemon that the move away from being a family enterprise was inevitable.

In 1991, Suzuki became chairman for the second time and the latest president, Yoshiyuki Saito, was a salaried manager who had worked his way up as a junior to Suzuki. When Jirozaemon was once again bumped upstairs, this time to the nonvoting role of chairman emeritus, the transformation to a managerial enterprise was now effectively complete. In 1993 the Matsuzakaya top-management lineup consisted of Suzuki as advisor, Saito as chairman, and Akira Itoh as president. Despite his name, Itoh was not from the Itoh clan but was a salaried manager promoted from within.

To summarize, the Matsuzakaya case was one where the Itoh family civil war resulted in their being ousted from the company's top management by salaried managers. The final cost of this war was that the family lost their company, which became a managerial enterprise. The cost of this family feud was priceless and irretrievable.[40]

Company Founders and Impediments to Growth

The Unusual Exception of Y.K.K.

The phrase "impediments to growth" used in this section heading refers to the impediments of growth within family enterprises. It might, therefore, seem that the idea of a company founder inhibiting growth in a family enterprise is a contradiction in terms because a company does not change from founder enterprise to family enterprise until the founder either fully retires or dies. Contrary as it may seem, however, cases like this do actually happen—as we shall see.

The company Y.K.K. is one such case.[41] Returning to table 4.1, we can see that Y.K.K. is not included as one of the eight family enterprises that remained unlisted on Japan's stock markets. The reason Y.K.K. was not included is that, as of 1978, the founder of Y.K.K., Tadao Yoshida, was still running the show and, as such, the company should be considered a founder enterprise and not a family one. In 1986, however, Yoshida was felled by a cerebral thrombosis and underwent treatment until he finally passed away in July 1993. During this treatment period Yoshida used to receive company updates twice a week but was unable, as might be expected, to take part in any top-level management meetings or make any related decisions. Chairing the meetings in Yoshida's place was Yoshida's eldest son, Tadahiro Yoshida, but since hope was being held out that the senior Yoshida would one day return to take over the helm, he did not resign his position as president.

Other representatives at Y.K.K.'s top-level management meetings during this time were the company chairman, Hisamatsu Yoshida (Tadao's older brother), Vice President Takahisa Yoshida (Hisamatsu's eldest son), Senior Director Masahiro Yoshida (Tadao's nephew), Hiroshi Yoshida (another of Hisamatsu's sons) as executive director, and Tadahiro Yoshida, mentioned above, as vice president. Besides these family members, there were a number of salaried managers present, and all key decisions concerning the running of the company were made by this group (founding family members and salaried managers). It was this inner circle, made up of close relatives and loyal salaried managers trained by the ailing Yoshida, who put forward and held the view that, until Yoshida's health issue was resolved, there would be no change in the president's office or the key principles by which the company was run. As we can see, although the company was no longer run by the founder, the senior Yoshida was still heading the company in name; more important, his continued shadow of a presence stopped the company from becoming a full-fledged family enterprise. Unlikely as it may be, here was a company that was essentially neither a founder enterprise nor a family enterprise.

With all due respect to the senior Yoshida, it is almost certain that the situation was not helping the company move forward and was probably detrimental to the firm's prospects. Two years before the Y.K.K. founder became ill, Y.K.K. was already heading for trouble, being passed in the marketplace for aluminum venetian blinds by arch-rival Toyosashi. Although the company was still performing reasonably well in its other business areas, such as zippers and fasteners, it was understood that reorganization was badly needed and the firm was gearing up to head off further troubles before they occurred.

Vice President Tadahiro was one of the leading proponents for the business restructuring, and he expended major efforts to get his fellow directors on board. Yet some of Tadahiro's proposals ran counter to the rather staid business policies established by founder Yoshida, and the younger Yoshida found himself up against a solid wall. The company's business issues were myriad and vexing. First, there was a financial crunch because of the company's unwillingness to go public. Second, the company's top management was becoming almost incestuous, with over half the board members coming from a single family. Third, the company was incredibly overdependent on creating everything in-house, from precision production machinery, to zippers, fasteners, to the production of raw materials for manufacturing aluminum blinds, to PCs—to whatever! The disadvantages were obvious: with so many production lines they could not mass-produce anything and take advantage of economies of scale; they were thus highly inefficient and cost-heavy. With this emphasis on production, marketing was also not what it could have been. Another problem was that, since the sales and marketing of building materials was left up to the regional branches, the head office was not getting enough information, resulting in shortages and other distribution problems. Moreover, the company considered itself too pure-blooded to even look at the issue of mergers and acquisitions. From this perspective, it's easy to see why Tadahiro felt that changes were in order.

Even though Tadahiro failed to realize his ultimate goal of a major corporate overhaul, he did achieve some minor successes. But minor triumphs were not enough to turn the company around and the inherent internal problems began to show up in the company's results. In the 14 years from 1980 to 1994, sales increased only a meager 7.5 percent (to 213 billion yen). The profitability picture looked even worse. During the same period, profits dropped almost 19 percent to 8.17 billion yen.

As we have learned, however, Y.K.K.'s founder Tadao Yoshida finally succumbed to his illness in 1993. Tadahiro then stepped into the president's job. Starting with the retirement of Chairman Hisamatsu, other top-management members from the Yoshida family were slowly being phased out and, at last count, the only relatives remaining were Tadahiro as president and Takahisa as vice president. The restructuring of the company had finally begun in earnest and full-scale changes started taking place. Although no one can predict Y.K.K.'s future prospects, for the time being the signs are positive.

The more successful a founder enterprise is, the greater the risk that the company will decline when the founder dies or leaves the business. Most founders are driven visionaries, and the ability to carry on the founder's policies and business style is often difficult. When a founder becomes ill but neither improves nor dies, the transition from founder enterprise to family enterprise is particularly difficult and can, as we've seen with Y.K.K., lead to top-management paralysis and a noticeable decline in company performance. This is the tragedy of a founder enterprise unable to become a family one.

A Paradigm Shift in a Founder Enterprise: Sony

My original plan was to include Sony in this section on "Company Founders and Impediments to Growth." Sony, however, is a difficult case because it is a business that does not fit neatly into either the founder enterprise or the family enterprise category. Sony was essentially established as a venture business created in cooperation with a number of technology experts, spearheaded by Akio Morita and Masaru Ibuka. The year 1979 brought great changes to Sony. At age 57, Ibuka shifted over to the largely ceremonial position of chairman emeritus and left Morita to run things his way, which he did with such a personal style that the company began to resemble a founder enterprise. Most recent figures indicate that the Morita family is a major shareholder in Sony with their company, called Reikei K.K., holding 4.1 percent interest and total family holdings representing about 10 percent of Sony's stock.

As for the makeup of Sony's top-management team, the real power still lay with Morita, who held the post of director/chairman. Morita's hand-picked choice as president was the former baritone singer Norio Ohga, and Morita's younger brother, Masaaki, is vice president. There are other family connections as well. Sony's president prior to Ohga was Kazuo Iwama, who was Morita's brother-in-law, and the president of Reikei K.K. is Kazuaki Morita, another of Morita's younger brothers. With this sort of lineup—and also taking into account the influence of Morita's extremely well-connected wife, Yoshiko—I had intended to write that Sony, as a founder enterprise, was headed for potential future problems.

But in November 1993 nature intervened, bringing huge changes at Sony. Akio Morita suffered a serious stroke, forcing him to resign as chairman a year later. In Morita's place Ohga became chairman, and other new appointments included Tsunao Hashimoto as vice chairman and Nobuyuki Idei (a regular director up this time) as president and CEO. Many had pegged Masaaki Morita to replace Ohga as president, but instead Masaaki took this opportunity to retire. Currently, the only Morita connection on the Sony board is Kazuaki Morita, who holds the position of auditor.

This flourish of boardroom changes, and the reasoning behind the changes, caused a rash of speculation—but unfortunately the true answers remain unknown. From the outside, however, the changes look like healthy ones. Sony avoided having a long-term disabled (or dictatorial) chairman running things his own way, and the appointment of a new president was not put off interminably as it was with Y.K.K., as we've seen. Sony's reputation remained solid and unscathed by what, from today's perspective, seems to have been only a temporary setback.[42]

The Process of Collapse in Family Enterprises

Initial Considerations

As explored in chapter 2, family enterprises have essentially intrinsic limits on their growth potential. First, family enterprises face the difficult task of finding management talent from within family ranks that even approaches that of the founder. What's more, founders are usually successful because they are driven people who have their finger on some aspect of society's pulse. Since they are usually raised in wealthy environments, the children of these founders have neither the need to be driven nor an understanding of how most people really live. Although this is not always the scenario, it is often the case. The fundamental limits on the growth of a family enterprise essentially stems from the factors mentioned above. But this view is only a general framework and it is probably necessary to provide a more detailed analysis. It should first be noted that the following discussion is limited only to family enterprises. More specifically, it should be mentioned that founder families that make the transition to family enterprises but soon recognize the lack of family management talent are a different subject because these companies soon become managerial enterprises.

The real defect in family enterprises occurs when founder families labor under the false impression that they are up to the task of running their own shows—when, in fact, they often are not. This is the beginning of the end and the start of a collapse. Below is a list of theories as to why and how some family enterprises fail to succeed and bring about their own collapse:

1. The family ignores plans and recommendations put forth by their salaried managers.
2. Arbitrary decisions and other factors lead to conflict with the family's salaried managers.
3. The family treats the company as their personal possession and mix private and professional matters instead of recognizing their societal obligations and intrinsic partnership with other investors and employees.

Let's now take a look at how some of the above theories have been realized in real-life situations.

The Case of Tobishima Construction

The Tobishima Construction Company was founded in 1920 as the Tobishima Group. Succeeding as heir to the company was Hitoshi Tobishima, who took over in 1947. Although Tobishima is not strictly the founder of the firm, he essentially rebuilt the company after the war and is generally credited with growing the company far beyond its modest origins. In 1985, it was finally time for Hitoshi to move aside. On becoming chairman, Hitoshi set up his son Akira as the new president. Although Akira had worked in the Mitsubishi Trading Company for three years and was a 12-year veteran of Tobishima Construction, he was still only 37 when he assumed the president's spot. The appointment of this young and relatively inexperienced president was the start of the Tobishima Company's troubles; the blame must rest squarely, however, on the shoulders of the man who made this appointment happen: father and chairman, Hitoshi.[43]

Akira was intent on changing the company's image from its previous incarnation, one in which the company was so focused on public works that the company was known as "Tobishima, the Public Works Company." Akira believed that public construction projects invariably have limited funds and thus little growth potential.

He therefore wanted to shift his targets and aim for the private sector. Akira also felt that the company's sales tactics were old-fashioned and not strategic enough, so he made plans to make the firm's marketing more aggressive and proactive.

It was at this point that the company began to run into trouble. Whether it was because Tobishima went into debt to fund these new plans or because of questionable real estate entanglements remains unclear, but the results were the same. And the results were not good. Tobishima's misfortunes became colossal when it agreed to guarantee a loan of 120 billion yen to the company's former finance director, who had formed a real estate venture called Nanatomi. Nanatomi then proceeded to go bankrupt and Tobishima was dragged into a related scandal, which sent the company spiraling downward at a dizzying rate. At the root of this trouble was President Akira's inexperience. He had guaranteed the loan to Nanatomi in return for future orders, which, of course, never materialized. His naïveté cost the company dearly.

We have just seen a perfect example of one of the key dangers of family-run companies: inexperienced family managers ignoring the advice of their salaried managers and creating new and untenable business policies. The other side of this double-edged sword is, of course, that if they take the advice of salaried managers they are in danger of losing the family-run company to the salaried managers. The Tobishima decision to guarantee the huge Nanatomi loan was taken at a Tobishima top-management meeting attended by Akira and four salaried managers. But because Akira's name was on the company letterhead, his view carried the day and the hired hands could do nothing more than carry out their boss's orders. Moreover, since Chairman Hitoshi had given full responsibility to son Akira, the salaried managers were essentially helpless in the face of Akira's solo run.

In 1991, Akira took his lumps and resigned as president, embarrassingly replaced by his father who, under the direction of the Fuji Bank, set about trying to nurse the business back to health. Tobishima then used up its total reserves for bad debts and took an extraordinary one-time loss in their March 1992 accounts to the tune of 44.3 billion yen, allowing them to temporarily escape financial ruin. Despite these measures, the company was left holding its real estate loan guarantee valued at 663.9 billion yen. To service this debt the firm had to take out additional loans of 218.5 billion yen (as an aside, as of March 1995, the company was capitalized at 30 billion yen).

It is said that misfortune comes in bunches, and this adage proved true for Tobishima Construction. In 1994, the firm was implicated in a payoff scandal with the Ibaraki Prefectural government and the Tobishima president, Hitoshi, was forced to resign. Worse, the company was then banned from bidding on public works contracts and was also hit by a downturn in the construction industry, crippling sales results even further. As of this writing, prospects for the company look grim, with not even a hint of light showing at the end of its long, dark tunnel.

The Problems Inherent with Successors to Top-Management Positions

The first, but by no means only, problem inherent with family successors to top-management positions is that these successors are not founders. In other words, they have not had to work for their supper but instead have been given it on a plate complete with silver spoon. The problems with being raised in luxury are manifest in any number of ways.

The case of the Yonezawa Company (formerly Yonezawa Toys) points out the problems with successors in sharp but grim detail. After the predecessor of Yonezawa retired, he was replaced as president by his 38-year-old son, Shigeru Yonezawa. In a relatively short time, the young Yonezawa managed to incur debts amounting to 8 billion yen. As a result, in July 1994 the company was forced to transfer its undertakings to game powerhouse Sega Enterprises. (To be more specific, it was actually a subsidiary of Yonezawa's called Espar that took over the undertakings with Sega buying control in Espar. Yonezawa functioned as a type of holding company.)

At the time of the Sega takeover, Shigeru Yonezawa was still only 48 years old. He had proved that he was unable to manage the company his father had founded, and his 10-year reign seems to have left a sorry legacy. As to why the debt was incurred, magazine reporters or journalists tell the story, although they are probably best taken with a grain of salt since the comments mainly originate with Shigeru Yonezawa himself.[44] According to these documents, the main failures can be attributed to the company's missing the boat on the TV-game boom and the residual opportunities for marketing game-character merchandise. Taking these statements at face value, however, leads me to think that Yonezawa's true failure was his inability to get the company and its employees behind his vision for the firm. In a market glutted with TV games, surely there must have been opportunities for other, original products. His decision not to get into the huge TV-game market was not wrong; where he failed was in the implementation of his policy.

Research indicates that one of Yonezawa's key problems was that he did not have the support of his employees. One of his plans was to promote party-related merchandise for university students, but apparently only 5 or 6 of some 120 employees thought the idea was a good one. The result was nonparticipation, a general lack of cooperation, and—apparently—even acts of harassment by the staff. To say that Shigeru, the successor president, was disliked seems, in the face of such evidence, to be an understatement of the first order.

Yet even such insubordination seems hardly enough reason for a company with 61 years of experience and subsidiary income from real estate interests to fall so badly into debt. Reports also indicate that the Yonezawa books, unbeknownst to young Shigeru, were often just window-dressing and that losses of 300–400 million yen were actually disguising debts that amounted to 8 billion yen, mainly incurred through margin losses in the stock market. This gross mismanagement is probably the true reason for the company's major setbacks.

Shigeru Yonezawa was the third president in the company's history. After the founder died in 1972, the president's post was held by the founder's brother-in-law, who remained in that position for 11 years, until Akira took over. Akira's early initiatives, according to him, did not go as planned. He wanted to change the firm's lawyers, tax consultants, and notaries to people he trusted, but his plans were turned down flat by the board of directors, which included his uncle (the former president) as chairman.

Although Shigeru granted that his uncle was more of a visionary than he was, he complained that, as past president and company chairman, his uncle had an obligation to support the son of the founder, an obligation in which he showed not the slightest interest. There was no evidence to implicate Shigeru's uncle in the accounting scandal that so adversely affected the company, and the uncle was not found culpable. That the former president and chairman of the company could remain untainted while malfeasance of the scale described took place, however, is unbelievable.

As president, Shigeru devoted most of his energies to product development and sales-related activities, and he sometimes spent as much as half the year overseas. One can only conclude that Shigeru trusted his uncle, the company chairman, to mind the shop while he was away. If that indeed was the case, his trust seems to have been seriously misplaced. Whether it was because of his privileged upbringing or some other reason, Shigeru's naïveté seems boundless and one does not know whether to criticize or pity him.

Ultimately, it seems, it was Shigeru's trust in others that did him in. Raised as he was, he had no street smarts or businessman's guile, and he seemed to see everything through rose-colored glasses. Otherwise, he would not have relinquished the president's power of attorney so readily. After the scandal broke, a bank official reportedly said the following to the shamed Shigeru: "What you failed to do was to keep the president's seal firmly in your hand every day. And for everything and everyone that you doubted, you should have refused your approval until all your doubts were removed." The same banker also reportedly said, "Even if you'd done nothing more than hold on to that seal all day every day and gone drinking every night in Ginza, you would have been a lot better off." Shigeru's reported reply? "You're absolutely right." One can only conclude that by this time, Shigeru was beyond tears.

The Yonezawa case is a sad one but by no means unusual. Family enterprises have always faced this kind of problem, and probably always will.

The Case of Saison

Seibu Department Stores and the Seiyu chain of retail outlets are the core businesses of the Saison Group. The group's companies were under severe financial pressures owing to a business downturn, particularly since the group's purchase of Intercontinental Hotels. Although pressure being applied to the group by the banks for loan repayments was enormous, Saison was still not ready to collapse. Therefore, although including Saison in this section might be stretching the definition of *collapse*, the subject of Saison has enough in common with other family enterprises that have collapsed for me to insert it here.

Seibu Department Stores and the Saison Group are business branches that sprang from the Seibu Railways Group founded by Yasujiro Tsutsumi. Yet despite its origins, the Saison Group and its component companies received little assistance from the parent corporation. As such, most, if not all, of these companies could be thought of as having been started from scratch under the guidance of Seiji Tsutumi, Yasujiro's son. Therefore, many business observers believe that Seiji Tsutsumi, as the builder of the Saison Group and

Seibu Department Stores, should be considered a founder in his own right and not part of a family enterprise started by his father.

I concur with the theory that the younger Tsutsumi is more a founder than a member of a founder family. That Tsutsumi took a run-down wooden retail outlet in Ikebukuro and turned it into the Saison empire is a measure of his considerable business talents—talents that deserved to be acknowledged. Be that as it may, to say that Seiji Tsutsumi received no help from his father or brother, Yoshiaki (who succeeded his father in heading up Seibu's railway interests), would be inaccurate. When father Yasujiro died, Seiji naturally received his share of the inheritance and the banks must also have kept in mind that, with Yoshiaki as the head of Seibu Railways, Seiji was a good credit risk for the loans granted to the Saison Group.

After Yasujiro's death, the family was in the unusual situation of having two family enterprise groups within it. The two brothers stubbornly kept their own operations independent and there were reports of conflicts between the siblings. Therefore, it is probably safe to say that the businesses grew with little cooperation between them.

As time went on, it was Seiji's side of the business that faced a major business crisis. Whether the group is on the verge of collapse or not is far from certain, but it's probable that the Saison Group and Seiji himself face one of their most testing crises ever. A feature of this crisis is that its origins seem not to spring from anything that Seiji could not control, but instead from the depths of his personality, one formed by being a member of the founder's family.

Much has been written about Seiji Tsutsumi. A penetrating book called *Tsutsumi Seiji to Saison Group (Seiji Tsutsumi and the Saison Group)*, written by Yasunori Tateishi and published by Kodansha, provides ample background on Tsutsumi and puts forward some interesting theories.[45] Another book, called *Saison no Rekishi—Henkaku no Dynamism (The History of Saison: The Dynamism of Change)* by Tsunehiko Yui, deals with similar themes but does not really go beyond accounts taken from Saison company records.[46] Tateishi's writings are particularly illuminating, especially where he writes about the collapse of family enterprises and how these collapses can be related to the unique lifestyle of families with remarkably able founders. Below is a list of my own interpretations of Tateishi's description concerning Seiji Tsutsumi's actions and motives. To place a time frame on things, let us go back to 1982, which was the first time that Seibu Department Store's Ikebukuro branch achieved its distinction of top sales outlet (for a single store) in Japan. Around this time, certain elements of Seiji Tsutsumi's behavior started to become somewhat mysterious—and became even more so as time went on.

1. There was a sudden rash of new store openings.
2. There was an unexpected startup of other new businesses in the following fields: finance, insurance, restaurants, helicopters, theaters, resorts, hotels, home constructions, real estate.
3. The startup of such large and complicated businesses required an equally complex control system that, as the businesses got under way, was far from perfect. The result was a decrease in employee morale (reported incidents included department store clerks serving customers while wearing portable stereos) and a scandal involving fictitious medical equipment contracts.
4. Frequent, internal management conflicts involving Seiji Tsutsumi and a large number of managers (including Yoshiaki Sakakura, Toji Masuda, Kohei Ueno, and Shigeki Hiraoka).
5. An accumulation of debt with repayments of interest and capital leading to a significant downward trend in profits, as exemplified by the Intercontinental Hotels purchase. Of the purchase price of $2.15 billion, the Saison Group companies reportedly paid only $750 million down, with the rest financed through bank loans. Worse, since a large portion of the group companies' funds used for the down payment came in the form of bank loans, debt and interest payments became astronomical. When taking into account the money used to purchase Intercontinental, the Saison Group reportedly had outstanding loans put conservatively at a trillion yen, or $100 billion.
6. Tsutsumi's business concepts were becoming increasingly idiosyncratic. In his early days, Seiji Tsutsumi successfully described his business theories and goals as relating to "culture," "information," and "sensitivity," among others. However, the more complicated his business empire became, the more difficult it was to apply these concepts—or even to understand them. In the sections of Tateishi's book titled "Tsukashin," "The Tsukuba Store," and "The Yurakucho Store," Tateishi describes the problems encountered and goes into great detail about the miseries suffered by the Saison Theater's general manager, Go Okochi, mainly owing to the problem of Tsutumi's unclear business concepts. We could surmise that not only Tsutsumi's subordinates found it increasingly unable to follow his abstract concepts; it's also possible that Tsutumi himself was becoming lost in his spiraling abstractions.

7. As Tsutsumi's business became more multifaceted, with even more demands made on his time and attention, it was more difficult for him to concentrate and focus. There are reports of his telling the same person different things at different times, first emphasizing the cultural aspect of a project, the next minute stressing that profit was the key. Tsutsumi was living on the edge and, intellectually, he seemed near exhaustion. When looking at Tsutsumi's almost unbelievable range of activities, however, it's easy to understand why he seemed tired. Besides running his business empire, Tsutsumi was also leading a literary life under the pen name Takashi Tsujii; he was a media commentator on politics, economics, and business, and he had an incredibly active social life with friends from all walks of life. Tsutsumi was, in short, trying to be a superman, but one whose human frailties were at last catching up with him. Yet no one asked him to be superhuman. It was a role he chose freely for himself.

The key to understanding Seiji Tsutsumi and the events described here is to know that he was both the successor to a rich, company founder and a company founder in his own right. Although Seiji was not the main heir in name to Yasujiro's inheritance because he was illegitimate, the fact is he was given control over one area of the family's business. Seiji was born into an unhappy family situation. His youth was, it seems, neither joyous nor particularly nurturing. Although probably suffering from emotional poverty, he was born into considerable material wealth, which carries its own high social position. In these two areas he could be described as having been spoiled. He was also a gifted student who did well at school. Even from a young age, his literary talents were considerable and well recognized. It is from such circumstances that inner confidence is born. During his student days, Tsutsumi flirted with Marxism and was even involved with the international arm of the Japan Communist Party and a related lynching scandal. But none of these experiences seemed to have had a profound effect on Tsutumi or set him back at all. On the contrary, his confidence seemed to grow as a result. He thought he could do anything and everything. Moreover, he thought he could do it all himself. He would prove to his father and his brother that he could do something different, on his own, and make it work—and work very well.

The sudden rash of new store openings, the sudden rush of other new business startups, the lack of concern for control and monitoring systems, the numerous personnel conflicts, the loan-based nature of his businesses, the stubbornness and increasing abstraction revolving around his business concepts, the finger-in-every-pie approach to elite life—all of these elements have their roots in Tsutsumi's upbringing and are traps easily fallen into by those rich sons who inherit successful family legacies. It is this all-embracing self-confidence and large-scale dreaming on the part of Seiji Tsutsumi that eventually led the Seibu Department Stores/Saison Group into crisis. It is with great interest that we watch how Tsutsumi might extract himself from these severe problems. Will he surrender himself and his company to the Seibu Railways group? Will the Saison Group be able to right himself on its own? As one can imagine, there is intense speculation concerning Tsutumi's possible courses of action.

The September 1, 1995, edition of the *Nihon Keizai Shinbum* newspaper describes one such strategy. According to this article, the Saison Group's developer, Seiyo Kankyo Kaihatsu (Seiyo Environmental Development), had been restructured through the transfer of Saison's subsidiary companies' stock and real estate deeds to Seiyu's eight main banks. The banks, in turn, agreed to reschedule repayments and to help lower the interest burden. Although this plan looked like it might work, Tsutsumi's role after all the dust has settled is unclear. Regardless of the result, the story of Seibu, Saison, and Seiji Tsutsumi is a tale unique to founder families, one that would seem unimaginable in other contexts.

A Final Word

The purpose of this chapter has been to show different types of family enterprises that have arisen in past and present Japan. More specifically, only large, leading family enterprises have been examined. Although my goal is to tell both positive and negative stories, the darker tales seem to have arisen more frequently, probably since the objective nature of case studies tends to reveal such things. My research has also shown how bottlenecks affect the development of family enterprises and has pinpointed the frequent problems associated with succession in founder enterprises.

Despite the evidence we have looked at, one cannot conclude that all the families of large, leading enterprises face the same problems. We have seen examples of solid and impressive growth from such firms and we should be careful not to overgeneralize. To aid our understanding, it might be useful to categorize successful, large, leading family enterprises into four categories:

1. Families that succeed by transferring major business responsibilities and power to salaried managers (or cooperate with the salaried managers) as a matter of business strategy. Examples: Ito Yokado (Seven Eleven Japan) and Ajinomoto.
2. Families that produce a large number of successful managers or technical people from within the family ranks and that foster a spirit of cooperation, not competition, within the family. Examples: Toyota and Casio.
3. Families where a second-generation leader is able to successfully take over from a charismatic founder and keep the company operating effectively by maintaining high morale. Example: Taisho Pharmaceuticals.
4. Families that come up with innovative products or that assess market opportunities effectively and capitalize on market booms and grow as a result. It should be noted, however, that these characteristics are not exclusively related to family enterprises. This kind of success is also found in managerial enterprises and other types of businesses. Examples: Nintendo, Nisshin Foods.

Despite taking the above factors into consideration, my persisting view is that future prospects for family enterprises are not optimistic. The first reason for my rather pessimistic outlook is that successful family enterprises, as in the examples above, are the exception rather than the rule. Also, even successful family enterprises find it difficult to have continued success over long periods of time owing to the problem of continually finding and training new and capable top managers from within the family. The same problem exists to an even greater degree with less successful family enterprises. These two issues should have been amply demonstrated in the examples shown earlier and strengthen the argument that family enterprises are intrinsically limited in their future prospects.

It would be difficult to overstress the importance of these two limiting factors on the future destinies of family enterprises. For family enterprises there is essentially no escaping these issues, just as there is no way around the other factors that cast a shadow over these companies.

Another limiting factor facing family enterprises is inheritance tax. When a company makes the transition from a founder enterprise to family enterprise, the founder family can be hit so hard by inheritance taxes that the family's wealth is greatly depleted or even totally lost. This tax can also cut into a family's ownership of their firm, particularly in terms of their stock holding. In order to avoid this devastating tax, founder families can often flirt with lawlessness, which can of course cause its own problems. Another problem with inheritance tax is that it strikes with each change to a new generation. Consequently, the founder family's stock holdings are almost always depleted with each inheritance levy, particularly when the company is unlisted on the stock exchange. Ironically, the longer a company is family owned, the less so it becomes. From a business standpoint, members of the founder family are also less likely to hold top-management positions, and this vicious cycle forebodes a bleak future except for the very lucky few who find some way to put off what seems inevitable.

Also of importance when analyzing the long-term problems facing family enterprises is changes in public perception and social mores about the companies and their ownership. Society now questions the legitimacy of hereditary rule and whether someone deserves to succeed to a position as a company's CEO strictly on the basis of family background. In the public mind, the role of company president is not just a symbolic one. That a position of real power should be awarded by succession on an exclusionary basis is increasingly frowned upon, a shift in thinking which, to my mind, is a healthy and natural one.

Once the egalitarian ideas discussed above infiltrate the body politic of a family enterprise, the raison d'être of the business may get called into question. This position is a difficult one for the founder family. This does not mean, of course, that founder families should or will radically turn their companies into public corporations at the behest of a critical labor union. Rather, the issue should probably be whether or not the family successor is able to work effectively within the framework of the company (both inside and outside the business), which is certainly a positive move toward meritocracy.

The issue of succession is, of course, a key one for a company's employees. Although they may not do anything overtly mutinous and pay lip service when presented with a new and uninspiring family president, it is almost a given—and probably normal—that employee morale will decline. And once morale is on a downward track, it is highly likely that company results will soon follow, which is another reason family enterprises are hostages of their own structure.

Proof that employee opposition to an incoming family-member president is not merely theory can be seen in the case of the Okuma Company. In 1988, Takeo Okuma (the third head of the main branch of the family) decided to resign as president after 10 successful years at the helm. Okuma planned to step aside for his son, Hajime, but encountered such opposition from the company's union (who accused Okuma of trying to run a private fiefdom) that the ensuing dispute not only forced him to give up his succession plans but even led to his resignation.[47]

Employee views have changed along with the rest of society. The idea of a family enterprise continuing unchanged generation after generation is, to today's worker, no longer a matter of course. Instead, each new successor must pass an unwritten test with the employees as adjudicators about whether or not he or she is capable of building on a company's existing skills network and successfully leading the company into the future. This kind of thinking on the part of the labor force is likely only to increase and is yet another reason the family enterprise is more at risk than ever before.

CHAPTER FIVE

The Conquest of the Managerial Enterprise

Theories of Corporate Governance

The Trend toward Increased Criticism of Managerial Enterprises

As the various tables in chapter 3 show, the development of managerial enterprises among large, leading enterprises in the post-Meiji era accelerated after World War II. Moreover, since 1970, the transformation has been such that the majority of large, leading enterprises are managerial enterprises and, in fact, this period could well be called the "era of managerial enterprises."

Having said that, however, managerial enterprises, which have been instrumental in growing the Japanese economy and making it truly international, are now finding themselves increasingly criticized. This change in perception can be attributed to the increasing importance of investors in the business process. These investors expect and demand impressive results from their investments and the top-management teams who oversee them, particularly when some of the top managers are investors themselves.

The first thing to consider in discussing the role of investors is that in the 1970s and 80s, there was a trend toward institutional investment in the United States, the unquestioned leader in managerial enterprises. Institutional investors were looking for high dividends, and the resulting pressure fell squarely on the shoulders of the salaried managers leading these managerial enterprises. When desired levels of returns were not reached, replacing directors became an accepted practice in the quest for ever-improving profits. These actions have led to a counterrevolution on the part of investors who have wrested back true control of the businesses from top management. Japan, too, has not been immune to this phenomenon and the relationship between owners and managers is undergoing a major reevaluation.

Although these issues are perhaps worthy of their own section in this book, their significance is underlined by recent Japan–U.S. talks on the trade imbalance between the two nations. At these talks, the relationship between investors and management was one of the key items on the table. More specifically, there were complaints on the U.S. side that large Japanese corporations were muddying the true picture of their ownership because of the numerous, almost incestuous, relationships among parent companies, subsidiaries, and associated firms. These accusations contended that institutional stockholders were essentially protecting other companies in the same group through unfair business practices and by cutting the legs out from under true managerial enterprises and the managers trying to run them. Boiling the issue down to its essence, the question then becomes "who are the true owners of joint-stock companies?"

Another factor in the changing face of managerial enterprises was the September 1985 agreement that led to the strengthening of the yen, which in turn generated large-scale speculation and gave birth to the bubble economy. In the 10-year span of the bubble economy and the post-bubble recession, many large, leading Japanese enterprises (led by the managerial enterprises) engaged in business practices that were in many ways scandalous. The intense speculation in land and the stock market led to frequent bankruptcies, and many companies relied on equity financing to service the growing bubble markets and build facilities through relatively low-cost financing schemes. These policies, based on greed, frequently ended in financial disaster, illegal activities, and an unprecedented level of scandal.

Although these activities were not limited to managerial enterprises, by virtue of their size and influence, these large, leading enterprises bore the brunt of criticism. More than ever, enterprise managers were held accountable for their actions. What kinds of checks and balances, it was asked, were being used to ensure that these salaried managers were acting ethically and prudently with the resources with which they were entrusted?

Yet another area in which large, leading enterprises were viewed as having failed was their inability to recover from the post-bubble long-term recession. Innovations that might have helped recovery were in short supply, and these businesses were held accountable as never before. Disappointment after disappointment led many to believe that large, leading enterprises were no longer capable of innovation. Instead, the public looked to small and medium-sized companies and to venture businesses for energy and creativity. Salaried managers, many now said, were only bureaucrats interested in protecting their own positions and fiefdoms, and true innovation had to come from entrepreneurs and companies controlled by capitalists. This type of thinking had become entrenched and represented the new paradigm.

I would now like to offer my own views concerning the trend toward increased criticism of managerial enterprises. In some areas, I believe the criticism is justified, but in others it may not be. Looking at the situation from the perspective of corporate governance should provide some interesting insights.

Does Stockholder Sovereignty Really Lead to Corporate Profit?

Regardless of who really controls a company's top management—be it salaried managers or someone else—it is essentially impossible for anyone to hold total sway over a firm's direction. The society in which a company operates effectively puts limits on how companies can be managed, with controls usually related to some legal principles. Below is a list of restrictions that affect how corporate bodies operate.

1. Regulations imposed by law through national or regional political processes.
2. Demands placed on directors' meetings by commercial law to approve of and consent to certain procedures.
3. As in (2), certain procedures that must be approved at general stockholder meetings.
4. Approval for personnel-related issues by labor unions.

Yet, whether these rules and regulations are carried out to the letter of the law or merely given lip service often depends on arbitrary interpretations of these restrictions by a company's top-management team. To my mind, the issue of how corporate governance is imposed is an urgent one that deserves much more intense public debate.

Any debate on such important issues concerning restrictions on the discretionary powers of a company's top management has to address the laws that grant these powers. Putting it another way, although there are laws and guidelines already in place, do they really do what they are supposed to do? And do these same laws and guidelines effectively limit the broad discretionary powers of a company's top executives? These are crucial questions. Also of importance is the longstanding idea that stockholder investments should be protected at all times and at all costs. Recently, the status quo has shifted so that many believe the true owners of joint-stock companies are its individual investors and that protecting their rights (financial or otherwise) is now the true job of management.

What this shift in thinking means is that the trend that created managerial enterprises is being reversed, and that investment and management responsibilities and rights are being reunified after a period during which they were essentially separated. There are any number of ways in which the sovereignty of stockholders is protected, and the following list outlines the most common methods:

1. Companies must disclose information and seek the opinions of their stockholders relating to the company's profit, whether this profit is withheld or dispersed, and company investments.
2. Stockholders have the means to launch takeover bids to oust managers who fail to meet their requirements and bring in replacements. Moreover, to ensure that this process cannot be derailed by the same corporate group stockholders, there should be a law prohibiting mutual joint-stock ownership by the same group companies.
3. If, in the exercise of their management responsibilities, a company's top management puts the company into a money-losing situation, stockholders have the right to not only demand their resignation but also to seek compensation for losses incurred. This right essentially validates the idea that, as far as managers are concerned, there is no line between personal and management liability.
4. By obligating companies to have outside directors (for the theoretical purpose of protecting stockholder rights), individuals who are nonemployees are given significant influence over a company's behavior and actions.
5. By separating German-style *Aufsichtsrat* from director meetings, stockholders are given an independent system whereby they can control their profits.[1]

What all these measures mean, of course, is a total rethinking of managerial enterprise management theory. Why have major-shareholder-run enterprises replaced managerial enterprises as the main form of capitalism? Also, why have managerial enterprises conquered major-shareholder-run ones? Investors who become stockholders of a *kabushiki kaisha*, or joint-stock company, don't usually have detailed information about the company or companies they have invested in. Nor do they necessarily have experience in the company in which they have invested. And nor are they usually interested in the long-term interests of the company. Company founders, of course, are a different story. Even though they are investors in their own right, they, along with any salaried managers they may bring into the firm, have the management skills and experience to help grow the company.

Professional investors have their own agendas—and they are usually short-term ones. Their concerns are for the security and growth of their investment, and thus they are interested in stock prices, dividends, profit allocation, hidden profits, and other short-term gains. In order to achieve their goals, investors will, of course, put pressure on a company's management. This pressure might take the form of delayed infrastructure investment, selling off of key but valuable assets, and disposal of any company nest eggs—or combinations of the above. In short, anything and everything may be sacrificed to the sacred cow of increased returns on investment. In contrast, however, company founders and their families do not go to such extremes because it is not in their self-interest to do so.

Yet, according to the theory behind stockholder sovereignty, it is only the shareholders who matter because it is they who are the true owners of a company. Any profits accrued are their profits alone, and the only purpose of management is to service stockholder needs and protect and grow their investments. But if this theory is to hold true as a guiding business principle, why is it that major-shareholder-run companies have never dominated the business scene in the way that managerial enterprises have? Although the advocates of the stockholder-primacy theory are increasingly vocal and visible, it is worth looking to past examples of how this concept affected company management and what negative factors came about as a result.

If the question of establishing verification systems is at issue, the first thing that should be done is to ask whether or not current regulatory controls are appropriate and practical. Do such controls, in fact, work? As another first step to go along with this soul searching, a wide range of regulatory options should be examined as to whether they will affect a business's ability to perform competitively. Yet having raised these questions, trying to discuss verification of regulatory systems within the context of stockholder sovereignty seems slightly ridiculous. The stockholder as the be-all and end-all of business is an idea tarnished by age and abuse of power and, in my view, is a throwback to the bad old days when checks and balances were unheard of.

The Problem with Salaried Managers

The recent trend toward stockholder sovereignty is in itself a form of corporate governance. Part of the blame for this trend (in Japan, anyway) can be attributed to Japan's rash and frivolous mass media, who have jumped on this bandwagon even though it bears little relation to the Japanese business scene. It is not the first time this has happened, and those smart enough to realize the role that the media play are surely saying, "not again." What we are seeing is nothing more than fashion, the latest flavor of the month.

Like many business fads that hit Japan, this one started in the United States. Regardless of the results of a stockholder sovereignty revolution in the States, there were fundamental reasons for its start in America. In the Japanese model, stockholders became annoyed because their opinions were ignored by management at stockholder meetings and they had their dividends diverted. The Japanese and American models differ in that American stockholders became more than annoyed; they were angry and out for blood.[2]

The problem of shareholder anger in the United States originated with America's CEOs. Regardless of their companies' performance, these executives were at the top of the world's compensation table. Even as their firms experienced restructuring and mass layouts, top management was feeding at the trough, sometimes even padding their earnings as their companies suffered. According to a 1990 survey, over 400 American CEOs at the time were earning at least $1 million per year. Even more astonishing was the fact that large numbers of chief executives had compensation packages topping $10 million per annum! Even though these huge figures included performance bonuses and stock options, the largest and most profitable Japanese companies were paying nothing like these figures to their equally able top-management players.

According to another survey done around the same time, the average American CEO's remuneration was 85 times that of the average blue-collar worker. In contrast, the Japanese figure was 10 times or less. Another measure of the CEO feeding frenzy was that, in the 10-year period from 1980 to 1990, the average American CEO's compensation package increased a whopping 212 percent in comparison to 53 percent for factory workers, 73 percent for engineers, and 95 percent for teachers. What's more, the lifestyle of the American CEO became visibly flamboyant—CEOs flying around the world in luxurious private jets became almost commonplace. These planes became increasingly common and highly prized status symbols for American CEOs, albeit ones unimaginable to Japanese heads of companies.

One example of American corporate excess occurred at Abbott Laboratories (a well-known pharmaceutical manufacturer), where the chairman's wife reportedly held huge, expensive parties at the company's expense, a fact which became known only after the chairman resigned. This unethical mix of business and personal affairs strikes the average Japanese person, I must add, as essentially incomprehensible. It would be hard to imagine such an issue ever reaching a stockholder meeting in Japan. Instead, it is more likely that when the problem would be addressed within the company before the stockholder meeting, the chief executive would be forced to resign.

As the above examples show, it is easy to conclude that a significant number of American top executives often use their considerable authority for personal gain. The public response to such corporate waste and extravagance has been, as might be expected, highly negative, with employee performance and morale plummeting. It's therefore no wonder that stockholders justifiably railed against such abuse of the system and became increasingly critical of how top executives handle themselves and their responsibilities. As much as we can understand the anger on the part of American shareholders to what amounts to a "CEO disease," however, the knee-jerk move toward stockholder sovereignty seems illogical and misguided. In having stockholders replace a CEO as a company's de facto leader, even worse abuses of the system are not only possible but even likely.

An article taken from the American magazine *Business Week* and published in Japanese in *Nikkei Business* reinforces this view with this telling statement: "The last defense for a company against CEO problems is its stockholders since shareholders not only have the right but the responsibility to choose company directors who are talented and responsible. The problem is, of course, that most stockholders couldn't care less—what they are really after are excellent, short-term returns on their investment." The preponderance of CEO disease in Japan is, in my opinion, far less than in America. Yet, due largely in part to irresponsible media, Japan is now mindlessly mirroring the American move toward a stockholder-led business climate, even when the need is fundamentally nonexistent. If the situation weren't so serious it would almost be laughable.

Let's now look at an example. In 1980, a company called National Intergroup (NII) appointed an executive named Howard Labb as its CEO. Citing a depressed economy, Labb made plans for a major reorganization of the company's steel division that would become the blueprint for corporate diversification. Based on these plans, the company then moved into wholesale pharmaceutical distribution, oil, retailing, savings and loans, and a number of other new fields. After 10 years of this diversified business, the company had lost $700 million.[3]

These sorts of business decisions, unfortunately, seem all too common to overseas observers of the U.S. business scene. Japanese commercial law prohibits executives acting alone by making a company's board of directors equally responsible for (1) the transfer and acquisition of major company assets; (2) applications for major loans; (3) the hiring and firing of key staff and executives; and (4) the establishment, reorganization, and closing of company departments and facilities. Although there are other important decisions that must be taken by the board as an entity, suffice it to say that the board is the organization that directs the company, not one individual. If Article 260 of Japan's commercial law is strictly followed, such unilateral decisions by a CEO like the one in the NII case are not possible, since all major policy decisions must be approved at directors' meetings. Even though a board decision may prove wrong, the system prevents an outbreak of the CEO disease that has plagued American business in recent years.

Newsweek magazine reports: "The most effective way of curing CEO excess is to hire outside directors who have both an understanding of a company's operations and financial position and the time in which to assist the company."[4] Although the theory discussed in *Newsweek* seems to make sense at first glance, in practice things are often different. Take, once again, the case of NII. One of the reasons given for the company's catastrophic losses of $700 million is that, despite the poor economic climate in which the company was operating, the CEO was so busy serving as an outside director for other companies and charities that he lost touch with his own business. Instead of solving the CEO disease, I believe that outside directors just make it worse. Interestingly, the United States is now moving toward the Japanese model as a new method of corporate governance. If Japan continues to mindlessly ape America's business practices, I see nothing but trouble ahead.

Employee Empowerment—Moving toward an Improved System of Checks and Balances

The idea that a company is the sovereign property of its shareholders by virtue of their investment alone is an oversimplified one. The natural sovereigns of a company are its employees. Nobody knows a company and its business better than its workers, and no one has the power to influence the growth and profitability of a company as much as its staff. For these reasons, I support and expand on the theory of employee empowerment and sovereignty put forward by Hiroyuki Itami.

Itami's view on employment empowerment is that, in the business world of today where investment money is not that difficult to come by, a company's employees have replaced money as a business's most important resource. When taking into account the difficulty and time involved in assembling and training a workforce, as well as its ability to influence a business's results and its future, Itami makes a strong case for employees being more important than shareholders. Employees, says Itami, need to rise to the top of the hierarchy of what is important to any business.[5]

Although I agree with Itami's assessment that employees are *the* key resource for company and that their empowerment represents the best model available, I believe with equal conviction that Japanese companies are nowhere close to achieving employee sovereignty. Even if only large, leading enterprises are considered, Japanese firms are a long way indeed from achieving employee empowerment in either of two key areas—assisting management in running the company and income distribution.

Although Japanese employees may have benefited from the rising salary-base at the peak of Japan's economic growth period, in the current climate of restructuring and downscaling the situation has moved further and further from the model espoused by Itami and others. In the area of employee participation in company management, the situation remains unchanged: the status quo has been maintained and employees are as far from the real management of their companies as they have ever been. Itami postulates that employee views reach top management through the promotion of workers as they become salaried managers. I remain, however, skeptical on this point and wonder about its validity.

One must grant, however, that salaried managers (who are usually experienced, senior employees who have managed the company's skill sets at various levels) who rise through the ranks to CEO *do* reflect employee viewpoints better than top-management people who come to the firm through other routes such as stockholder appointees, as members of the founder family, or from government agencies. But even having a salaried manager CEO who has worked his or her way up through the company does not mean that there is an employee representative sitting in the boardroom. By virtue of their position, those who become CEOs have a natural barrier between them and their employees. For a truer model of employee empowerment, it is probably best to look outside Japan to the German system of the labor/management consultation meeting, where employee participation in company management is far greater.

Although I have to disagree with Itami's views and interpretations on many fronts, I believe the model he offers is better than that represented by stockholder sovereignty. Any move toward employee empowerment is a good one, and although the ideal may be difficult to achieve, movement in that direction is extremely positive. It strikes me as strange that societies that espouse democracy can also espouse the rights of shareholders over the rights of employees. It is hard to see how companies controlled by a shareholder's right to seek maximum profit is democracy in action.

It should be stressed that, to date, no one in the Japanese business establishment is taking employee empowerment seriously enough to put concrete plans into action. Interestingly, the same could probably be said for shareholder sovereignty. Contrary to press coverage, the system remains largely a theory that is not being put into practice. I cannot feel, however, that this is a bad thing. Before putting into place a concept that doesn't allow for employee participation in management and profit-sharing, there needs to be a lot of hard thought and soul searching—something that has yet to be done.

Regarding an improved system of checks and balances, any move toward a democratically based system in which employees have more power and rights is bound to be an improvement on what currently exists. Such systems, as we have already pointed out, exist in a number of countries, and Japan can learn from these countries' experiences. To conclude, giving more power to stockholders or outside directors evades the deep issues and is a sure recipe for disaster.

The Worst Failings of Japanese Business

Listing the Failures

The Japanese business scene and the country's economy have long been dominated by large, leading enterprises, and we shall limit our analysis to these types of firms. Within this group, it is also generally acknowledged that managerial enterprises have provided the leadership and have been the engine that has driven the vast economic machine that is Japanese business. Yet for all their successes, it is the highly educated top management of these companies, along with the shihonka keieisha (owner manager), who have helped engineer some of the worst failures in the history of Japanese business.

The origins of these failures can be traced to the Plaza Accord of 1985. Owing to the combination of a strengthened yen, adjusted international balance of trade (related to Japanese superfluous international liquidity), unusually low interest rates, and the promotion of domestic consumption by the Japanese government, intense speculation in real estate and the stock market resulted. This speculation and the resulting crash, known worldwide as the bubble economy, can be seen as the basis for Japan's economic decline and can be described as the first Japanese economic failure.

The bubble was not only a failure in terms of speculation-associated problems. Most Japanese businesses, misreading the illusory quality of the boom, made huge investments in facilities, infrastructure, and sales capabilities. Without the bubble, these investments would never had been made, since most of them were equity financed. Companies were shamelessly attempting to take advantage of unrealistically low interest rates. The boom mentality led to excess production capabilities and was behind what is called the Heisei recession. This investment-led debacle was the second Japanese economic failure.

The third failure is related to land and stock speculation. Banks seemed to almost gleefully finance corporate bubble speculation, which led them on a downward spiral that resulted in the huge banking scandal that has become familiar to us all. The scale of the scandal was not the only surprise. As the matter unfolded, it became apparent that large Japanese companies were deeply involved with mobsters, to a degree that astonished and shocked the general public. As the media uncovered story after story of improper loans, corruption, and other illegal acts committed by the banking industry, the country reeled, aghast at the financial world that had come tumbling down so far and so quickly.

Let us now take a more in-depth look at the failures described above.

The Origins of the Bubble

The first cause of the bubble economy can be traced to a lack of usable land in Japan and the resultant large-scale increase in land speculation by real estate companies. Starting in the early 1980s, Japan experienced a brisk trade in the buying and selling of real estate and banks were heavily involved in financing this volatile land trading.

As a result, land prices soared and the latent value of land-based assets skyrocketed. Banks then found themselves with hypertrophied collateral in the form of real estate and the banks seemed blithely unaware of the hidden dangers of overvalued land collateral. In the nine years from March 1980 to March 1989, the value of bank loans backed by land collateral increased a whopping four times. From March 1986 to March 1989 alone, the value of these loans more than doubled.[6] Loans based on the real estate collateral were used for any number of speculative purposes: housing developments, the stock market, funds and trusts, golf club memberships, even purchases of works of art. There can be little doubt that most loans were for speculative purposes and therein lay the greatest danger.

The early returns on these speculative investments were spectacular. The real estate and stock markets were both booming. With the yen at sky-high levels, surplus liquidity was also being achieved, one of the goals of the 1985 economic accord. Although it is no surprise that land values soared owing to increasing demand, that the Japanese stock market (despite yielding low returns on investment) continued to boom was a surprise to domestic and international observers alike. This phenomenon seemed directly linked to the newly achieved surplus liquidity, a shaky basis at best on which to build financial stability.

With the rise in the stock market and the increase in the latent value of shares and paper profits came a splurge of equity financing. A large proportion of companies caught this fever and became finance-driven. Using whatever cash was available, companies began to invest in stocks, bonds, trust funds, and the like at an ever-increasing pace. Money management became the game everyone wanted to play. And the money management game in and of itself became a boom. One well-known commentator even appeared on TV and said, "companies that have the money to invest and don't are throwing away opportunities and are nothing short of stupid." Not everyone was tricked by this illusonary profiteering, however. Despite the urgings of their finance people, some company presidents decried the trend, saying that it was the wrong path for companies to take and that the boom wouldn't last. Unfortunately, however, such prudent views were all too few and were the exception rather than the rule.

Yet the myth of ever-escalating land values was destined, like all myths, to be revealed as unreal: there had to be a ceiling. There were limits to what people and companies would pay for land. For the stock market, too, what had gone up had to come down. With the fall in the market, paper profits began rapidly turning into real losses. By the autumn of 1990, the superheated economy had significantly cooled. The bubble had burst.

Why, one is forced to ask, did the salaried managers and top management of large corporations fail to foresee the end of the bubble economy? Why did they follow one another like lambs to the slaughterhouse? Although the intense speculation that had defined the bubble economy had been criticized with both government agencies and some financial institutions, the criticism seemed to be after the fact.

In the aftermath, the wretched state of the Japanese business world was fully revealed.[7] The fund-based losses incurred by Japan's trading giants were staggering: Marubeni, 80 billion yen; Itochu, 70 billion yen; Mitsubishi, 60 billion yen; Nissho Iwai, 50 billion; Sumitomo, 40 billion. Mitsui Bussan was the only major trading company to escape unscathed, the second time this century that the company had avoided major losses by refusing to follow the herd. It is believed by some that Mitsui's successful escape from the economic collapse after World War I had taught the company an important lesson. Some critics, however, take a more jaundiced view and say that Mitsui failed to invest in the bubble economy because they were short of cash after the IJPC scandal.

For the accounting period ending in March 1992, the assessed value of securities-based losses by banks and brokerage houses almost defies imagination. The combined losses of city banks, long-term credit associations, and trust companies reached 1.297 trillion yen. For brokerage houses, the figures were 213.2 billion yen, 130 billion of which was from the four biggest firms. For the banks, however, the aftershocks didn't stop there. Their outstanding loans were huge, with default after default staring them in the face.

Almost all of the major manufacturing companies had fallen victim to the speculation madness that gripped the country. The results reflected the degree to which they had been caught unprepared. Conspicuous in the scale of their losses were Yanmar, Sekisui Kagaku, Mitsubishi Kasei, Tobishima Kensetsu, and Daishowa Seishi. Although not a manufacturer, Hanwa Kogyo was also considered to be one of the biggest losers in the money-management debacle.

It is hard to underestimate the scale of economic failure that was the bubble economy and its subsequent collapse. It is therefore essential that the causes and results are well understood in the hopes that history will not repeat itself.

The Huge Overestimation of Domestic Demand

In the last section, I stated that the bubble economy was based on rising land values and rising stock prices. But there are other, secondary causes that also need examination. As the bubble was expanding, the Japanese economy was also being inflated through private investment.

The yen started to strengthen in 1984 and is credited with slowing down the economy for a short time. The Plaza Accord of 1985 then increased the speed at which the economy was declining, to the point where in 1986 actual growth was estimated to be a mere 2.5 percent—a far cry from the 5.1 percent of 1984. After hitting bottom, the economy recovered and registered growth of 5.7 percent, Japan's highest level since the oil crisis.[8] This period of economic growth was driven mainly by domestic demand in the form of private investment in facilities and equipment. Investment in private and corporate facilities was, in 1984, 16.7 percent (in actual terms), growing to 21 percent in 1988. In terms of overall economic growth, these investments represented 43.3 percent of the total expansion. Although private investment as a percentage of the total expansion was less than the private fixed capital—expenditure of 56.8 percent and the final consumer outlay of 48.2 percent—it was significantly higher than the 12.8 percent increases for exports and 8.9 percent for public spending.[9]

It is important to realize that this expansion of private investment was also linked to the bubble economy: money for the investments was coming from low-interest loans and from financial market gains. According to Juro Hashimoto, the ratio between the value of cash and short-term and regular negotiable securities held by companies in proportion to their monthly sales grew dramatically between 1985 and 1988. For all businesses, the average ratio was 1.41 in 1985, while three years later it was 2.25. More specifically, for the manufacturing industry during the same period, the ratio rose from 2.18 to 2.93.[10] Extrapolating from these figures, it is easy to see that equity financing is what led to such huge private investment in facilities and equipment.

The next question to ask is, were there reasons other than the availability of cheap financing that caused Japanese corporations to invest at this particular time in more facilities and equipment? To help us answer this question, there is some useful information in table 5.1, which shows private facilities and equipment investment from 1985 to 1992 and the amount of growth from year to year.

The first explanation as to why Japanese companies decided to undertake such investment is easily arrived at. Faced with a strong yen and rising labor costs, Japanese firms had no alternative except to improve the efficiency of their production capabilities in order to meet increasingly stiff international competition. Using microelectronics as the new building block, Japanese companies set out on a high-tech mission to do what they had always done best: build and sell a wide range of products in knowledge-intensive fields through just-in-time production, thus creating new niches and new areas for expansion. To accomplish this high-tech mission, investments in new facilities were clearly essential.

To deal with the strong yen, rising labor costs, and tougher international competition, companies found that new investment in industrial facilities had a cost beyond its equity-financed price tag. Firms should have been forced out of small-scale production, to close their less competitive plants, or take other severe mea-

Table 5.1. Changes in Actual Private Facilities Investment from 1985 to 1992 (totals for manufacturing and nonmanufacturing industries combined)

Year	Facilities Investment (in billions of yen)	Change from Previous Year (%)
1985	127,44	
1986	125,01	−1.9
1987	123,00	−1.6
1988	149,87	+17.9
1989	170,74	+12.2
1990	209,63	+18.5
1991	217,85	+3.7
1992	192,25	−13.3

Source: The Ministry of International Trade and Industry yearly publications: *Shuyo Sangyo no Setsubi Toshi Keikaku—Sono Genjo to Kadai (Plans for Major Industry Facility Investment: Conditions and Themes)*

sures. Although major restructuring seemed to be the order of the day, it was not undertaken. Why not? After industrial demand had bottomed out in the fall of 1986, there were signs of improvement that led corporate Japan to believe it could stimulate and increase demand without the painful process of major restructuring.

Another possibility is that companies, confident in their ability to create new demand, chose to increase market share and profits. Regardless of the true motivations, however, let there be no mistake that Japanese facilities investment in this period came about because of equity financing. Because of the scale of failure in misreading the ability to create new demand, it is impossible to list all the examples. Instead, let's just look at two of the most shocking failures as graphic representatives of those equity-financed times.

In the automobile industry, Toyota and Nissan built new extensions to their assembly plants in Fukuoka (with Nissan even building a second factory). Matsuda built a second assembly plant in Bofu, while Honda added a second assembly-line plant in Suzuka. Toyota also built parts plants in Tomakomai and Sendai, which along with their Fukuoka plants was part of their plan to move facilities away from where they had been concentrated in central Japan. The results were disastrous.

> Each of these companies had taken the bold step of using their abundant investment capital to build dream factories, ones in which working conditions and facilities were second to none. The majority of these factories, however, were not completed till 1992 or 1993, well after Japan's economic bubble had burst. As a result, even now these sparkling new factories are still not operating at full capacity because of falling demand. The real output of these factories, however, is neither automobiles nor parts but, sad as it is to say, huge depreciation costs and not much more.[11]

What is conspicuous about these new, excess factories is that, despite their existence, Japanese domestic automobile production dropped year-on-year from 1991 to 1995. The combination of declining exports owing to the strong yen and competition from foreign imports meant that domestic car production was on a long, downhill slide. The car industry, however, was not the only industry that had misread long-term demand. All the planning had been nothing more than a huge gamble, and bubble-era investments in facilities and equipment left all manner of corporations with nothing but a mountain of debt. Some observers say that if the same money had been spent on research in new intelligence-based fields, Japan would have been ahead by leaps and bounds of other countries at the start of the new millennium.

Our second example of an industry that got it wrong is the petrochemical industry. In 1967, the Japanese Ministry of International Trade and Industry (MITI) issued directives to the industry that a company had to produce a minimum of 300,000 tons of ethylene annually in order to get government authorization. The result was a disaster: the industry geared up for production levels that were, as it turned out, excessively over actual market demands. In order to maintain market share, keep up with the competition, and meet the MITI demands for the increased production of 300,000 tons, companies were forced to take out bank loans. Little did they know that MITI had gotten it totally wrong.[12]

The first step in expanding these ethylene production facilities was getting past a 1983 law that limited production to demand, something which had been achieved in 1987 when supply and demand were well matched. Post-1987, the door was opened for investment in new production capabilities and the ban on new facilities was lifted. The timing of these events coincided with the start of the bubble economy. These two factors combined to make the industry players giddy with euphoria and they went to town, blissfully unaware of the hangover that would greet them as they woke in the morning.

Table 5.2 outlines actual and predicted facility investments for the petrochemical industry, ethylene production capacities, and the degree to which their production facilities were operating. As the economy expanded, so did demand, so did production, and so did investment in production. By 1991, however, demand had dropped and the industry found itself once again with excess production capabilities.

Bubble-Related Scandals

So much has already been written about bubble-related scandals that there is really little researchers like myself can add. What's perhaps most surprising about these scandals is that the top management of Japan's leading companies—graduates of Japan's best universities—could get themselves so entangled with mobsters. This subject is one that needs greater investigation. In some respects, it's perhaps vaguely understandable that companies were attempting to increase market share and take advantage of unprecedented business opportunities through real estate speculation in a rising land market. It's also understandable that, to handle these land deals, they needed people considered to be experienced and knowledgeable in real estate matters—who, it turned out, just hap-

Table 5.2. Changes in the Petrochemical Industry from 1985 to 1993

Year	Actual or Estimated Investment in Production Facilities (in billions of yen)	Maximum Ethylene Production (in thousands of tons)	Percentage of Total Ethylene Production Facilities Used (%)
1985	177 (est.)	4,227	88
1986	152.1 (act.)	4,291	91
1987	194.5 (act.)	4,481	98
1988	259.3 (est.)	5,057	103
1989	350.1 (est.)	5,603	103
1990	406.5 (est.)	5,810	101
1991	514.9 (est.)	6,142	97
1992	372.7 (est.)	6,103	91
1993	233.8 (est.)	5,772	85

Source: The Ministry of International Trade and Industry yearly publications: *Shuyo Sangyo No Setsubi Toshi Keikatu—Soro Genjo to Kada* (Plans for Major Industry Facility Investment: Conditions and Themes)

pened to be gangsters. But is that all there was to it? Perhaps an answer can be found in the following example.

Itoman Trading, a company specializing in textiles trading, went to the Sumitomo Bank looking for management assistance in 1975. The Sumitomo executive in charge at that time, Ichiro Isoda (a vice president), responded by sending one of his most trusted staff, executive director Yoshihiko Kawamura, to Itoman with the plan to have Kawamura become the struggling company's president. This strategy met with success, and the Isoda-Kawamura team was able to rejuvenate Itoman's business. At the same time, Sumitomo set about merging a company called Sugiyama Trading (which was in debt to Sumitomo to the tune of 250 billion yen) into the Itoman Group with the aim of setting up Sugiyama (whose name changed to Itoman Total Housing) as the real estate arm of Itoman.

The new head of Itoman's real estate business was an individual named Suemitsu Itoh, whose background was in land deals that often required strong-arm tactics. In 1990, Itoh was appointed as an Itoman director, soon rising to become an executive director. By this time, Isoda had become Sumitomo Bank's chairman, and he reportedly considered Kawamura and Itoh to be two of his closet confidantes. Itoh, however, had a different agenda and used his trusted position for shameless personal gain. Along with his backroom manipulator, one Kyo Eichu, Itoh managed to arrange a huge "investment loan" from Itoman. Then, using this money, the duo purchased real estate and art works that they then resold to Itoman at highly inflated prices. In Itoman, Itoh and his accomplice had finally found the goose that laid the golden egg. Reports indicate that Itoh and his associates milked Itoman for somewhere around 100 billion yen—money that seemed to disappear into thin air. Sumitomo too was a loser. Itoman by then had outstanding debts to Sumitomo and other banks (which Sumitomo took over) amounting to a staggering 553 billion yen. As if this weren't enough, Isoda was forced to resign over another scandal, one involving his actions as an intermediary for one of his branch managers and a suspect loan of more than 20 billion yen. Itoh was also forced to resign and Kawamura was dismissed as Itoman's president. Later, both Itoh and Kawamura were arrested.

This scandal involving Itoman and the Sumitomo Bank is representative of others during the bubble economy. But it is by no means unique, which is the real tragedy of this black period in Japan's economic life. Most of my information about the Itoman scandal came from a book published by the *Nihon Keizai Newspaper* titled *Document—Itoman/Sumigin Jiken (Document: The Itoman/Sumitomo Affair)*.[13] The most gripping parts of this book are the interviews conducted by the Nikkei journalist with Sumitomo's Isoda. In a February 1990 interview, Isoda, then still Sumitomo's chairman, is unyielding in his support for Kawamura and Nishi, one of Sumitomo Bank's vice presidents. Neither Kawamura nor Nishi were career climbers; instead, they both seemed more interested in getting things than in playing office politics. Interestingly, both were also rumored to have links with shady characters in the Japanese underworld, something that Isoda must have known. Despite this knowledge, Isoda still backed Kawamura and Nishi. The educated corps of Japanese salaried managers had changed, and changed for the worse.

From March onwards, Chairman Isoda began showing his anxieties to the Nikkei reporter. His concerns focused on the fact that, according to Isoda, Itoh was showing new and negative sides to his character in his manipulation of Itoman that were causing Isoda to worry. Complaints and accusations from within the company had started surfacing and were making Isoda anxious.

By the end of March, Isoda began intimating that the company should cut its losses at 100 billion yen and disassociate itself with Itoh and his cronies. Despite these intimations, Isoda seemed paralyzed and action still wasn't taken. In May, Itoman was starting to rebel against the Sumitomo Bank for the way things were—or weren't—being handled. There were even reports of telephone tirades against Kawamura, but despite the appearance of anger, still no decisions or actions were forthcoming. The calls to investigate further and wait for more information were becoming tiring in the face of the bank's paralysis.

Before the Itoh situation could be resolved, however, Isoda's role in the Aobadai Branch Manager loan scandal was uncovered, and the Sumitomo chairman resigned in disgrace in October 1990. This situation and the processes that led to it can only be described in the harshest terms possible. When looking for reasons behind Isoda's actions, we see that in the early stages he seemed to be acting for the good of his company by placing Kawamura in Itoman and merging Sugiyama with Itoman. Itoman's recovery seemed to work and the conversion of Sugiyama into Itoman's real-estate arm also seemed to make reasonable business sense. Although it is stretching credibility, it is even almost understandable that Isoda gave his tacit permission for Kawamura to bring Itoh on board. But the line should have stopped there. Once Isoda knew of Itoh's mob connections and learned that Itoman was being ransacked by Itoh—a traitor within the ranks—Isoda's endless investigations which led nowhere showed a regard for his company, his responsibilities, and moral courage.

Yet, as disturbing as Isoda's lack of ethics were, even more troubling is that, as we shall see, he could hardly resolve the situation alone. As much as one tries to find excuses for Isoda's behavior, even in the early stages, the Sumitomo Bank appointed untrustworthy personnel to positions of authority. These appointments alone say something about the nature of the company's top management. The first duty of anyone in a top management position is to make responsible decisions; in this respect, Isoda and Sumitomo were sadly lacking. The scandal cast a huge shadow over the highly educated elite corps employed as Japan's salaried managers. But, sadly, there were plenty of other scandals blackening the Japanese corporate map.

The Reasons behind the Failures

Business's Main Responsibilities

The sorts of failures just described are highly unusual in the history of Japanese business and management. Why did they occur? The reasons lie not in the business environment nor in the economic policies of the times. In my field, the history of management, scholars agree that other reasons were the causes for these dark happenings. For the answers to the troubling questions of why and how business in this period was so badly tainted, it is necessary to look within the companies' management structures. Once again, the explanation of business environment and economic policies is an untenable one. Every period has its set of unique circumstances and they do not always lead to such gross failures in terms of result and behavior.

Another disturbing characteristic of the bubble mess is that a large proportion of Japanese corporate leaders were quick to blame others for their problems. Blame, according to them, should be placed on the government and finance ministry for following America's economic lead and guidance after the Plaza Accord, which caused the strong yen. Responsibility has also been shirked by top management, who blame the mass media and some top economists for jumping so quickly onto the bubble bandwagon. This lack of willingness to take responsibility for their actions seems just another sign of the ethical erosion of Japan's top managers.

Putting these distractions aside, it is time to look at the true reasons for the ruinous failures of Japanese companies during and after the bubble economy. We must not avert our eyes from the true cause, painful as it may be, for failure to understand the cause may well lead us down the same road again.

The Reasons behind the Failures: The Paralysis of Company Systems

There is no one true cause of the Japanese failures described above; instead the reasons are multiple and multifaceted. Moreover, among the reasons we shall discuss, there is no single cause that can be said to be the ultimate or definitive one, and there is even justification for argument about whether the reasons given are the true ones.

Regardless, for the time being let us outline three important causes. The first is that the fundamental way in which Japanese businesses operated in the developing postwar Japanese economy no longer applied to the rapidly changing world of business in the modern and postmodern eras. The main bank system is a good example. Although Japan's main banks should have been able to prevent the bubble economy, they instead were a major contributor to the ensuing fiasco.

Juro Hashimoto has aptly described a major bank's relationship with its corporate clients as "the family doctor."[14] According to this interpretation, a main bank is a company's pipeline that supplies capital and information. Banks are also adept at taking long-term views and acting as interested but objective outside parties to provide companies with a necessary system of checks and balances. This synergetic relationship, when it works (as it did in Japan's period of continued postwar growth), has allowed Japanese companies to grow successfully and dynamically and has been key to Japanese success. But, over time, the family doctor changed. The doctor started to give only brief, insubstantial examinations to its patients and instead began giving them dangerous medicine while charging ever-higher fees. But, some scholars might say, capitalism works like this and investment capital should be managed by the new style of family doctor. Regardless of which style is best, it's interesting to speculate as to why, some ten years ago, banks transformed from benevolent institutions into hungry organizations whose quest for profits led to the scandals that occurred in and post-1985.

The Reasons behind the Failures: The Sudden Loss of Foresight

The second reason behind the Japanese business failures we have outlined was the inability of companies to estimate the actual levels of market demand during the bubble economy. Moreover, large firms were unable to predict the limits to which land and stock prices would rise, and these two factors combined to create a grim picture indeed—as we already know. Of course, no company can be expected to consistently predict the future, particularly during times of great economic turbulence; in fact, in times of massive economic swings, it is probably rarer to find companies that guess right instead of wrong. The history of Japanese business is littered with companies that failed because of wrong predictions.

The period after World War I is one example of a turbulent economic time. Although the financial picture first seemed to be good, the economy was not on a firm footing or based on true demand. In 1920 things fell apart, and in Japan alone, there was a rash of bankruptcies and business failures. A situation that had once seemed promising collapsed in disaster and caused untold human misery. The Kuhara Zaibatsu, Kawasaki Shipyards, the Asano Zaibatsu, Suzuki Shoten, the Murai Zaibatsu, Mogi Gomei, Takada Shokai, the Fujita Bank, and other large companies and powerful *zaibatsu* were all dealt terrible blows and bankruptcies abounded.

When compared with the number of major company bankruptcies in the period following Word War I, the bubble failures seem relatively minor. Although it may be hard to judge whether the financial system imposed by Japan's bureaucracy after the Showa-period panic helped reduce the number of potential bankruptcies in the latest round of economic mishaps, some observers give it at least partial credit for somewhat mitigating the disaster. The financial disaster after World War I was rooted in the particular circumstances that gripped Japan and the world after the war. The bubble debacle is not notable for the circumstances surrounding it but instead for the number of large Japanese companies that got it wrong. Yet even though large firms such as Mitsui, Mitsubishi, and the Sumitomo Zaibatsu made it through the tumult after World War I with only minor damage owing to adroit top management, it's telling that during this later round of failures almost no one was unaffected, despite the absence of a major social upheaval such as a world war. The more we know about them, the uglier the bubble scandals get.

The Reasons behind the Failures: Scandal and Vanishing Ethics

The questionable loans made by some banks, the Itoman case, the whitewash by securities companies of huge losses incurred by companies' special clients, the fictitious accounting of Marubeni and Seibu Department Stores—these were not crimes perpetrated by individuals acting alone. Even if the individuals who committed the criminal acts did profit from their actions, they were not acting purely for personal, individual gain. Instead, unethical acts were undertaken to boost company profits or gain market share; in other words, illegal acts were done for the "good of the company." Press conferences held after the arrests of the individuals involved were notable for their common chorus: "We were doing it for the company." Frighteningly, they were probably telling the truth.

In the September 23, 1991, issue of *Nikkei Business*, survey results were published based on questionnaires sent the previous month to section heads of companies listed on the Japanese stock exchanges. Here are some of the questions and responses.[15]

Q: In your industry, is the general feeling that questionable bank loans and the way that stock market customers were compensated for losses considered illogical or out of the ordinary?

Yes	42.9%
No	48.6%
Undecided:	8.5%

Q: In what circumstances would these illogical actions be taken?

If pressured to do so	38.1%
If confident they would not be made public	26.7%
If and whenever the chance presented itself	15.2%
Never	11.4%
Unsure	8.6%

Q: If ordered by a superior to improve company performance using dishonest means, what would you do?

I would always refuse	30.5%
I would complain to the appropriate department within the company	28.6%
I would try to dissuade but would ultimately comply	18.1%
If I thought it would not be revealed I would do it	10.5%
Undecided	8.5%
I would follow orders	3.8%

Q: For example, if you learned that your firm was acting dishonestly on a company-wide basis, what would you do?

I would complain to the company's top management	49.5%
I would prohibit anyone in my department from acting dishonestly	17.1%
I would not follow the company's directives	13.3%
Undecided	10.6%
I would follow orders	9.5%

One might suppose that having more than half of the respondents say they would act in an honest and ethical way, regardless of how the question is phrased, is a good—albeit expected—response. Learning about the other group, however, is discouraging. Fully 42.9 percent of respondents said they essentially accept dishonest behavior, whereas 41.9 percent said they would consider unethical methods if the chance presented itself and they had assurances that their actions would not be discovered. If ordered by their superiors to engage in such actions, 28.6 percent said they would complain but then do it, or would do so if they were confident that they wouldn't get caught. If the people who said they'd do it uncomplainingly are added, the previous figure jumps to 32.4 percent. As these figures show, the concepts of honesty and ethical behavior in large Japanese companies vary, but the percentages are, most would agree, far from comforting.

Experiencing Success and the "Fat Cat Syndrome"

The paralysis of the economic system that helped coddle Japan's postwar growth economy, the mass inability of Japanese companies to forecast the downturn in land and stock prices, the fall in ethical standards—all of these events are recent phenomena previously unseen in the history of Japanese business and management and are events that were noticeably absent during Japan's period of high economic growth.

One guess as to why these blots occurred on the Japanese business record is that the events are attributable to the period of long economic growth experienced by Japanese companies. In other words, companies grew so much, for so long, that they lost their edge and essentially became "fat cats," confident of ample food and comfortable surroundings without really having to work for them. Although this speculation is hard to prove, it is one worth considering. Another way to describe this syndrome is to posit the idea that the top management of large Japanese companies became drunk on their own success and grew to believe their own headlines. Overconfident, these executives started to dismiss the United States and Europe as real competition and began taking success for granted. This self-satisfaction then transformed into a general malaise that, during the bubble economy, seemed to grip an entire generation of business leaders. Books maligning American and European business while lauding Japan seemed to suddenly sprout in bookshop windows everywhere and they sold briskly in this new mood of self-satisfaction.

At the apex of this mood, between 1980 and 1990, Japanese business seemed to fall into a monkey-see, monkey-do culture. There seemed to be no essential difference from one Japanese company to the next, whether in terms of policy, views of the chief executive, or even language and expressions used by management. While everyone was looking over his shoulders to see what everyone else was doing, no one wanted to be seen as doing anything extraordinary or unusual. The climate was decidedly conservative, which makes it even more surprising that companies plunged so fast and so headlong into the turbulent world of low-interest loans, skyrocketing real estate values, and high-yielding funds. To this day I shake my head in wonder at it all.

The results of the overconservative and overconfident mood were many and essentially negative. There was a stiffening of personnel policies and organizations. Corporate "groups" became common and led to a decrease in the kind and quality of the exciting new R&D that characterizes new businesses and enterprises. At this time, Japanese companies were also experiencing a labor shortage. To accommodate new employees, companies became soft, forgoing formerly rigorous training programs and farming out any jobs considered "dirty, dangerous, or demanding." Unfortunately, the "fat cat syndrome" was not limited to the business world, and its ramifications were felt throughout society. Japan, for example, became less interested in anything outside its own borders. Introspection and navel-gazing became the order of the day. As long as Japan's economy was growing by leaps and bounds, that was all that counted. Success had brought with it blinders that shut out new ideas, essentially everything except growing economic conservatism. Instead of sitting back self-contentedly, there should have been plans made to deal with a rejuvenated America, a new and dynamic EU, and the burgeoning economies of South Korea, Taiwan, China, and other countries in Southeast Asia. Instead of scenario building and contingency planning, inertia became the order of the day.

To put it simply, there was no fostering of a culture whereby new industries and business could be developed. The ability to build a new, competitive edge had been lost. It was not only business that was at fault. Universities and society at large were lacking in the effort to constantly improve. The work ethic had been lost and no one knew—or cared—where to find it. Worse, this status quo seems to be continuing even now. Hunger to succeed seems a thing of the past, a fact as true in the Japanese universities of today as it is in the corporate world. It's a very sad situation all around.

Although it may be impossible for me or other researchers to use real examples to quantify and qualify the true effects that the "fat cat syndrome" has had on Japan, I feel certain that it exists, and that it is one of the reasons Japanese businesses fell into the quagmire known as the bubble economy. The question then becomes, Where to go from here? The answer, we can only hope, will be forthcoming.

NOTES

CHAPTER ONE

1. Alfred D. Chandler, Jr., "The United States: Seedbed of Managerial Capitalism," in A. D. Chandler and H. Daems, eds., *Managerial Hierarchies* (Harvard University Press, 1980): 13–14. Alfred D. Chandler, Jr., *Scale and Scope—The Dynamics of Industrial Capitalism* (Cambridge: Harvard Belknap, 1990): 201.

2. Jurgen Kocka, *Industrialization, Organization, and Bureaucracy—Enterprises and Society of Modern Germany* (a compilation of Kocka's seven monographs [1990]), trans. Sachio Kaku (Nagoya University Press, 1992): 40.

3. Hidemasa Morikawa, "Nihon ni Okeru Professional Kigyojin no Keisei" (Formation of Professional Entrepreneurs in Japan), in *Soshiki Kagaku (Organizational Science)* 14, No. 4 (1980): 39ff.

4. Terushi Hara, "France ni Okeru Keieishakigyo no Konnan na Tanjo" (The Difficult Birth of Managerial Enterprises in France), in Hidemasa Morikawa, ed., *Keieisha Kigyo no Jidai (The Age of Managerial Enterprises)* (Yuhikaku Publishing, 1991).

5. Shigeaki Yasuoka, "Shoyu to Keiei no Kokusai Hikaku Shiron" (International Comparison of Ownership and Management), in Doshisha University Commerce Division *Shakai Kagaku (Social Science)* 55 (1995): 7–8.

6. Ibid., p. 9.

7. A. A. Berle, Jr., and G. C. Means, *Kindai Kabushiki Gaisha to Shiyu Zaisan (The Modern Corporation and Private Property* [New York: Mac-

millian, 1933], trans. Tadao Kitajima (Bungado Ginko Kenkyusha, 1958).

8. Chandler, "The United States: Seedbed"; A. D. Chandler, Jr., "Managers, Families, and Financiers," in K. Kobayashi and H. Morikawa, eds., *Development of Managerial Enterprises* (University of Tokyo Press, 1986).

9. Ibid.

10. Ibid.; Chandler, *Scale and Scope*, p. 71.

11. Alfred D. Chandler, Jr., *Keieisha no Jidai (The Visible Hand: The Managerial Revolution in American Business* [Cambridge: Harvard Belknap, 1977]), trans. K. Toba and K. Kobayashi (Toyo Keizai Shinposha, 1979), vol. 1, pp. 16–17, 19; vol. 2, p. 843.

12. Chandler, "Managers," p. 38.

13. Ibid., Chandler, *Scale and Scope*, pp. 71, 161, 194.

14. H. Morikawa, "Naze Keieisha Kigyo ga Hatten Suru no ka" (Why Do Managerial Enterprises Develop?), Morikawa, ed., *Keieisha Kigyo no Jidai (The Age of Managerial Enterprises)*, p. 2.

15. E. Abe, "Chandler Moderu to Morikawa Hidemasa-shi no Keieisha Kigyo Ron" (Chandler Models and H. Morikawa's Views on Managerial Enterprises), in *Keieishi Gaku (Management History)* 28, no. 4 (1994).

16. H. Morikawa, "Kabushiki Shoyu no Bunsan to Keieisha Kigyo—Abe Etsuo-shi no Hihan ni Kotaete" (Distribution of Stock and Managerial Enterprises—in Response to the Criticism of E. Abe), in *Keio Keiei Ron Shu (Keio Management Review)* 12, no. 3 (1995).

17. Chandler, "Managers," p. 38.

18. Harold C. Livesay, "Entrepreneurial Persistence through the Bureaucratic Age," *Business History Review* L1, no. 4 (1977).

19. Ibid., Chandler, *Scale and Scope*, p. 523.

20. Takao Sugiyama, *Heishi ni Kike (Listen to the Soldiers)* (Shinchosha, 1995): 139.

21. K. Kobayashi and H, Morikawa, eds., *Managerial Enterprises*, pp. 282–285.

22. In this book I use the word *skill* to mean human ability that can be obtained through knowledge and experience.

CHAPTER TWO

1. Matao Miyamoto, "Nihon Gata Kigyo Keiei no Kigen—Edo Jidai no Kigyo Keiei" (The Origins of the Japanese Management of Enterprises—Management of Enterprises in the Edo Era), in Matao Miyamoto et al., eds., *Nihon Keieishi (History of Japanese Management)* (Yuhikaku, 1995): 53; Matao Miyamoto; *Osaka no Kenkyu (Study of Osaka)* 3 (1964).

2. Ibid., pp. 53–55.

3. Tamio Hattori, "The Relationship between *Zaibatsu* and Family Structure: The Korean Case," in Akio Okochi and Shigeaki Yasuoka, eds., *Family Business in the Era of Industrialized Growth: Its Ownership and Management* (University of Tokyo Press, 1984).

4. Katsuyuki Ozawa, *DuPont Keieishi Reki (Management History of DuPont)* (Nihon Hyoronsha, 1986): 9.

5. Ibid., p. 32.

6. Frederick Morton, *Rothschild's Okoku (Rothschild's Kingdom)*, Tomiyasu Takahara trans. (Shincho-sha, 1975): 22, 26.

7. Geofferey Jones and Mary Rose, eds., *Family Capitalism* (Frank Cass, 1993).

8. Leslie Hannah, "Introduction," in *From Family Firm to Professional Management: Structure and Performance of Business Enterprise*, 9th International Economic History Congress, B9, Budapest, 1982.

9. A. D. Chandler, Jr., *Scale and Scope*, Etsuo Abe et al., trans. (Yuhikaku, 1993): 244, 286, 292.

10. Roy Church, "The Family Firm in Industrial Capitalism: International Perspectives on Hypothesis and History," in G. Jones and M. Rose, eds., *Family Capitalism*.

11. Ibid., p. 28.

12. A. D. Chandler, *Scale and Scope*, pp. 430–431.

13. A. D. Chandler, Jr., "Foreword," in H. Morikawa, *Zaibatsu: The Rise and Fall of Family Enterprise Groups in Japan* (University of Tokyo Press, 1992).

14. R. Church, "Family Firm," pp. 34–36.

15. R. Church, "Family Firm," pp. 34–36; P. L. Payne, "Family Business in Britain: A Historical and Analytical Survey," in A. Okochi and S. Yasuoka, eds., *Family Business*.

16. Yasunao Nakata, *Takatoshi Mitsui* (Series of People) (Yoshikawa Kobun Kan, 1959); Compilation Committee of the Story of Hachiro Uemon Mitsui, "Foreword," in *The Story of Hachiro Uemon Takamine Mitsui* (University of Tokyo Press, 1988).

17. "Tora-ya—A Unique Enterprise," in *Nikkei Business*, March 25, 1991.

18. K. Ozawa, *DuPont Keieishi (Management History of DuPont)*: 126.

19. Ibid., p. 267.

20. Ibid., pp. 204–206.

21. Examples of the conflict can be found in Etsuo Abe's, *Industrial Supremacy of the British Empire—The Rise and Fall of British Steel Enterprises* (Yuhikaku, 1993): 53.

22. Both discussions are introduced in J. Kocka, *Industrialization, Organization, and Bureaucracy*.

23. William Lazonick emphasizes this point in discussions on family enterprises in the U.K. For example, William Lazonick, *Business Organization and the Myth of the Market Economy* (Cambridge, 1991).

24. H. C. Livesay, "Entrepreneurial Persistence through the Bureaucratic Age," *Business History Review*, 51, no. 4 (1977).

25. Jurgen Kocka, "Entrepreneurs amd Managers in German Industrialization," in *The Cambridge Economic History of Europe*, Vol. VII: The

Industrial Economies: Capital, Labour, and Enterprise, Part I, P. Mathias and M. M. Postan, eds. (Cambridge, 1978).

26. A. D. Chandler, Jr., "Managers, Families, and Financiers," in K. Kobayashi and H. Morikawa, eds., *Development of Managerial Enterprises* (University of Tokyo Press, 1986): 38.

27. Ibid., pp. 38–51.

28. A. D. Chandler, *Scale and Scope*, pp. 514–515.

29. Hidemasa Morikawa, *Zaibatsu: The Rise and Fall of Family Enterprise Groups in Japan* (University of Tokyo Press, 1992).

30. H. Morikawa, "Prerequisites for the Development of Managerial Capitalism," in K. Kobayashi and H. Morikawa, eds., *Managerial Enterprises*, pp. 14–15.

31. Examples of British family enterprises can be seen in Abe.

32. G. Jones and M. Rose, "Family Capitalism," in G. Jones and M. Rose, eds., *Family Capitalism*, p. 11.

33. Ryuichiro Inoue, *Asian* Zaibatsu *and Enterprises,* Nihon Keizai Shinbunsha, 1987.

34. Ibid., p. 36.

35. Ibid.

36. Ibid., p. 38.

37. Ibid., p. 39.

38. Akira Suehiro, "Ownership and Management of Business Groups in Thailand," in *Report of the 29th Management History Study Council*, 1993.

39. R. Inoue, *Asian Zaibatsu and Enterprises*, p. 114.

40. Akira Suehiro and Makoto Nanbara, *Zaibatsu in Thailand—Family Business and Management Reform* (Dobunkan, 1991): 96–98.

CHAPTER THREE

1. Naozo Nitta, ed., *Kikuchi Kyozo O Den (Kyozo Kikuchi)* (Denki Hensan Jimsho [Biography Editorial Office], 1948): 84, 161, 666.

2. Ibid., p. 201.

3. Ibid., pp. 157, 164–165, 175–176, 199–201.

4. M. Miyamoto and T. Abe, eds., *Nihon Keieishi 2-Keiei Kakushin to Kogyoka (Management History in Japan II—Managerial Innovation and Industrialization)* (Iwanami Shoten, 1995): 284.

5. *Mitsui Jigyoshi (Mitsui Business History)*, Vol. 1 (Mitsui Bunko, 1980); Jun Kawada, *Sumitomo Kaisoki (Recollection of Sumitomo)* (Chuo Koronsha, 1951): 133.

6. T. Abe has criticized my evaluation of Minomura's and Hirose's views. Hosei Daigaku Sangyo Joho Center (Hosei University Industrial Information Center), Juro Hashimoto and Haruhito Takeda, eds., *Nihon Keizai no Hatten to Kigyo Shudan (Development of the Japanese Economy and Corporate Groups)* (University of Tokyo Press, 1992): 36.

7. Kazuo Yamamoto, "Sumitomo Sohonten" (Sumimoto's Head Office), Vol. 1: 1909–1912, in *Sumitomo Shiryokanpo (Sumitomo Shiryokan Report)*, 26 (1995):104.

8. Hidemasa Morikawa, *Zaibatsu: The Rise and Fall of Family Enterprise Groups in Japan* (University of Tokyo Press, 1992): 52–54.

9. Ibid., pp. 77–78.

10. Miyamoto and Abe, eds., *Management History in Japan II*, p. 5.

11. Yujiro Nishihara, *Fujiyama Raita Den (A Biography of Raita Fujiyama)* (The Fujiyama Family, 1939), Chapters 10, 11, 15.

12. Kota Akiyama, *Soukamanshitsu (Comic Ramblings from Under the Widow)*, private issue, 1932, p. 157.

13. Morikawa, "The Family Multisubsidiary," *Zaibatsu*, Chapter 7.

14. Shigeaki Yasuoka, *Zaibatsu no Keieishi (Management History of Zaibatsu)* (Gendai Kyoyo Bunko, Shakai Shisosha, 1990): 16.

15. Takeo Kikkawa, "*Zaibatsushi* to Kigyo Shudanshi no Ronri" (The Logic of the History of *Zaibatsu* and the History of Corporate Groups), in *Keieishigaku (Management History)*, 30, no. 2. (1995).

16. Morikawa, *Zaibatsu*, pp. 218–19.

17. Hosei Daigaku Sangyo Joho Center (Hosei University Industrial Information Center), eds., *Japanese Economy and Corporate Groups*.

18. Hidemasa Morikawa, *Gijutsusha—Nihon Kindaika no Ninaitetachi (Engineers—Supporters of Modernization in Japan)* (Nihon Keizai Shinbunsha [Nikkei Shinsho] 1974); H. Morikawa, "Nihon Gijutsha no *Genba Shugi" (Emphasis on Sites by Engineers in Japan*—Examination from the Viewpoint of Management History), in *Yokohama Keiei Kenkyu (Yokohama Management Study)*, 8, no. 4 (1988).

19. Tetsuji Okazaki and Masahiro Okuno, eds., *Gendai Nihon Keizai System no Genryu (Roots of the Modern Japanese Economic System)* Series Gendai Keizai Kenkyu 6, Modern Economy Study Series # 6 (Nihon Keizai Shinbunsha, 1993): 103.

20. Hidemasa Morikawa, *Nihon Keieishi (Japan's Business History)* (Nikkei Bunko) (Nihon Keizai Shinbunsha, 1981): 157.

21. Tetsuji Okazaki and Masahiro Okuno, eds., *Roots of Modern Japanese Economic System*, p. 106.

22. Kamemichi Takahashi, *Kabushiki Gaisha Bokoku Ron (The Ruination of a Country by Stock Companies)* (Manrikaku Shoba, 1930): 48.

23. Tsunehiko Yui, "Gaisetsu : 1915–1937" (Overviews: 1915–1937), in T. Yui and Eisuke Daito, eds., *Nihon Keieishi 3—Daikigyojidai no Torai (Management History in Japan 3—Arrival of the Time of Large Enterprises)* (Iwanami Shoten, 1995): 75.

24. *Nihon Keizai Nenpo #55 (Annual Report on the Japanese Economy no. 55)* (Toyo Keizai Shinposha. 1944): 56–66.

25. Osamu Nagashima, "Senji Keizai Kenkyu to Kigyo Tosei" (Study of Economic Situations during the War and Corporate Control), in Masahiro Shimotani and O. Nagashima, eds., *Senji Nihon Keizai no Kenkyu (Study*

of Economic Situations during the War) (Koyo Shobo, 1992), Introduction, pp. 15–18.

26. *Tonen 15 Nen Shi (Fifteen Years of Tonen History)* (Toa Nenryo Kogyo K.K., 1956): 23.

27. *Nakahara Nobuhei Nikki (Diary of Nobuhei Nakahara)*, Vol. 2 (Tonen, 1994): 23.

28. Ibid., p. 25.

29. Hideaki Miyajima, "Zaibatsu Kaitai" (Dismantling of the *Zaibatsu*), Hosei Daigaku Sangyo Joho Center (Hosei University Industrial Information Center), eds., *Nihon Keizai no Hatten to Kigyo Shudan (Development of the Japanese Economy and Corporate Groups)*. After this book was written, Dr. Miyajima's excellent report titled "Senmon Keieisha no Seiha —Nihongata Keieisha Kigyo no Seiritsu" (The Supremacy of Salaried Managers—Establishment of Japanese-style Managerial Enterprises), in *Nihon Keieishi 4—Nihonteki Keiei no Renzoku to Danzetsu (Management History in Japan 4—Continuation and Discontinuation of Japanese-style Management)* by H. Yamazaki and T. Kikkawa (Iwanami Shoten, 1995) was published subsequently.

30. Ryoichi Miwa, "Sengo Minshuka to Keizai Saiken" (Post-war Democracy and the Restructuring of the Economy), in Takahide Nakamura, ed., *Nihon Keizaishi 7—Keikakuka to Minshuka (Management History in Japan 7—Planning and Democracy)* (Iwanami Shoten, 1989).

31. Okazaki, Okuno, eds., *Roots of Modern Japanese Economic System*, p. 121.

32. Takeo Kikkawa, "Kigyo Shudan no Seiritsu to Sono Kino" (Establishment and Functions of Corporate Groups), in H. Morikawa, ed., *Businessmen no Tame no Sengo Keieishi Nyumon (Guide of Post-war Management History for Business People)* (Nihon Keizai Shinbunsha, 1992), Chapter 3, pp. 69–73.

33. Kunio Suzuki, "From *Zaibatsu* to Corporate Complexes," in Takao Shiba and Masahiro Shimotani, eds., *Beyond the Firm: Business Groups in International and Historical Perspective* (Oxford University Press, 1997).

34. Ibid.

35. Compared to the reorganization of Mitsubishi Corp. in July 1954, that of Mitsui Corp. came much later, in Feburary 1959. The reason for this is described in *Kohon Mitsui Bussan Kabushiki Kaisha 100 Nenshi (Mitsui Corp.'s 100 Years of History)*, Vol. 2 (1978), Chapter 2, Sections 3 and 4.

36. T. Kikkawa, Establishment and Functions of Corporate Groups, pp. 74–77.

37. Masahiro Shimotani, *Nihon no Keiretsu to Kigyo Shudan (Affiliated Firms and Corporate Groups in Japan)* (Yuhikaku Publishing, 1993), Chapter 4.

38. T. Kikkawa, Establishment and Functions of Corporate Groups, pp. 83–84.

39. Ryuichiro Inoue, *Kyodai Kigyo no Botsuraku (The Decline of Giant Enterprises)* (Asahi Shinbunsha [Asahi Bunko], 1994): 63–70.

40. Takeo Kikkawa and Izumi Nonaka, "Kakushinteki Kigyosha Katsudo no Keiki—Honda Giken to Sony no Jirei" (Movements of Innovative Entrepreneurs—The Examples of Honda and Sony), Tsunehiko Yui and Juro Hashimoto, eds., *Kakushin no Keieishi—Senzen Sengo ni Okeru Nihon Kigyo no Kakushin Kodo (The History of Innovative Management—Innovative Movements in Japanese Enterprises before and after the War)*, (Yuhikaku Publishing, 1995): 168.

41. H. Morikawa, *Japan's Business History*, pp. 170–171.

42. Takeo Kikkawa, "Sengo Nihon Keieishi Kenkyu no Shoten" (Focus of the Study of the Post-war Management History in Japan), H. Morikawa, ed., *Keieisha Kigyo no Jidai (The Period of Managerial Enterprises)* (Yuhikaku Publishing, 1991): 227.

43. Ibid., p. 225.

44. *Tokyo Gas 100 Nenshi (Tokyo Gas's 100 years of History)*, (Tokyo Gas, 1986), related data.

45. Katsuto Uchihashi, "Hikigiwa no Kenkyu" (Study on the Timing of Retirement), Vol. 1 *Nikkei Business*, October, 24, 1988.

46. Ryuichiro Inoue, *Decline of Giant Enterprises*, pp. 169–175.

CHAPTER FOUR

1. Quotations taken from the following: Derek F. Channon, *The Strategy and Structure of British Enterprise* (Macmillan, 1971): 161; P. L. Payne, "Family Business in Britain: An Historical and Analytical Survey," in A. Okochi and S. Yasuoka, eds., *Family Business in the Era of Industrial Growth* (University of Tokyo Press, 1984): 178.

2. Sazo Idemitsu, *Waga Yonjugo Nen Kan (My Forty-five Years)*, private publication, 1956, p. 519.

3. Ibid., p. 347.

4. Ibid., pp. 346–347.

5. Ken Hayashibara, "21 Seiki E No 100 Nin" (100 Individuals to Take Us Into the 21st Century), *Nikkei Business*, January 20, 1992.

6. Yasunori Tateishi, "Sekai Ichi no Okane Mochi Tsutsumi Yoshiaki—Kokudo no Kenkyu: Naze Kokudo Wa Zeikin wo Harawanai ka" (The World's Richest Man, Yoshiaki Tsutsumi—Researching Kokudo and Why Kokudo Pays No Taxes), *Bungei Shinju*, September 1994.

7. Ibid.

8. Hidemasa Morikawa, *Chiho Zaibatsu (Regional Zaibatsu)* (Nihon Keizei Shimbunsha, 1985), Chapter 2, Part 2.

9. Yoshinari Satoh, "Fukugo Dozoku Keiei Kikkoman no Kokei Rule" (The Kikkoman Extended Family Business and Their Rules of Succession), *President*, July 1980.

10. Tomie Kondo, *Tabata Bunshi Mura (Tabata Literary Village)* (Chukoku Bunko/Chuo Koronsha, 1983), Chapter 7 and others.

11. *Kashima Kensetsu 100 Nen Shi (100 Years of Kashima Construction)*, Vol. 1 (Kashima Kensetsu Kabushiksi Kaisha, 1971), Chapter 1, 2.

12. Kondo, *Tabata Literary Village*, p. 132.

13. *100 Years of Kashima Construction, Volume 1, Chapter 2. Also, Masami Kita, Kokusai Nihon wo Hiraita Hitobito—Nihon to Scotland no Kizuna (The Individuals Who Established Internationalized Japan—The Bonds between Japan and Scotland*) (Dobunkan, 1984): 205, 207. It should be noted, however, that author Kita confuses Ryuzo Kashima and Seiichi Kashima (same book, pp. 207, 213).

14. Kondo, *Tabata Literary Village*, pp. 132–133.

15. Ibid., pp. 136–140.

16. Makiko Arima, "Kashima Ume to Yonnin no Musko Tachi" (Ume Kashima and Her Four Sons), *Kikan Chuo Kuron Keiei Mondai*, Special Spring Issue, 1978.

17. According to personnel directories.

18. Yasuo Mishima, *Zosen O Kawasaki Shozo no Shogai (The Life of Shozo Kawasaki, the Shipbuilding King)* (Dobunkan, 1993).

19. Makiko Arima, "Mikimoto Ke San Dai—Shinju O no Eikou wo Otte" (The Three Heads of the Mikimoto Family: The Shouldered Glory of the Pearl King), *Kikan Chuo Koron Keiei Mondai*, Winter Issue, 1979.

20. Ibid., p. 361.

21. *Mistui Ginko Shiryo 4 (The Historical Records of the Mitsui Bank, Volume 4)* (Zaidan Hojin Nihon Keieishi Kenkyusho, 1987): p. 805.

22. Information on the Bridgestone case was taken from *Bridgestone Tire 50 Nen Shi (50 Years of Bridgestone Tire)*, Bridgestone Tire K.K., 1982.

23. Ibid., pp. 22–29.

24. From the author's own materials.

25. *Matsushita Denki 50 Nen no Ryakushi (A Short History of Matsushita Electric's First 50 Years)*, Matsushita Denki Sangyo K.K., 1968, p. 89.

26. Material for the Matsushita case study was based on Yasunori Tateishi's "Fukushu Suru Shinwa—Matsushita Konosuke no Showa Shi" (The Konosuke Matsushita Showa Years: A Tale of Revenge), *Bungei Shinjuu* (Bunshun Bunko, 1992). A paperback version was also published by the same company in 1988.

27. Ibid., Chapter 2.

28. Ibid., Chapter 14.

29. Ibid., p. 366.

30. Ibid., pp. 388, 390.

31. *Nikkei Business*, combined December 20 and December 27, 1993, issue.

32. For the Shimizu Construction Company case study, *Shimizu Kensetsu 180 Nen (Shimizu Construction: 180 Years)*, published in 1984, was a useful reference.

33. Ibid., p. 41.

34. Eisuke Daito, "Tokei Kogyo no Hatten to Hattori Tokeiten no Shoyu to Keiei" (The Development of the Watch Industry and the Ownership and Management of the Hattori Timepiece Store), in *Keieisha Kigyo no Jidai (The Era of the Managerial Enterprise)*, Hidemasa Morikawa, ed. (Yuhikaku, 1991), Chapter 3.

35. Ryutaro Kobayashi, *Shirarezaru Kigyo Shudan Seiko Group (The Unknown Seiko Enterprise Group* (Nihon Kogyo Shimbunsha, 1987).

36. *Nikkei Business*, March 20, 1992, p. 20.

37. Ibid., pp. 11–14.

38. *Nihon Keizai Shimbun*, Morning Edition, August 28, 1995.

39. For the history of Matsuzakaya and the Itoh family, see H. Morikawa, *Regional Zaibatsu*, Chapter 2, Part 8.

40. For material and information on the history of the inner conflicts relating to the story of Matsuzakaya and the Itoh family, an excellent source is Katsunori Morita's doctoral thesis, "Waga Kuni Hyakkaten Gyokai ni Okeru Senmon Keieisha no Hatten Katei" (The Development Process for Salaried Managers in the Japanese Department Store Trade), Keio University Business School, 1995.

41. Source material for the Y.K.K. section was adapted from *Nikkei Business*, April 23, 1990.

42. As part of my research for the Sony case study, I examined the personnel records as listed in the *Kaisha Shiki Ho (Seasonal Company Report)*.

43. My major reference for the Hishima case study was *Nikkei Business*, July 15, 1991.

44. My reference for the Yonezawa case study was *Nikkei Business*, September 26, 1994.

45. Yasunori Tateishi, *Tsutsumi Seiji to Saison Group (Seiji Tsutsumi and the Saison Group)* (Kodansha Bunko/Kodansha, 1995). It should be noted, however, that this book is an expanded version of Tateishi's previous book, *Hyoryu Suru Keiei (Management Adrift)* (Bungei Shinju, 1990).

46. Tsunehiko Yui, ed., *Saison no Rekishi/Henkaku no Dynamism (The History of Saison: The Dynamism of Change)*, 2 vols. (Libroport, 1991).

47. Source material for the Okuma case study was taken from Nikkei Business, ed., *Yoi Kaisha (Good Companies)* (Nihon Keizai Shimbunsha, 1989): 131–133.

CHAPTER FIVE

1. "Corporate Governance—Kabunushi no Fukken ga Kaisha wo Kaeru" (The Restoration of Corporate Governance to Stockholders and the Changes to the Company), *Nikkei Business*, June 15, 1992.

2. The April 1, 1991, issue of *Nikkei Business* introduced excerpts from the May 13 edition of the American edition of *Business Week*.

3. Ibid.

4. Ibid.

5. Hiroyuki Itami, *Jinponshugi Kigyo (People-centered Businesses)* (Chikuma Shobo, 1987), Chapter 2.

6. "Tochi ni Mirareta Ginko" (The Banks Spellbound by Real Estate), *Nikkei Business*, January 29, 1990.

7. Tomoaki Saitoh, *Kigyo Zaimu no Hensen—Kansetsu Kinyu kara Chokusetsu Kinyu e (Changes in Corporate Money Management: From Indirect to Direct Financing)*, quoted in Hidemasu Morikawa, ed., *Businessman no Tame no Sengo Keieishi Nyumon (Guide of Postwar Management History for Business People)* (Nihon Keizei Shimbunsha, 1992), Chapter 11.

8. Juro Hashimoto, *Nihon Keizairon—20 Seiki System to Nihon Keizai (Views on the Japanese Economy: 20th Century Systems and the Japanese Economy)* (Mineruba Shobo, 1991): 239.

9. Ibid.

10. Ibid., pp. 250–251.

11. Toshiichi Takamura and Hiroshi Koyama, eds., *Nihon Sangyoshi 4 (The History of Japanese Industry)* (Nihon Keizei Shimbunsha, 1994): 113.

12. Iwao Iwanaga, "Sekiyu Kagaku—Nihonteki Kato Kyoso no Ronri" (The Petro-chemical Industry: The Logic of Japanese-Style Over-Competition), Editorial Department of *The Economist*, supervised by Hidemasa Morikawa, in *Sengo Sangyoshi e no Shogen 2-Kyodaika no Jidai (Testimonies on the History of Post-war Industry: The Expansion Period)* (Mainichi Shimbunsha, 1977), article.

13. Nihon Keizai Shimbun, ed., *Document—Itoman/Sumigin Jiken (Document: The Itoman/Sumitomo Affair)* (Nihon Keizai Shimbunsha, 1991).

14. Juro Hashimoto, "Gendai Nihon Kigyo no Soshiki to Kodo" (The Organization and Behavior of Modern Japanese Businesses), in Hosei Daigaku, *Keiei Shirin 27, no 1* (1990): 127. Also, by the same author, "Dai Kigyo no Keizai Kozo" (The Economic Structure of Large Businesses), Tokyo Daigaku Shakai Kagaku Kenkyusho, ed., in *Gendai Nihon Shakai 5—Kozo (Modern Japanese Society 5: Structure)* (University of Tokyo Press, 1991), Chapter 2, p. 99.

15. "Yogoreta Elite Tachi" (The Dirty Elite), *Nikkei Business*, September 23, 1991.